LIVENESS

Liveness: performance in a mediatized culture addresses what may be the single most important question facing all kinds of performance today. What is the status of live performance in a culture dominated by mass media?

Liveness begins with an overview of the cultural position of live performance in a media-dominated culture. Philip Auslander shows that media technology has encroached on live events to the point where many, like the sports events and concerts that feature huge video screens, are hardly live at all. He proposes a way of understanding the history of this development based on an analysis of the relationship between early television and the theatre.

Auslander goes on to a detailed analysis of what live performance has meant in rock music culture, arguing that live performance has been devalued here, as it has been in the culture at large. The final section of the book examines one social realm in which live performance seems to have retained much of its traditional value: the legal arena. Through an examination of American jurisprudence Auslander shows how the live trial continues to be central to the legal process.

By looking at live performance, *Liveness* offers penetrating insights into media culture. Auslander also takes issue with those who see live performance as a means of commenting on media culture from the outside. This book will provoke debate on a rarely addressed issue that is essential to our understanding of both performance and the culture within which it takes place – what is live performance and what can it mean to us now?

Philip Auslander teaches Performance Studies and Cultural Studies at the Georgia Institute of Technology, USA. His other books include *From Acting to Performance* (Routledge, 1997).

LIVENESS

Performance in a mediatized culture

Philip Auslander

London and New York

First published 1999
by Routledge
11 New Fetter Lane, London EC4P 4EE

Simultaneously published in the USA and Canada
by Routledge
29 West 35th Street, New York, NY 10001

Typeset in Goudy by Routledge
Printed and bound in Great Britain by Clays PLC

British Library Cataloguing in Publication Data
A catalogue record for this book is available from the British Library

Library of Congress Cataloging in Publication Data
Liveness: performance in a mediatized culture/Philip Auslander.
Includes bibliographical references and index.
1. Performing arts – Social aspects.
2. Rock music – Performance.
3. Trials. I. Title.
PN1590. S6A88   1999   98–43440
791'.0973'0904–dc21   CIP

ISBN 0–415–19689–2 (hbk)
ISBN 0–415–19690–6 (pbk)

Why would you make live work in an age of mass communications? Why work in more or less the only field which still insists on presence? For artists interested in "the contemporary" this area of live performance seems like a bit of a backwater. Do you have something against mass-reproduction? Do you work from some quaint notion about immediacy and real presence?

I don't know.

Answer the question.

(Forced Entertainment 1996:87)

Like most art critics, I get my best ideas from television.

(Dave Hickey 1996:43)

CONTENTS

ACKNOWLEDGEMENTS

I would like to thank Talia Rodgers for her enthusiasm and unflagging support of this project from the moment I first told her about it over a modest dinner in Philadelphia, through our discussion of it over a much nicer lunch in London, and beyond.

The material of this book has been the basis for numerous papers and presentations over the last six years. I want to thank all the organizers of conferences, panels, and public lectures who provided me with platforms. The responses I got on all occasions were stimulating and instructive; the influence of those occasions and audiences is reflected here.

A number of colleagues, both inside and outside the academy, made significant contributions to the ideas expressed here. I would like to thank Mike Jones, Richard Neupert, Matthew Starr, Leslie Taylor, and all my colleagues in the School of Literature, Communication, and Culture at Georgia Tech for invaluable dialogue. Special thanks to Margery M. Fernald and Michael Landau for helping me with legal research and for talking law with me.

And thanks to Evie (The Dog) Sirlin whose live presence made the work on this book so much more pleasant.

Parts of Chapters 2 and 3 appeared in "Liveness: performance and the anxiety of simulation," in *Performance and Cultural Politics*, edited by Elin Diamond (London and New York: Routledge, 1996); part of Chapter 2 was published as "Against ontology: making distinctions between the live and the mediatized," *Performance Research*, 2, 3 (1997); part of Chapter 3 appeared as "Seeing is believing: live performance and the discourse of authenticity in rock culture," *Literature and Psychology: a journal of psychoanalytic and cultural criticism*, 44, 4 (1998);

and part of Chapter 4 was published as "Legally live: performance in/of the law," *TDR: The Journal of Performance Studies*, T154 (1997). I would like to thank the editors and publishers of these journals for permission to use these materials here.

1

INTRODUCTION:

"An Orchid in the Land of Technology"[1]

The prospectus for a conference entitled "Why Theatre: Choices for the New Century"[2] posed a question that goes straight to the heart of the matter that concerns me here: "Theatre and the media: rivals or partners?" My own answer to this question is unequivocal: at the level of cultural economy,[3] theatre (and live performance generally) and the mass media are rivals, not partners. Neither are they equal rivals: it is absolutely clear that our current cultural formation is saturated with, and dominated by, mass media representations in general, and television in particular.

In an essay on theatre and cinema, Herbert Blau (1982: 121) quotes Marx's *Grundrisse*:

> In all forms of society, there is one specific kind of production which predominates over the rest, whose relations thus assign rank and influence to the others. It is a general illumination which bathes all the other colours and modifies their particularity. It is a particular ether which determines the specific gravity of every being which has materialized within it.

Although Marx is describing industrial production under bourgeois capitalism, for Blau, "he might as well be describing the cinema." I would argue, *pace* Marx and Blau, that Marx might as well be describing

---

1 The title of this chapter is taken from Walter Benjamin's celebrated essay "The work of art in the age of mechanical reproduction" (1986 [1936]: 40).
2 The conference, which took place in the fall of 1995 in Toronto, was sponsored by the University of Toronto and Humboldt University in Berlin.
3 I use the phrase "cultural economy" to describe a realm of inquiry that includes both the real economic relations among cultural forms, and the relative degrees of cultural prestige and power enjoyed by different forms.

television: Marx's allusions to a general illumination and an ether (a word frequently used in early discussions of broadcasting to describe the medium through which electronic waves pass) are even more appropriate to that medium than to the cinema.

As for the cultural dominance of television and its productions, Cecilia Tichi (1991: 3–8) has suggested that television can no longer be seen just as an element in our cultural environment, one discourse among many, but must be seen as an environment in itself. Television has transcended its identity as a particular medium and is suffused through the culture as "the televisual."

> What the televisual names…is the end of the medium, in a context, and the arrival of television as the context. What is clear is that television has to be recognised as an organic part of the social fabric; which means that its transmissions are no longer managed by the flick of a switch.
>
> (Fry 1993: 13)

In other words, if television once could be seen as ranking among a number of vehicles for conveying expression or information from which we could choose, we no longer have that choice: the televisual has become an intrinsic and determining element of our cultural formation. As Tony Fry indicates, it is indeed no longer a question of thinking about television in various cultural contexts but of seeing it as *the* cultural context. Clearly, this issue and the related question of the nature of television culture could be (and have been) the subjects of books in themselves. The project of describing the position of other cultural discourses within our mediatized environment is as pressing as the project of describing that environment itself. Because live performance is the category of cultural production most directly affected by the dominance of media, it is particularly urgent to address the situation of live performance in our mediatized culture.

Investigating live performance's cultural valence for the present volume, I quickly became impatient with what I consider to be traditional, unreflective assumptions that fail to get much further in their attempts to explicate the value of "liveness" than invoking clichés and mystifications like "the magic of live theatre," the "energy" that supposedly exists between performers and spectators in a live event, and the "community" that live performance is often said to create among performers and spectators. In time, I came to see that concepts such as these do have value for performers and partisans of live performance. Indeed, it may even be necessary for performers, especially, to believe in them. But where these concepts are used to describe the relationship between live performance and its present mediatized environment, they yield a reductive binary opposition of the live and the mediatized. Steve Wurtzler summarizes this traditional view well:

> As socially and historically produced, the categories of the live and the recorded are defined in a mutually exclusive relationship, in that the notion of the live is premised on the absence of recording and the defining fact of the recorded is the absence of the live.
>
> (Wurtzler 1992: 89)[4]

In this tradition, "the live comes to stand for a category completely outside representation" (Wurtzler 1992: 88). In other words, the common assumption is that the live event is "real" and that mediatized events are secondary and somehow artificial reproductions of the real. In Chapter 2, I will argue that this kind of thinking persists not only in the culture at large but even in contemporary performance studies.[5] The arguments of that chapter are intended both to exploit and to challenge the traditional way of thinking about liveness and its cultural position by employing its terms (that is, taking the binary opposition for granted), then opening those terms themselves to critique. Chapters 3 and 4 depart from a different premise – that liveness must be examined not as a global, undifferentiated phenomenon but within specific cultural and social contexts.

Perhaps because of my impatience with the conventional wisdom, I have sometimes been mistaken for someone who does not value – who is even antagonistic toward – live performance. This is very far from being the case: my interest in the cultural status of live

---

4 Wurtzler (1992: 89–90) challenges this binary opposition by asserting that "the socially constructed categories live and recorded cannot account for all representational practices." He offers a chart in which various kinds of events are positioned according to spatial and temporal vectors. Two categories of representations that are neither purely live nor purely recorded emerge: those in which performance and audience are spatially separate but temporally co-present (e.g., live television or radio) and those in which performance and audience are spatially co-present but elements of the performance are pre-recorded (e.g., lip-synched concerts, instant replays on stadium video displays).
5 I have found that scholars working in mass media studies, particularly those interested in television or popular music, have dealt more directly and fruitfully with the question of liveness than most scholars in theatre or performance studies.

performance derives directly from my sense of living in a culture in which something I continue to value seems to have less and less presence and importance. Despite my own commitment to the theatre and other forms of live performance, I have tried here to take a fairly hardheaded, unsentimental approach. The resulting assessment of the situation of live performance in a culture dominated by mass media has not made me optimistic about its current and future cultural prestige, as understood in traditional terms. It has also enabled me to see, however, that those terms may no longer be the most useful ones.

Performance artist Eric Bogosian, for example, describes live theatre as:

> medicine for a toxic environment of electronic media mind-pollution....Theater clears my head because it takes the subtextual brainwashing of the media madness and SHOUTS that subtext out loud....Theater is ritual. It is something we make together every time it happens. Theater is holy. Instead of being bombarded by a cathode ray tube we are speaking to ourselves. Human language, not electronic noise.
>
> (Bogosian 1994: xii)

Bogosian's perception of the value of live performance clearly derives from its existence only in the moment ("every time it happens"), and its putative ability to create community (if not communion) among its participants, including performers and spectators. These are both issues I address in the chapters to follow. Most important for the present discussion, he sets live performance in a relationship of antagonistic opposition to mediatization and imputes to live performance the social, perhaps even political, function of opposing the oppressive regime of "electronic noise" imposed upon us by the mass media. This opposition, and live performance's ostensible curative powers, presumably derive from significant ontological distinctions between live and mediatized cultural forms. This perception of an oppositional relationship between the live and the mediatized animates my own discussion, for I wish both to exploit and to deconstruct that opposition in my discussion of the ontology of live performance in Chapter 2.

Several important premises are implied by my use of the word "mediatized," which I have borrowed from Jean Baudrillard. Its emphasis on a conventional concept of mass media marks a limit of my inquiry. Although I discuss the impact of digital information technologies on the issues at hand, especially in Chapter 3, my primary concern here is with the relationship between live performance and what may now be called "old media" (e.g., television, film, sound recording). Others have already begun the project of theorizing performance in the environment of advanced information technologies more specifically than I do here (see Case 1996, Causey [forthcoming], McKenzie 1997, Saltz 1997).

I often employ the term "mediatized," admittedly somewhat loosely, to indicate that a particular cultural object is a product of the mass media or of media technology. "Mediatized performance" is performance that is circulated on television, as audio or video recordings, and in other forms based in technologies of reproduction. Baudrillard's own definition is more expansive: "What is mediatized is not what comes off the daily press, out of the tube, or on the radio: it is what is reinter-preted by the sign form, articulated into models, and administered by the code" (1981: 175–6). For Baudrillard, mediatization is not simply a neutral term describing products of the media. Rather, he sees the media as instrumental in a larger, socio-political process of bringing all discourses under the dominance of a single code. Although I ignore Baudrillard's admonishment that the word "mediatized" does not define modes of cultural production, I hope I have retained in my use of the term Baudrillard's characterization of the mass media as the cultural dominant of contemporary, western/ized societies. (I believe my description here can be generalized to this extent, though my focus is admittedly on the United States.) I intend to describe both live performance's cultural–economic competition with other forms and the position of live performance in a culture for which mediatization is a vehicle of the general code in a way that live performance is not (or is no longer). Although this book is not generally in service to Baudrillardian politics, I do follow Baudrillard's line in my discussion of rock music in Chapter 3, both to extend his analysis into that cultural realm and to critique that analysis.

In the sense that I am treating live and mediatized performance as parallel forms that participate in the same cultural economy, my usage of "mediatization" follows Fredric Jameson's definition of the term as: "the process whereby the traditional fine arts…come to consciousness of themselves as various media within a mediatic system" (Jameson 1991: 162). Susan Sontag (1966: 25), in her essay on theatre and film, contrasts the two forms by saying that: "theatre is never a 'medium'" in the sense that "one can make a movie 'of' a play but not a play 'of' a movie." Part of my argument in Chapter 2 is intended to prove Sontag wrong: there have long been plays "of" movies and television programs, and live performance can even function as a kind of mass medium. Whereas the traditional view represented by Sontag's comment sees theatre and the live performance arts generally as belonging to a cultural system separate from that of the mass media, live forms have become mediatized in Jameson's sense: they have been forced by economic reality to acknowledge their status as media within a mediatic system that includes the mass media and information technologies. Implicitly acknowledging this situation, a number of theatres have displayed signs similar to the banner that flew outside the Alliance Theater in Atlanta declaring that its offerings are "Not Available on Video," demonstrating that the only way of imputing specificity to the experience of live performance in the current cultural climate is by reference to the dominant experience of mediatization.

There is no question that live performance and mediatized forms compete for audiences in the cultural marketplace, and that mediatized forms have gained the advantage in that competition. Broadway producer Margo Lion's observation about the position of theatre within this competitive cultural economy can be applied to live performance generally: "we have realized that we are all competing for the same entertainment dollars in a climate where theater isn't always first on the list" (quoted in Rick Lyman, "On stage and off," *New York Times*, December 19 1997: B2). Blau elaborates:

> [The theater's] status has been continually threatened by what Adorno named the culture industry and...the escalating dominance of the media. "Do you go to the theater often?" That many have never gone, and that those who have, even in countries with established theater traditions, are going elsewhere or, with cable and VCRs, staying home, is also a theatrical fact, a datum of practice.
>
> (Blau 1992: 76)

As Blau recognizes, theatre and other forms of live performance compete directly with mediatized forms that are much more advantageously positioned in the marketplace. Blau's calling the pressure of live performance's competition with the mediatized "a datum of practice" suggests that performance practice inevitably reflects this pressure in the material conditions under which performance takes place, in the composition of the audience and the formation of its expectations, and in the forms and contents of performance itself.

An important consequence of thinking about live and mediatized performance as belonging to the same mediatic system is the inscription of live performance within the historical logic of media identified by Marshall McLuhan (1964: 158): "A new medium is never an addition to an old one, nor does it leave the old one in peace. It never ceases to oppress the older media until it finds new shapes and positions for them." Jay Bolter and Richard Grusin (1996: 339) have refined this analysis with their concept of "remediation," "the representation of one medium in another." According to their analysis, "new technologies of representation proceed by reforming or remediating earlier ones" (ibid.: 352).[6] My discussion in Chapter 2 of the relationship between theatre and early television and the consequent displacement of live performance by television is an attempt to describe how this historical logic plays out in that instance. To put it bluntly, the general response of live performance to the oppression and economic superiority of mediatized forms has been to become as much like them as possible. From ball games that incorporate instant replay screens, to rock concerts that recreate the images of music video, to live stage versions of television shows and movies, to dance and performance art's incorporation of video, evidence of the incursion of mediatization into the live event is available across the entire spectrum of performance genres.

This situation has created an understandable anxiety for those who value live performance, and this anxiety may be at the root of their need to say that live performance has a worth that both transcends and resists market value. In this view, the value of live performance resides in its very resistance to the market and the media, the dominant culture they represent, and the regime of cultural production that supports them. This is the position Peggy Phelan has elucidated in her influential *Unmarked: The Politics of Performance* (Phelan 1993a). For many reasons (which will be elaborated in the following chapters), I find this view untenable. The progressive diminution of previous distinctions between the live and the mediatized, in which live events are becoming more and more like mediatized ones, raises for me the question of whether there really are clear-cut ontological distinctions between live forms and mediatized ones. Although my initial arguments may seem to rest on the assumption that there are, ultimately I find that not to be the case. If live performance cannot be shown to be economically independent of, immune from contamination by, and ontologically different from mediatized forms, in what sense can liveness function as a site of cultural and ideological resistance, as Bogosian, Phelan, and others claim?

6 Noël Carroll (1998: 187–8) also discusses this process, with specific reference to the ways in which some popular art forms were incorporated into art forms based in technologies of mass reproduction.

Chapter 2 presents an overview of these issues and a general consideration of the status of live performance in a culture dominated by mass media. I begin with a discussion of the relationship between theatre and early television in the United States to show that television originally modeled itself on the live form. This historical narrative serves as an allegory for the general cultural tendency of mediatized forms to displace and replace live ones. I then examine the more recent phenomenon of live events modeling themselves on mediatized representations, in a reversal of the previous historical pattern. I then turn to the way in which the issue of live performance is treated in contemporary performance theory and challenge its grounding of the distinction between the live and the mediatized in ostensible ontological differences between live and mediatized forms. Against that formulation, I argue that the relationship between live and mediatized forms and the meaning of liveness be understood as historical and contingent rather than determined by immutable differences. To conclude this chapter, I examine several of the conventional explanations for why people still value live performance and raise the question of how much longer this will remain the case.

Chapter 3 offers a case study of the meaning of liveness within one particular cultural formation, that surrounding rock music. Because rock exists primarily as recorded music and only secondarily as live performance (see Gracyk 1996), this cultural context is a particularly interesting one in which to examine the functions and values attributed to live performance. My task, then, is to offer an explanation of what functions live performance once served within rock culture, and to show how those functions changed following the expanded mediatization of rock represented by music video. Considering these issues leads me to discuss some of rock's institutional discourses especially that of the Grammy awards, and the crisis precipitated by the Milli Vanilli scandal. The chapter concludes with a Baudrillardian analysis of Milli Vanilli in the context of the technological and legal changes affecting the music industry in the 1980s.

Chapter 4 resumes the critique of liveness as a site of cultural and ideological resistance begun in Chapter 2, this time by way of a discussion of the status of live performance in two fields of American jurisprudence. I begin with an examination of the effort in the early 1970s to instate prerecorded videotape trials and discuss the failure of that effort in terms of the law's preference for live courtroom proceedings, a preference that is deeply rooted in constitutional and procedural issues. My purpose there is to show that the legal arena has proved more resistant to the incursion of mediatization than the other cultural sites examined here. I then turn to copyright law. I discuss copyright in Chapter 2 in the context of the music industry; in Chapter 4, it is pivotal to a discussion of the legal status of live performance. After showing that live performance does, in fact, escape legal control in the context of copyright, I argue that, nevertheless, this escape does not make performance a privileged site of resistance to the law. Whereas an influential strain of performance theory suggests that live performance's disappearance and persistence only in spectatorial memory make it a site of resistance to the authority of law, I argue that those very same qualities make performance available and useful to the law as both a policed site and a mechanism of regulation. Live performance and its putative ontology of disappearance (which I challenged on other grounds in Chapter 1) are in fact central to the theory and practice of American law. Indeed, the legal arena may be one of the few remaining cultural contexts in which live performance is still considered essential.

I hope this study will be received in the speculative spirit in which it is offered. Drawing on a mixed bag of disciplines, including media theory, cultural theory, sociology, performance studies, and legal studies, it is the product of what Jacques Attali (1985: 5) calls "theoretical indiscipline." Although I have made some effort to ground my arguments in material realities, I have not hesitated to invoke barely supported (or supportable) generalizations. I have also not tried to impose a strict consistency on the book's three main sections. Although certain issues recur, arguments that may be important in the context of the broad overview offered in Chapter 2 may not carry as much weight in the more specific contexts examined in the other two chapters, and vice-versa. Above all, I am aware of a certain tendentiousness in my arguments, which leads, as Attali (1985: 4) says of his own work, to "unusual and unacceptable conclusions." I trust, however, that there is a sense in which these unacceptable conclusions articulate some small truths of our cultural situation

2

LIVE PERFORMANCE IN A MEDIATIZED CULTURE

In his autobiography, John Densmore (1991), the drummer for the rock group the Doors, recounts an anecdote concerning an early television appearance by the group, probably in 1967. Having taped an appearance on a variety show, the Doors wanted to be able to watch themselves on television. They therefore requested that a set be placed in their backstage dressing room the night their performance was to be broadcast. Because their segment had not yet come on when they were ready to begin their concert, they took the television set onstage with them, perching it atop an amplifier with the volume turned off. When the Doors finally appeared on the television, they stopped playing mid-song, turned up the television volume, and sat on the floor of the stage watching themselves, their backs to the audience. When their segment was over, they resumed playing.

By staging their relationship to television in this way in 1967, the Doors revealed their prescience concerning what would be happening in the relationship between live and mediatized performance. There are several harbingers to be noted in this anecdote, particularly the presentation of a previously recorded event as live; the incorporation of video into the live event; and the precedence of the mediatized over the live, even for the performers themselves. Now, thirty years later, we are well into a period of cultural history defined by the domination of mediatized representations. My concern here is with the situation of live performance within that mediatized environment. I begin with an historical account of the early relationship between television and theatre in the United States, which I present as an allegory for the general relationship of live to mediatized forms within our cultural economy. Initially, mediatized events were modeled on live ones. The subsequent cultural dominance of mediatization has had the ironic result that live events now frequently are modeled on the very mediatized representations that once took the self-same live events as their models. After presenting this allegory, I will turn to the present day to describe what I see as a pattern of increased incursion of mediatization into live events themselves. I go on to discuss the way in which performance theory continues to characterize the relationship between the live and the mediatized as one of opposition, despite the erosion of the differences between them.

Although I have stated that the relationship between the live and the mediatized is one of competitive opposition at the level of cultural economy, I do not see that opposition as deriving from the intrinsic characteristics of live and mediatized forms but, rather, as determined by cultural and historical contingencies. Through an examination of what may be called the ontological characteristics of live and mediatized performances, an examination which begins with the discussion of early television and theatre that opens the chapter, I will argue against intrinsic opposition and in favor of a view that emphasizes the mutual dependence of the live and the mediatized and that challenges the traditional assumption that the live precedes the mediatized. Throughout this chapter, I emphasize large contextual and cultural issues in the hope of creating a theoretical and historical framework for understanding the current relationship of the live and the mediatized.

Teevee's playhouse

Although I stated in the previous chapter that I consider television, not film, to be the dominant cultural medium of the second half of the twentieth century, the historical relationship of theatre to film provides a precedent for the pattern of development I am describing and is therefore worthy of some attention. Early film modeled itself directly on theatrical practice. As A. Nicholas Vardac shows in his classic study *Stage to Screen* (1949), the narrative structures and visual devices of cinema, including the close-up and the fade-in/fade-out, and parallel editing, had all been fully developed on stage before becoming the foundations of the new medium's language, at least in its narrative forms. Steele MacKaye, for example, embarked on a series of technical innovations, beginning in the late 1870s, that brought greater flexibility to the stage in ways that anticipated cinematic techniques. To cite but one example, his "proscenium adjuster," a device that instantly changed the shape and size of the proscenium opening, enabled smooth transitions between scenes and among different views of the same setting. "In this way, MacKaye could control the type of stage picture offered, in the fashion of the motion picture with its long or medium shot, its panoramic or tracking shot" (Vardac 1949: 143). In their more recent look at the relationship between early film and the stage, Ben Brewster and Lea Jacobs disagree with Vardac's character-ization of nineteenth-century theatre as: "'proto-cinematic,' as attempting to be cinematic without the appropriate technology" (Brewster and Jacobs 1997: 214). But they agree with Vardac concerning the profound influence of theatrical practice on early cinema: "The development of cinematic staging and editing in the 1910s were not attempts to lay the basis for a specifically cinematic approach to narration, but the pursuit of goals well-established in nineteenth-century theatre with new means" (ibid.: 210). "[T]he cinema," they conclude, "strove to be theatrical" (ibid.: 214). Early cinema took over and reformed a theatrical vocabulary and also rapidly usurped the theatre's cultural position as the dominant form of enter-tainment. Indeed, film had so thoroughly routed the theatre by 1926 that there was little left to pillage when television arrived in force some twenty years later (Poggi 1968: 85–6). In these respects, the historical relationship between television and theatre, and the general situation of live performance in our mediatized culture, merely recapit-ulate this earlier history.

There can be no question that the advent of film had a devastating cultural–economic impact on the theatre, but that fact, taken by itself, leaves an important question unanswered. If the theatre as a popular form had been so thoroughly usurped by film in the 1920s that it was hardly even a force to be reckoned with when television came around, *why* did television "[embrace] the theatre as a model for representa-tion" (Spigel 1992: 142) as the cinema itself had done in its earliest days, rather than model itself on film? As a camera-bound medium, television might well have striven to be cinematic; in fact, it strove to be theatrical. The answer to this question lies in the way in which the essence of the televisual was understood, from television's earliest appearances, as an ontology of liveness more akin to the ontology of theatre than to that of film. Television's essence was seen in its ability to transmit events as they occur, not in a filmic capacity to record events for later viewing. Originally, of course, all television broadcasts were live transmissions. Jane Feuer (1983) argues that the definition of television as an ontologically live medium remains part of our funda-mental conception of the medium – even though television ceased long ago to be live in an ontological sense, it remains so in an ideolog-ical sense. Rick Altman (1986: 45) has made a similar observation: "whether the events transmitted by television are live or not, the tele-vision experience itself is...sensed as live by the home viewing audience."[1] The fact that television can "go live" at any moment to convey sight and sound at a distance in a way no other medium can remains a crucial part of the televisual imaginary even though that way of using the medium is now the exception rather than the rule.[2]

It is my contention that this ideologically engrained sense of television as a live medium makes its historical relationship to the theatre different from that of film, and enabled television to colonize liveness, the one aspect of theatrical presentation that film could not replicate. Vardac shows how film remediated theatre by adopting the narrative structures and visual strategies of nineteenth-century melodrama. Whereas film could only remediate the theatre at these structural levels, television could remediate theatre at the ontological level through its claim to immediacy. It is also significant in this context that television not only remediates live performance, it remediates film in a way that film has never remediated television.[3] Although

---

1 Steve Wurtzler makes the point that:

> the textual practices of American television present themselves as, or are experienced in ways similar to, the fully present live....even the recorded programs of broadcast television are assigned a sense of spatial co-presence and temporal simultaneity in that, once a program has aired in its scheduled time slot, there is little or no chance of viewing it outside of its initial temporal and spatial (channel) context.
>
> (Wurtzler 1992: 91)

Wurtzler (ibid.: 259) implies in a note that time-shifting by means of VCRs has made this effect even more pronounced. The impulse to tape programs for later viewing only emphasizes the extent to which we think of them as fleeting, one-time, quasi-live events.

2 Margaret Morse observes that the imaginary developing around interactive computer technologies also entails an ideology of liveness whose source lies in our interaction with the machine itself rather than the interaction with the outside world permitted by the machine.

> Feedback in the broadest sense…is a capacity of a machine to signal or seem to respond to input instantaneously. A machine that thus "interacts" with the user even at this minimal level can produce a feeling of "liveness" and a sense of the machine's agency and – because it exchanges symbols – even of a subjective encounter with a persona.
>
> (Morse 1998:15)

3 There are very few cases in which television becomes film in the same way that film becomes television when it is broadcast or played on a video cassette. One such instance is the film *The Groove Tube* (1974), a counter-cultural parody of television shot originally on videotape then transferred to film. Clearly, there were stylistic reasons for doing this, as is often the case when film directors use video transfer as a

television was originally dependent on cinematic technology (the kinescope) for its own reproduction,[4] the advent of videotape liberated television and gave it the means of transforming film into a televisual discourse to the point that, by now, much of our experience of "film" is actually a televisual experience (of video). Television "does not simply 'transport' previous forms (theatre, film, radio) but rather translates them and recombines them," thus turning them into something different: television itself (Dienst 1994: 142).

Television broadcasting was inaugurated in the United States in 1939, when the National Broadcasting Company (NBC), the Columbia Broadcasting System (CBS), and Dumont all began broadcasting diverse programming in New York City. By 1940, there were twenty-three television stations actively broadcasting in the country (Ritchie 1994: 92). Along with the manufacture of radio receivers and sound recordings, television programming was curtailed in 1942 with the entry of the United States into World War II. Television experienced a resurgence after the war, beginning in 1946 when sets became widely available to the public. The first television era in the United States, then, occurred between 1939 and 1945, for although programming and the industrial development of television were truncated by the war effort, the discourse on television remained lively during the war years. This first phase of television was characterized by experimentation, speculation, and debate. From 1947 onward, television broadcasting coalesced into the industry we know today.

One of the central concerns of the discourse on television in the United States during its earliest phases was the relationship of televi-

---

technique. The historical context of this particular remediation is also important. Since the ideology of the counter-cultural audience it hoped to reach rejected television as a necessarily co-opted medium but found film to be credible, *The Groove Tube* had to look like television, the object of its satire, but also had to establish its identity as a *film* and thus distinguish itself from its source medium. I return to the counter-cultural rejection of television in another context in Chapter 3.

4 An early version of the kinescope was the Paramount Intermediate Film System, in which a television image was recorded on motion picture film, then processed and projected immediately (the delay from reception to projection was 66 seconds). Douglas Gomery (1985: 56–7) describes this process as an early form of projection television. Arguably, it can also be seen as a filmic remediation of television. Although the content shown derives from a television signal, the actual perceptual experience is of a filmed image, not a televisual one. By incorporating television technology, the Paramount system gave film nearly the same immediacy that was foregrounded as the essence of television in the early descriptions of that medium discussed here.

14

sion to other forms of entertainment and communication, particularly radio, film, and theatre. Television was often described as a hybrid of existing forms. One analyst characterized television as a "new and synthetic medium...radio with sight, movies with the zest of immediacy, theatre (intimate or spectacular) with all seats about six rows back and in the centre, tabloid opera and circus without peanut vendors" (Wade 1944: 728). The question, in the words of Hans Burger (1940: 209), was "whether or not television is...a new complex of existing arts, or an art in its own right. And if it is an art, what are its essential techniques and possibilities?" In the opinion of Kay Reynolds (1942: 121), "an authentically television form" had not yet been discovered.

Although the question of authentic television form remained unresolved, early writers on television generally agreed that television's essential properties as a medium are *immediacy* and *intimacy*. As Lenox Lohr, the president of NBC, put it, "the most utilitarian feature of television lies in broadcasting events *exactly when and as they happen*" (Lohr 1940: 52, original emphasis). Orrin E. Dunlap's later description is even more emphatic: "People now look upon scenes never before within their range; they see politics as practiced, sports as played, drama as enacted, news as it happens, history as it is made" (Dunlap 1947: 8). In an essay of 1937, Alfred N. Goldsmith, an industrial engineer, compares television, film, and human vision in these terms:

> As far as ocular vision is concerned, a real event can be seen only at the instant of occurrence....Accordingly all the historical past is lost so far as direct vision by human beings is concerned. The motion picture suffers from no such limitation. [T]he motion picture may be made at any time and shown at any later time....Television with direct pick-up of an actual event is as dependent on its time of occurrence as is the eye.
> (Goldsmith 1937: 55)

Here, film is represented as the realm of memory, repetition, and displacement in time. By contrast, television, like direct human vision (and also like theatre, as Goldsmith (1937: 56) observes later in his essay) occurs only in the now. Unlike film, but like theatre, a television broadcast is characterized as a performance in the present. This was literally the case in the early days of television when most material was broadcast live. Even now that most television programming is prerecorded, the television image remains a performance in the present in an important sense I shall discuss later in this chapter. Although the possibility of recording television broadcasts was available as part of television technology from quite early in its development, the capacity for rebroadcasting was seen then as ancillary to television's essence as a live medium. In the 1930s and 1940s, television was envisioned primarily as a medium devoted to the transmission of ongoing live events, not to reproduction. Not surprisingly, early television displayed a voracious appetite for all types of live presentations. A survey of the activity of one pioneering television station (WRGB in Schenectady, New York) between 1939 and 1945 lists among its offerings: variety shows and revues; sports; drama, including amateur and college theatricals; light opera; various musical groups; dance; news; panel discussions; educational presentations; fashion shows; puppet shows; quizzes and games; vaudeville acts, monologists, and magicians; children's shows; religious shows; and commercials (Dupuy 1945).

Television's intimacy was seen as a function of its immediacy – the close proximity of viewer to event that it enables – and the fact that events from outside are transmitted into the viewer's home. As Lohr (1940: 3) put it, "the viewer of the television scene feels himself to be on the scene." The position of the television viewer relative to the image on the screen was often compared with that of a boxing fan sitting ringside or a theatre-goer with the best seat in the house. Television "make[s] all the world a stage and every home a front-row seat for sports, drama, and news" (Dunlap 1947: 8). Television was thought to make the home into a kind of theatre characterized, paradoxically, by both absolute intimacy and global reach.

Given the domestic context in which television was envisioned,[5] it is important to sketch the social implications of the home theatre.[6]

---

5 Lohr (1940) treats television as a domestic technology, thus implying that the uses of the technology had been decided definitively that early. In fact, the situation was somewhat more complicated. As Gomery (1985) has shown, Hollywood's major motion picture corporations hatched a scheme in the late 1940s to co-opt television by installing television projection equipment in movie theatres and offering programming, including live coverage of sports and newsworthy public events, to a paying public in those venues. This experiment, known as theatre television, proved not to be cost-effective and was abandoned in the early 1950s.

6 Lynn Spigel (1992: 99, 106–9) traces the phrase "home theatre" and the concept it embodies as far back as 1912 and discusses how, in the period after World War II, suburban homeowners were encouraged to construct their television viewing areas on the model of a theatre. It is significant that throughout the first half of the twentieth century, the home theatre was imagined as a domestic version of the dramatic stage. Now, in the waning years of the twentieth century, that phrase is used to describe equipment intended to transport the experience of the cinema, not that of live theatre, into the home.

Spigel (1992: 110) argues persuasively that the new medium was associated with an existing cultural discourse, dating back to the mid-1800s, in which "electrical communications would defuse the threat of cultural difference by limiting experiences and placing social encounters into safe, familiar, and predictable contexts." By the early 1920s, "radio, like the telegraph and telephone before it, was seen as an instrument of social sanitation" that would make cultural objects more generally accessible, but in a way that would also keep "undesirables away from the middle-classes." In the postwar era, Spigel (1992: 111) goes on to say, "the fantasy of antiseptic, electrical space was transposed onto television." That the linkage between television and the discourse of antiseptic electrical space occurred in the context of the growing suburbanization of the postwar period is evident from the following quotation, from a 1958 book entitled, strikingly, A Primer for Playgoers, in which the author stresses:

> the tremendous personal comfort of relaxing at home in an easy chair and seeing some of the top names in the theatre world perform in a variety of three or four programs in a single evening. This involves a greater degree of physical comfort than to come home weary from the day's work, wash, dress, hurry, drive through heavy traffic, find a place to park, walk to the theatre, pay an ever-increasing admission, sit on the same seat for two hours, then fight traffic and arrive home very late.
>
> (Wright 1958: 222–3)

Here, the benefit of television-as-theatre over live performance is defined explicitly in terms of the suburban experience. Tichi notes that this understanding of television was frequently reiterated in advertisements for television sets:

> Numerous advertisements…showed couples in evening attire gathered in their living rooms as if in a private box at the theatre, and gazing in rapt attention at on-screen ballet, opera, or drama from the legitimate stage. Television in the living room was thus offered…as an excursion out of the household and into an expensive private box for an experience of high culture.
>
> (Tichi 1991: 94; see also Spigel 1992: 126)

Descriptions of drama on television from this period emphasize that television's immediacy and intimacy make the experience of televised

drama entirely comparable to that of drama in the theatre. (By televised drama, I mean plays written or adapted for television, not direct
broadcasts of theatre events. Although such broadcasts did occur, it
was generally conceded that direct transmission of a play in the theatre
yielded unsatisfactory television.[7]) In an article in *Theatre Arts*, Mary
Hunter (1949: 46) observes that "the audience experience in relation
to the performer is similar in television to the performer–audience relationship in the theatre: the audience is in direct contact with the
performer at the moment of his 'performance.' You see him when he
does it." Lohr (1940: 72), writing almost a decade earlier, actually
makes the immediacy of televised drama the basis on which to distinguish television from film: "the instantaneous nature of the broadcast
gives television drama a certain superiority over filmed drama. The
spectator knows that he is seeing something actually taking place at
the moment."[8] (Lohr (1940: 80–1) advances the same argument to
assert the superiority of televised news over the filmed newsreel.)
Spigel summarizes this discourse:

> Television, it was constantly argued, would be a better approx-
> imation of live entertainment than any previous form of
> technological reproduction. Its ability to broadcast direct to
> the home would allow people to feel as if they really were at
> the theatre....Whereas film allowed spectators imaginatively
> to project themselves *into a scene*, television would give people
> the sense of being *on the scene* of presentation – it would simu-
> late the entire experience of being at the theatre.
>
> ⸙ (Spigel 1992: 138–9, original emphasis)

I want to emphasize the implications of this last statement, as I shall go
on to argue that the goal of televised drama was not merely to convey a

---

7   For a useful overview of theatrical presentations on television from the 1940s
    through the 1980s, see Rose (1986).
8   The immediacy of televised drama was harrowing for actors. Even as seasoned a
    trouper as Jose Ferrer (1949: 47), writing of his first television appearance (as
    Cyrano de Bergerac on the Philco Television Playhouse in 1949), described the
    "'this-is-it' feeling" of performing on television as "a bad psychological handicap."
    This insecurity was apparently brought on by television's characteristically brief
    rehearsal period and the absence of a prompter. Television production manuals of
    the 1940s monotonously repeat the assertion that a basic requirement for television
    actors is the ability to memorize lines, leading one to speculate about the exact state
    of the art of acting in the United States at the time.

theatrical event to the viewer, but to recreate the theatrical experience for the home viewer through televisual discourse and, thus, to *replace* live performance.

As significant as this habitual representation of television as theatre and the notion that televised drama partakes of the immediacy of drama in the theatre is the suggestion that emerges from the early commentary that television production techniques themselves evolved in a conscious effort to reproduce the theatrical image. In commenting on the television actor, Lohr observes:

> In a theatre, each actor assumes that the audience has as wide-angle vision as he possesses, but he must be taught that a television camera does not see at such wide angles....For this reason, television producers have found it helpful to use more than one camera for studio productions. This enables a tele-viewer to see a continuous action.
>
> (Lohr 1940: 56)

The multiple-camera set-up enables the television image to recreate the perceptual continuity of the theatre. Switching from camera to camera allows the television director to replicate the effect of the theatre spectator's wandering eye: "the eye, while observing a stage set...makes its own changes to various parts of the scene to maintain interest, whereas in television the camera must take the eye to various points of interest in the scene" (ibid.: 55). One way of objecting to Lohr's characterization of television editing would be to say that televisual discourse fails to replicate the perceptual discourse of the spectator's eye because whereas in the theatre spectators direct their own vision, the television camera does not permit them to choose their own perspectives. In her article explaining why stage directors might make good television directors, however, Hunter implicitly responds to such an objection by suggesting that the spectator's gaze is always directed in the theatre by means of focal points in the staging that are equivalent to camera views. Hunter compares the stage director's manipulation of audience attention with the television director's use of the camera, saying that: "the [stage] director's approach to movement on the stage is to apply something of a 'psychological' camera eye. He must direct the audience's attention about the stage precisely as the camera moves from one point of interest to the next" (Hunter 1949: 47).

These observations are striking because they suggest that the multiple-camera set-up deploying three to five cameras simultaneously, still the standard way in which television studio productions are shot, evolved specifically out of a desire to replicate the visual discourse of the spectator's experience of theatre. In a provocative comparison of television and film editing, Burger explains in detail why the image produced by the multiple-camera set-up is theatrical rather than cinematic:

> This shifting between cameras has a purpose similar to cutting in the movies. It divides the scene into different views of the same object, thus affording a greater variety. Actually, however, the effect of television cutting is quite different. Since the cameras are placed almost in one line, and since the settings resemble bas–reliefs more than the three-dimensional sets of the films, the possibility for variety among the shots is strictly limited. If the angles of the cameras are changed they run the danger of catching each other or the low-hanging mike in their line of vision; and counter-shots are, as yet, almost impossible because there is no background for them. Therefore, although the television camera shifts, it does not show a *new* angle of the scene or tell *more* about the actors. What happens is essentially the same as in the occasional use of opera glasses in the theatre; the *frame* of the picture is changed, but the angle is the same.
>
> (Burger 1940: 209, original emphasis)

Susan Sontag contrasts theatre and film by asserting that whereas "theatre is confined to a logical or *continuous* use of space[,] cinema…has access to an alogical or *discontinuous* use of space" (Sontag 1966: 29, original emphasis). Burger suggests that the limited camera work possible in early television created an effect of spatial continuity more comparable to the theatre than to cinema. That television editing appears as a reframing of a single, continuous image from a fixed point of view, rather than a suturing of image to image or a shift in point of view, also asserts the immediacy, the sense of a continuous perceptual experience unfolding in real time, that television shares with theatre.

It is important to acknowledge that the resemblance of televisual discourse to theatrical discourse was strongest at this early stage of the development of broadcast television, when live presentation of drama and other televised events was the norm, and the technology itself was sufficiently clumsy that it could not easily replicate cinematic discourse. Because of their relative immobility, the cameras were arranged along a single axis parallel to the width of the playing area, and their movements were highly restricted. In an article on directing ballet for television, Paul Belanger (1946: 8–9), a director of dance programs for CBS, catalogues the types of shots available to television cameras: all are either pans, "tongues" (i.e., vertical pans), or trucking shots. In the diagrams that accompany the article, the two cameras are always placed outside and in front of the performance space. This set-up illustrates the fact that in this earliest phase of American broadcast television, all shows were shot "in proscenium" (see Barker 1987 [1985]); the cameras never entered the playing space to produce reverse angles (Burger's "counter-shots"). As a result, the television image was frontal and oriented toward the viewer in much the same way as a performance on a proscenium stage would be. This was reflected in the actors' playing, which Burger describes as "aimed...at the fourth wall" in front of the cameras "much as it is on stage" (Burger 1940: 209).

As television technology quickly became more sophisticated and television cameras more nimble, televisual discourse aspired less to the theatrical and more to the cinematic. To Murray Bolen, the author of a postwar book entitled *Fundamentals of Television*, immediacy was no longer clearly fundamental to the medium. Acknowledging that champions of televisual immediacy have a valid point, Bolen (1950: 190) nevertheless demurs that "we cannot be sure as yet that the instantaneous element of immediacy is really that much of television" and goes on to deduce from the success of prerecorded radio programs that "canned" television shows are quite likely to attract an audience. A television production textbook of 1953 makes the relationship between the changed capacity of television technology and the transition from a theatrical to a cinematic paradigm explicit:

> The question has been commonly asked: Why cannot the television medium transmit a stage play to the home audience, capturing the immediacy of the performance instead of attempting to simulate the motion picture? Perhaps if a play were televised in one continuous long shot with the proscenium arch of the stage constantly visible, the effect of a stage play would be retained. As soon as the cameras are brought onto the stage, however, and proceed to break the action down into close-ups, two-shots, reverse angles, and so forth, the show no longer resembles a play but has become a motion picture. The television medium is a medium of the camera and as such has departed almost as far from the live theatre as has the medium of film.
>
> (Bretz 1953: 3)

Once the cameras could enter the set and shoot from reverse angles, the syntax of televisual discourse became that of cinematic discourse, though it is probably not coincidental that these comments were made around the time (1951–2) when television production was beginning to switch over from live broadcasting to film production and, consequently, from New York City to Hollywood (Barnouw 1990: 133–4). For Bretz, who embraces the cinematic paradigm for television, to replicate theatrical discourse on television means to present a static television image. But, as we have seen, the more imaginative television conceptualists of the previous decades felt that replicating theatrical discourse on television meant replicating the discourse of the spectator's shifting eye, not that of the static proscenium.

As television production practice moved away from honoring the ontology of televisual immediacy and its links with theatrical discourse, televisual appropriations of theatrical discourse ironically became simultaneously more overt and more vestigial. Fictional shows shot cinematically still represented themselves as theatre through the use of dramatic convention rather than by using the camera to replicate the perceptual experience of the theatre spectator. The so-called "Golden Age" of television, which began after World War II and lasted through the 1950s, saw a spate of drama anthology shows with theatrical names, including The Kraft Television Theatre, Ford Theatre, Playhouse 90, The Philco TV Playhouse, and Goodyear TV Playhouse (see Barnouw 1990: 154–67). In the early 1960s, the practice of making episodes of such hourlong dramatic series as *The Fugitive* and *The Man from U.N.C.L.E.* into "plays" by giving each episode a title and dividing it into "acts" became prominent. Even as the American theatre moved closer to making the streamlined two-act play its normal product, television drama remained wedded to an Ibsenian four-act structure because of the segmentation imposed upon it by the requirements of advertisers. The laughtrack and the practice of announcing that programs are "filmed before a live studio audience" are more recent techniques of theatricalizing television. It is ironic that in the 1930s and 40s, when television practice was most faithful to the medium's ontological immediacy, television studios could not accommodate audiences; the programs were directed exclusively to the home audience. The current practice of taping before "a live studio audience" is a simulation, rather than a replication, of the conditions of live theatrical production. The presence of the studio audience on the television screen and soundtrack implies that the program is a record of a real event. Because the programs are edited, however, the home audience does not see the same performance as the studio audience, but sees a performance that never took place.

An important theme emerges from this glimpse at history. For Raymond Williams (1992 [1974]: 19), "when the question of [early television's] content was raised, it was resolved, in the main, parasitically." Television was imagined *as theatre*, not just in the sense that it could convey theatrical events to the viewer, but also in that it offered to replicate the visual and experiential discourse of theatre in the antiseptic space of the suburban home theatre. Television, as parasite, strangled its host by offering itself not as an extension of the theatrical experience but as an equivalent *replacement* for that experience. As the passage from A *Primer for Playgoers* I quoted above suggests, the implication of the cultural discourse surrounding television was that one should watch television *instead* of going to the theatre. The televisual experience is implicitly equated with the live theatrical experience, but is represented as better suited to the postwar, suburban lifestyle: the message is that nothing is lost, and much is gained, by staying home.

This assumption translated into very concrete economic effects on the market for live performance. In their pioneering 1966 study of the economic situation of the performing arts, Baumol and Bowen (1966: 245) analyze live performance's competition with television by pointing out that between 1948 and 1952, the years in which television became widely available, consumer spending generally rose by 23 per cent, but admissions to live performances rose only by 5 per cent. "In sum," the authors conclude, "it seems clear that the mass media have made inroads into the audience for live performance." Television's usurpation of the cultural–economic position formerly enjoyed by live media such as theatre was not simply the result of the generalized mediatization of our society. Television's specific ability to position itself as theatre's replacement has its origins in the claims of immediacy made on behalf of television throughout its development, and in television's claim to replicate theatrical discourse. What is true of the relationship between television and theatre is true, by allegorical extension, of the general cultural relationship of the televisual and mediatized to the live: the ideology of liveness that the televisual (the cultural dominant) inherited from television (the medium) has enabled it to displace and replace live performance in a wide variety of cultural contexts.

Is it live, or...?

To move from a discussion of the early relationship between theatre and television to an examination of the current situation of live performance is to confront the irony that whereas television initially sought to replicate and, implicitly, to replace live theatre, live performance itself has developed since that time toward the replication of the discourse of mediatization. This phenomenon is understandable in terms of the historical logic of remediation discussed in Chapter 1. While new technologies remediate older ones, as film and television both remediated theatre, "earlier technologies are struggling to maintain their legitimacy by remediating newer ones" (Bolter and Grusin 1996: 352).[9] The multiple ways in which live performance now endeavors to replicate television, video, and film provide vivid examples.[10]

Live performance now often incorporates mediatization such that the live event itself is a product of media technologies. This has been the case to some degree for a long time, of course: as soon as electric amplification is used, one might say that an event is mediatized. What we actually hear is the vibration of a speaker, a reproduction by technological means of a sound picked up by a microphone, not the original (live) acoustic event. Recently, however, this effect has been intensified across a very wide range of performance genres and cultural contexts, from the giant television screens at sports arenas to the video apparatus used in much performance art. The spectator sitting in the back rows of a Rolling Stones or Bruce Springsteen concert or even a Bill Cosby stand-up comedy performance, is present at a live performance, but hardly participates in it as such since his/her main experience of the performance is to read it off a video monitor.

---

9   Vsevolod Meyerhold, the Soviet theatre director, actively promoted this phenomenon. Noting in an essay of 1929–30 (Meyerhold 1969 [1930]: 254–6) that "the cinema is attracting far greater audiences than any other type of theatre," he called for the "cinefication" of the theatre: "Give us the chance to work in a theatre incorporating modern techniques and capable of meeting the demands which our conception of the theatrical spectacle will create, and we shall stage productions which will attract just as many spectators as the cinema." Meyerhold's analysis was based, however, in a faulty perception of film's position in cultural economy. He saw sound film as an attempt by the cinema "to compete with the theatre, with live actors [...by] furnishing the screen with dialogue." This attempt was doomed to failure, in his view, because film's strength – and its international appeal – was as a visual, not a verbal, medium. When film acquired language, Meyerhold believed, it lost its universality. He felt that once the theatre could offer visual spectacle comparable to the cinema, an audience craving both that spectacle and words would flock back to the theatre.

10   One amusing example of live theatre's replication of film (at least of a particular way of watching movies is the Wolfskill Theater in Los Angeles. The Wolfskill is a drive-in theatre that features live performance – audiences watch plays from the comfort of their cars and listen to the actors' voices over their car radios (Associated Press, "Car culture brakes for live theater," Atlanta Constitution, 18 August 1998: C9).

Spectators at many sporting events now watch significant portions of the games they are attending on giant video screens. The rhetoric of mediatization embedded in such devices as the instant replay, the "simulcast," and the close-up, at one time understood to be secondary elaborations of what was originally a live event, are now constitutive of the live event itself. The games – their scheduling, the distribution of time within them, their rules, and so forth – have themselves been molded by their entry into the economy of repetition, which demands that the form of the games as live events be determined by the requirements of mediatization. Given these conditions, "attending a live performance…these days is often roughly the experience of watching a small, noisy TV set in a large, crowded field" (Goodwin 1990: 269).

The theatre, too, has experienced this attenuated incursion of media technology. The set for the 1995 Broadway revival of *How to Succeed in Business without Really Trying*, for example, was "a wall composed of thirty-two projection cubes showing a video of computer-generated three-dimensional images" (von Hoffman 1995: 132). In the theatre, as at the stadium, you are often watching television even when attending the live event, and audiences now expect live performances to resemble mediatized ones. The celebrated helicopter effect in *Miss Saigon*, to choose but one small example, represents a direct importation of cinematic or televisual realism into the theatre. As theatre designer Wendall K. Harrington has said, "theatre-goers today have been raised on television. They have a cinematic vocabulary that one must deal with" (quoted in von Hoffman 1995: 132). This development lends credence to Patrice Pavis's claim that "the formation…of audience taste by television necessarily rebounds on the future audience for theatre, particularly in the demand for realism" (Pavis 1992: 121).

Not only are theatre audiences seeing live performances that resemble mediatized ones as closely as possible, they are also apparently modeling their responses to the live event on those expected of them by television. Ethan Mordden, quoted in an article analyzing the ubiquity of standing ovations on Broadway, offers the opinion that "audience reactions at live performances are so programmed as to seem canned, and…theatre audiences, emulating those in television studios, appear to applaud on cue" (Peter Marks, "Standing room only (and that's not good)," *New York Times*, December 8 1995, sec. H: 5). Of course, audience response has been the object of manipulation throughout the history of theatre; the organized claques employed from the ancient Roman theatre at least through the dawn of the twentieth century were a central mechanism of such manipulation (see Esslin 1977: 64 for a useful summary of this phenomenon). It is tempting to draw a parallel between claques and the "Applause" signs used in television studios as mechanisms for cuing audience response, but it is likely that the more recent model is the proximate cause of contemporary audience behavior. Even in the absence of "Applause" signs, contemporary spectators respond in a programmed fashion, as if they were a television studio audience. Arguably, theatre audiences today respond spontaneously to the same sorts of cues that would be signaled by means of the "Applause" sign in a television studio because the studio audience has become the culturally engrained model for what gets applause and how audiences behave.[11]

Just as mediatization is reflected in the presence of the apparatus of reproduction in the live setting, so too is it reflected in the forms and cultural positions of performance. In his book on the political economy of music, Jacques Attali offers a useful description of the cultural economy in which performance currently takes place. He distinguishes an economy based on *representation* from one based on *repetition*:

> Stated very simply, representation in the system of commerce is that which arises from a singular act; repetition is that which is mass-produced. Thus, a concert is a representation, but also a meal à la carte in a restaurant; a phonograph record or a can of food is repetition.
>
> (Attali 1985: 41)

In his historical analysis, Attali points out that although "representation emerged with capitalism" when the sponsorship of concerts became a profitable enterprise and not merely the prerogative of a feudal lord, capital ultimately "los[t] interest in the economy of representation" (ibid.). Repetition, the mass-production of cultural objects, held greater promise for capital because whereas "in representation, a work is generally heard only once – it is a unique moment[,] in repetition, potential hearings are stockpiled" (ibid.). By being recorded and becoming mediatized, performance becomes an accumulable value. Live performance exists within the economy of repetition largely either to promote mass-produced cultural objects – the primary economic

---

11 Altman (1986: 47) describes what he calls television's "internal audiences," which can be studio audiences, newscasters, announcers, commentators, or even characters on fictional programs. The reactions of the internal audiences focus viewer attention and response by functioning as a "sign that someone else thinks an important phenomenon is taking place on the screen," thus manipulating viewer attention.

function of popular music concerts is to promote the sales of recordings, for example – or to serve as raw material for mediatization, as
when live theatre productions are staged in order to be reproduced on
television.[12]

I first became aware of the imbrication of theatre within the
economy of repetition in the early 1980s when I noticed that a number
of the Broadway productions I was seeing had been underwritten in
part by cable television money with the understanding that taped
versions of the productions would appear later on cable networks.[13]
Whether by conscious intention or not, the productions themselves
(particularly their sets, but also their staging) were clearly "camera-
ready" – pre-adjusted to the aspect ratio, intimate scale, and relative
lack of detail of the television image – a suspicion borne out when I
later saw the televised version of one of them. This is a particularly
explicit example of the historical reversal I mentioned earlier. In a
process driven by the economics of cultural production, television,
which initially modeled itself on the theatre, especially in dramatic

---

12 To an ever greater extent, live performances are economically tied to mediatization.
In the case of professional sports, for instance, the live game can take place because
of the income the teams receive from the companies that broadcast the game, who
derive income, in turn, from advertising during the game. In many instances, the
same capital interests are behind both live and mediatized cultural objects. This is
true of the Broadway productions underwritten by cable television companies that I
discuss below. Disney's *Beauty and the Beast*, also mentioned below, is another
example: Disney has produced the same material as an animated film for theatres
and video cassettes, live productions, sound recordings, toys, and so on. In these
instances, the economic success or failure of any one cultural object is much less
important than the profit derived from the whole package. This has always been the
case for popular music concerts. In many instances, the concerts themselves do not
turn a profit (which is one reason why they are now usually underwritten by spon-
sors from outside the music industry). They do, however, serve to advertise
recordings that, if successful, will be enormously profitable and more than make up
for losses incurred by the concert tour. The current trend, which will continue for
the foreseeable future, is for highly capitalized cultural producers to envision
"projects" that can be realized in many different forms (as films, television programs,
video cassettes, live performances, sound recordings, toys, collectibles, etc.) rather
than individual cultural objects. As long as the project as a whole is profitable, none
of its particular manifestations need be.
13 For a useful overview of cable television's involvement in the presentation of
theatrical productions, see Rose (1986: 229–33). Although Rose does not discuss
the involvement of cable networks in the financing of live theatre, he does take
note of the fact that cable executives lost interest in theatre around 1982 when they
realized that an original television movie can be produced for less than the cost of
mounting a theatrical production for broadcast (ibid.: 231).

presentations, has become both model and *telos* for live theatre. In *The Post-Modern Aura*, Charles Newman (1985: 129) declares that "the adaptation...has become the primary literary convention of the age." As compared with those of television's Golden Age, the productions to which I refer here did not *need* to be adapted to make the journey from stage to television, because the live versions had been constructed to be seen *as television* – they were pre-adapted (so to say) to the demands of their new medium. Contrary to Newman's suggestion that the adaptation is the essential postmodern form, I would argue that the very fact that these productions required *no* adaptation in making the transition from representation to repetition is what defines them as postmodern. While I would not want to assert unconditionally that the live event I saw while sitting in the theatre was no different from its television counterpart, its identity as *theatre*, rather than television, and its specificity as a *live*, rather than mediatized, event had been called into question long before it actually showed up on the screen.

The incursion of mediatization into the live setting probably began earlier in avant-garde performance than in the commercial theatre and is currently manifest not only in the presence of video in much performance art, but also in the kind of performing characteristic of the avant-garde. Over twenty-five years ago, Michael Kirby (1984 [1972]: 100) characterized the kind of performance taking place in much experimental theatre and performance art as "nonmatrixed representation," in which the performer does not embody a fictional character but "merely carries out certain actions" that nevertheless can have referential or representational significance (ibid.). As Kirby observes, the decade from the early 1960s through the early 1970s saw a trend away from conventional acting and toward nonmatrixed performance in American avant-garde theatre (ibid.: 110). Although "character" did make something of a come-back in the performance art of the later 1970s and 1980s, the concept of nonmatrixed representation remains a useful (and underemployed) one for describing the kinds of performing evident in much performance art from the 1960s to the present. It also serves as a conceptual bridge from the experimental theatre of the 1960s, which was frequently ideologically opposed to the mass media, to subsequent mediatized performance.

The sense in which nonmatrixed representation provided a beachhead for mediatization within artistic practices that resisted mediatization may best be seen in Kirby's statement that "in nonmatrixed representation the referential elements are applied *to* the performer and are not acted *by* him" (ibid.: 100). In other words, the performance requires some form of mediation of the performer's actions to create meaning. Although that mediation was not usually techno-logical in the performances Kirby discusses, film acting seems to be a good example of nonmatrixed representation. There are, after all, many times when a film actor, like the avant-garde performers Kirby mentions, is called upon merely to carry out certain actions that acquire representational and characterological significance only in the editing room.[14] Clint Eastwood's squint, for example, becomes mean-ingful only through the mediation of the camera in close-up and editing. Prior to this mediation, it is just Clint squinting.

Wooster Group performer Willem Dafoe suggested the parallel between avant-garde performing and film acting when I interviewed him in 1985. He told me that from his point of view as a performer, what he does when performing in a Wooster Group piece is virtually identical with that of acting in films – to him, both are primarily nonmatrixed, task-based performing (Auslander 1997: 44). Dafoe is one of a growing group of American performance artists whose experi-ences in the avant-garde have enabled them to make a smooth transition into acting on film or television; the careers of Laurie Anderson, Spalding Gray, the late Ron Vawter, Ann Magnuson, Eric Bogosian, Steve Buscemi, and many others are noteworthy in this regard. More important, their more experimental work itself has found its way into mass-cultural contexts in many cases: Anderson's perfor-mances as rock concerts, films, and videos; Gray's and Bogosian's monologues as movies; Magnuson's pop performance extravaganzas as cable television specials, and so forth.[15] Daryl Chin (1991: 20) describes

14 Kirby (1984 [1972]: 107) acknowledges that "the film actor may do very little, while the camera and the physical/informational context do the 'acting' for him," and he characterizes film acting as "simple acting" which, for him, is at the "matrixed" end of the spectrum between completely nonmatrixed and fully matrixed performing. Although I employ Kirby's vocabulary, my own characterization of film acting is somewhat different in emphasis, since I wish to position film acting toward the "nonmatrixed" side of Kirby's performance continuum.
15 I summarize these activities in Auslander (1993: 62). A number of performance artists have had "specials" on cable networks or have appeared on public television and on the occasional network program, such as Saturday Night Live. Ann Magnuson has played characters from soap operas – one of her performances was entitled Christmas Special (1981); she has also appeared in films (Making Mr. Right (1987)) and on television (on Anything But Love), and toured with her satirical rock band, Bongwater. In 1990 she returned to solo performance, including an appearance at Lincoln Center in New York, in You Could Be Home Now. A number of these performers have achieved success in mass entertainment forms as a consequence of their notoriety as performance artists: Bogosian has acted in films and on television;

this trend disparagingly by saying that "much of what passes for performance art, experimental film, and 'advanced' visual art is more like an audition, a trial-run, a mock-up for work in television, commercial movies, or advertising." While I disagree with Chin's evaluation of this work, his point that it is now possible for a performer to move directly from the context of the avant-garde to that of mass culture is surely valid. I have proposed the expression "cross-over," a venerable music business term referring to popular songs that appear on more than one hit parade, to characterize this phenomenon, with the understanding that what is being crossed over – the distinction between the avantgarde and mass culture – is a distinction between received cultural categories that is more profound even than that between, say, rock and disco (which is not inconsiderable).[16] Ironically, one of the factors that contributed to the performance avant-garde's becoming ready for prime-time was its adoption of nonmatrixed performance, an approach originally meant to differentiate "performing" from conventional acting but that ultimately served as a training ground for the kinds of performance skills demanded by the mass media because, like film acting, it depends on mediation for its significance. In effect, the performance avant-garde had absorbed the phenomenology of mediatized performance even before it took up a position within the economy of repetition.

That mediatization is the experience to which live performance must refer and which it must seek to recreate is evident from examples drawn from a broad range of cultural contexts. The practice of staging live reenactments of televisual events began as early as the mid-1950s, when television plays like *Twelve Angry Men* and *Visit to a Small Planet* were presented on Broadway, and it has accelerated in recent times with the restaging of television programs as live performances (*The Real Live Brady Bunch*), animated films as stage musicals (Disney's *Beauty and the Beast*), and of music videos as concerts. As the personnel involved in staging Madonna's tours freely admit, the goal of

his play *Talk Radio* was made into a film released in 1988. Anderson records for a major label and has appeared in a film of *United States*, which she has also produced as a sound recording and a colorful book. Spalding Gray has also acted in films and on television, most recently in *The Nanny*; he has appeared in film versions of several of his monologues and has also published them in book form.

16 For a more detailed discussion of cross-over performance artists, see Auslander (1992b). The issue of distinctions between genres of popular music, to which I refer here merely in passing, is central to my discussion in Chapter 3 of the present volume.

their productions, like that of many rock and pop concerts, is to reproduce the artist's music videos as nearly as possible in a live setting on
the assumption that the audience comes to the live show expecting to
see what it has already seen on television. One could say that because
the music video sets the standard for what is "real" in this realm, only a
recreation of its imagery can count as "realistic." Reciprocally, the fact
that images from Madonna's videos can be recreated in a live setting
enhances the realism of the original videos.

Another performance genre in which that assumption operates is
stand-up comedy. From the advent of television until the 1980s, the
conventional wisdom was always that television used up in a few
minutes of broadcast time material it might have taken the comic years
to hone. With the stand-up comedy boom of the 1980s, however,
comics and comedy club owners discovered that audiences were only
too happy to come to a club to hear the same jokes they had already
heard on a comic's cable television special. (Indeed, they may have
been disappointed not to hear them.[17]) In these cases, the traditional
privileging of the "original," live performance over its elaborations and
adaptations is undermined and reversed: in an "inversion of the structural dependence of copies upon originals" (Connor 1989: 153) the
mediatized performance has become the referent of the live one.
"What irony: people originally intended to use the record to preserve
the performance, and today the performance is only successful as a
simulacrum of the record" (Attali 1985: 85). Vincent Canby ("Look
who's talking on Broadway: microphones," *New York Times*, January 22
1995, sec. 2: 1, 4–5) has argued that the use of sound systems and
mixing techniques that produce digital-quality sound at live performances of Broadway musicals encourages audiences to assess live
performances in terms of their resemblance to mediatized ones: "the
theatre is fast approaching the day when a Broadway show will be a
nearly perfect, if artificial, representation of a live performance." In all
of these contexts, live performance is now a recreation of itself at one
remove, filtered through its own mediatized reproductions. (I shall
make a similar argument regarding live performance of rock and music
video in Chapter 3.)

All of these instances, and a great many more that I could mention,
exemplify the way mediatization is now explicitly and implicitly
embedded within the live experience. I have described examples of the

---

17 See Auslander (1992b) for a discussion of the comedy boom and television in a
somewhat different context.

incursion of mediatization into a range of live performance events at some length to make the point that, within our mediatized culture, whatever distinction we may have supposed there to be between live and mediatized events is collapsing because live events are becoming more and more identical with mediatized ones. When I have presented this idea in public lectures, it has often been challenged by the claim that while what I say may be true of large-scale entertainment such as sporting events, Broadway shows, and rock concerts, it does not hold true for more intimate forms of theatre and performance art. However, I do not believe this distinction to be valid. I am not arguing that all instances of live performance reflect the incursion of mediatization in the same ways or to the same degree, and scale is certainly one differentiating factor. Some sectors of our cultural economy determine that if an event is to occur live at all, it must be mounted on a large scale. Connor (1989: 151–2) points out, for example, that the use of giant video screens at rock concerts provides a means of creating in a large-scale event the effect of "intimacy and immediacy" associated with smaller live events. In order to retain those characteristics, large-scale events must surrender a substantial measure of their liveness to mediatization. Ironically, intimacy and immediacy are precisely the qualities attributed to television that enabled it to displace live performance. In the case of such large-scale events, live performance survives as television.

More intimate live performances may not be mediatized in the same way or to the same effect. Inasmuch as mediatization is the cultural context in which live performances are now inevitably situated, however, its influence nevertheless pervades even these smaller-scaled events. I have already referred to the ubiquity of video in performance art, a phenomenon that speaks for itself. But mediatization is not just a question of the employment of media technology; it is also a matter of what might be called media epistemology. It "should not be understood as meaning simply that our world-view is being increasingly dominated by technical equipment. Even more important is the fact that we often perceive reality only through the mediation of machines (microscope, telescope, television). These frameworks...preform our perception of [the world]" (Bolz and van Reijen 1996: 71). Even small-scale, intimate live performances can be products of this preformed perception. In an earlier analysis (Auslander 1992b: 70–81), I pointed out that both Laurie Anderson's media-saturated performances and Spalding Gray's low-tech, intimate ones can be seen as *televisual*, even in live presentations. To those familiar with her performance work, Anderson's engagement of media technology is well-known (see Auslander 1992b: 105–24; I shall also have occasion to refer to one of her performances at the end of this chapter). Because Gray's relation to mediatization is less obvious, I will review that part of my argument briefly. I contend that Gray's monologue performances are televisual in two respects. First, their narrative structure, which follows the continuing adventures of a small group of central characters whose essential traits never change, is very close to that of the television serial. Second, and more important here, Gray has created a performance persona that:

> can crop up anywhere – as character and narrator in [his] monologues, whether live or recorded; as a television or film actor (I would insist here that when we see Gray acting on television, in film or on the…stage…what we are seeing is the "Spalding" persona as actor); as a character in, and the author of a book….the "Spalding" persona, which began as a fictional conceit of his performances, has become "real" by virtue of its continual reappearance in the cultural arena.… The blending of real and fabricated personae and situations that occurs when performance personae assume the same functions as "real" people in the media has the same disorienting effect as the flowing together of various levels and types of meanings on television [itself].
>
> (Auslander 1992b: 77–8)

That Gray's performance persona itself can be seen as a televisual entity, that the commercial theatre now frequently presents live versions of films and television and camera-ready productions of plays, that live concerts often recreate the imagery of music videos, that the nonmatrixed performing characteristic of avant-garde theatre proved a suitable training ground for television and film acting, all suggest that the incursion of mediatization into live performance is not simply a question of the use of certain equipment in that context. It also has to do with approaches to performance and characterization, and the mobility and meanings of those within a particular cultural context. What we are seeing in many cases is not so much the incursion of media-derived "technics" and techniques into the context of live performance but, rather, live performance's absorption of a media-derived epistemology.

Thinking about these phenomena has led me back to Walter Benjamin's crucially important essay, "The work of art in the age of mechanical reproduction" (1936); the focus of Benjamin's analysis in that essay is on the historical progression from unique, "auratic" cultural forms to mass-reproduced ones (Benjamin 1986 [1936]). Except in his brief discussion of Dada, Benjamin does not take note there of the kind of doubling back that I have described, in which older forms emulate and incorporate newer ones. Benjamin was remarkably prescient, however, and many of the terms of his analysis still shed light on the current situation.

I will begin by noting Benjamin's emphasis on the idea that "human sense perception…is determined not only by nature but by historical circumstances as well" (ibid.: 31). Many aspects of our relation to performance suggest that mediatization has had a powerful effect in shaping the sensory norm for the current historical moment. Roger Copeland (1990: 29) has explained the use of amplification in live theatrical performance in precisely these terms: "on Broadway these days even nonmusical plays are routinely miked, in part because the results sound more 'natural' to an audience whose ears have been conditioned by stereo television, high fidelity LP's, and compact disks." The use of relatively invisible microphones placed on the bodies of the actors only reinforces our perception of an amplified voice as "natural." Goodwin (1990: 266) has identified another intriguing case of the normalization of mediatized sound: that of the handclap effect used on many pop and dance records. Recordings of the 1970s frequently used a particular percussion synthesizer, the TR-808, as the source for this sound. After a decade of synthesized handclaps, when musicians in the 1980s wanted to sample a handclap effect from existing recordings, "they sampled their own electronic simulation from the TR-808 machine, rather than 'real' handclaps" because "the electronic hand-clap sounded so 'natural' to pop musicians and audiences" (ibid.). The degree to which our eyes and ears have been conditioned by mediatiza-tion was clear well before the advent of compact discs, stereo television, and sampling: think of the people who have long brought portable radios or television sets to the ballpark, or consider Evan Eisenberg's anecdote of stumbling upon a free jazz concert in Central Park in New York City, only to notice that some spectators were listening to the radio broadcast of the very concert they were attending (Eisenberg 1987: 85). An even more developed version of the latter scenario occurred at an Atlanta performance of the rock group Yes. The group's set-up included a system that permitted those attending the concert to listen to it on headphones plugged directly into the group's mixing board.

Benjamin describes the mode of perception he saw in an emergent mass culture in terms of overcoming distance (and therefore banishing aura, which can be understood as a function of distance). He refers to:

the desire of contemporary masses to bring things "closer" spatially and humanly, which is just as ardent as their bent toward overcoming the uniqueness of every reality by accepting its reproduction. Every day the urge grows stronger to get hold of an object at very close range by way of its likeness, its reproduction.

(Benjamin 1986 [1936]: 31–2)

Benjamin's notion of a mass desire for proximity, and its alliance with a desire for reproduced objects, provides a useful matrix for understanding the interrelation of live and mediatized forms that I have described. The people listening to the Central Park concert on the radio and those watching Yes with headphones clapped on their ears are trying to achieve a kind of aural intimacy that can be obtained only from the reproduction of sound. The use of giant video screens at sporting events, music and dance concerts, and other performances is another direct illustration of Benjamin's concept: the kind of proximity and intimacy we can experience with television, which has become our model for close-up perception, but that is absent from these performances, can be reintroduced only by means of their "videation". When a live performance recreates a mass-reproduced one, as in the case of the replication of music video imagery in concerts or cartoon images in theatre, an inverted version of the same effect takes place. Because we are already intimately familiar with the images from our televisual and filmic experience of them, we see them as proximate no matter how far away they may be in physical distance. If you know what Madonna's videos look like from MTV, you can read the images in her concerts as if you were in intimate relation to them, even from the last row. Whether the effect of intimacy results from the videation of the live event or from acquaintance with the live images from their prior reproductions, it makes live performances seem more like television, and thus enables live events to fulfill the desire for reproduction that Benjamin notes. Even in the most intimate of performance art projects, in which we may be only a few feet away from the performers, we are still frequently offered the opportunity for the even greater intimacy of watching the performers in close-up on video monitors, as if we can experience true proximity only in televisual terms. This points to another of Benjamin's postulates: that "the quality of [the original's] presence is always depreciated" by reproduction. Steve Wurtzler's analysis of this effect in the context of sports may be generalized to many other cultural contexts:

> Over time, as the conventions of the televisually posited live come to constitute the way we think of the live, attending the game...becomes a degraded version of the event's televisual representation. This degradation of the live is itself compensated for by the use of Diamondvision and instant replays on elaborate stadium score boards....In other words, the degradation of the live is compensated for by the inscription into the "real" of its representation.
>
> (Wurtzler 1992: 92)

The ubiquity of reproductions of performances of all kinds in our culture has led to the depreciation of live presence, which can only be compensated for by making the percepetual experience of the live as much as possible like that of the mediatized, even in cases where the live event provides its own brand of proximity.

I will conclude this section with a brief consideration of mixed-media performances,[18] in the cultural/perceptual environment I have described. There has been a critical discourse surrounding the concept of mixed-media performance and the possibilities of incorporating film into theatre since at least the early 1920s.[19] Robert Edmond Jones declared: "*In the simultaneous use of the living actor and the talking picture in the theatre there lies a wholly new theatrical art, whose possibilities are as infinite as those of speech itself*" (Jones 1941: 17, original emphasis). Whereas film, for Jones, is "the perfect medium for expressing the Unconscious," live actors express conscious reality. Therefore, the combination of the two media "will reveal simultaneously the two worlds of the Conscious and the Unconscious...the objective world of actuality and the subjective world of motive" (ibid.: 18). Implicit in Jones's calling for this form of mixed-media performance is the assumption that live and filmed representations can be combined as complementary and equally compelling languages. He does not take cultural economy into consideration or raise the question of how live performance juxtaposed with film would be perceived by an audience that had been deserting theatres in favor of movie houses for over

---

18 By "mixed-media performances" I mean events combining live and mediatized representations: live actors with film, video, or digital projections, for instance.

19 In 1923, Sergei M. Eisenstein directed a stage production that incorporated filmed sequences. He discussed the possibilities of combining film with theatre, and of making the theatre more cinematic, in "The montage of attractions" (Eisenstein 1988 [1923]).

twenty years.[20] Would such an audience perceive the live aspects of the kind of mixed-media production envisioned by Jones as equally compelling as its filmed components, or would they see the live as an uninteresting, degraded version of the filmic?

Twenty-five years later, the actor Roberts Blossom, who was combining live actors with film in a series of experiments he called Filmstage,[21] explicated his activity in terms very similar to Jones's. Whereas Jones saw film as representing the unconscious and live actors as representing consciousness, Blossom (1966: 70) saw film as representing consciousness and the live actors as representing corporeality, physical existence. Unlike Jones, who saw theatre and film as portraying complementary aspects of the psyche, Blossom saw the live and filmed elements of his productions as competing with one another. Blossom acknowledged that the competition between the actors' live bodies and the filmed images in these mixed-media performances was intrinsically unfair because the filmed images were inevitably more compelling. By comparison with the films, the actors appeared as "fifty-watt bulbs waiting to be screwed into their source and to shine with the light that is perpetual (behind them, around them) but which they can only reflect at fifty watts" (ibid.). In terms of psychic economy, we might interpret Blossom as saying that physical existence is only ever a pale reflection of the consciousness underlying it. But Blossom's statement can also be read in terms of the cultural economy. In those terms, the live actors are only pale reflections of the mediatized representations that dominate the cultural landscape. Although Blossom (1966: 72) may be implying the possibility of existing as pure consciousness when he concludes that "our presence as bodies begins to be suspect," that statement also summarizes the devaluation of live presence in mediatized culture.

20 Movies had been stealing American audiences from theatre both in New York and on the road since the early 1920s. By 1930, about twenty Broadway theatres "were alternating motion pictures with plays"; many of these theatres soon became movie houses (Poggi 1968: 83). Poggi comments: "the motion pictures could not have crushed the legitimate theatre if there had been a real preference for live drama. Theatre managers would never have turned their buildings over to the movies if they could have made more money by booking plays" (ibid.: 43). I assume that Jones was aware of these developments. It is possible, therefore, that his proposal for mixed-media performance was a covert way of recuperating theatre's enemy.

21 Filmstage was but one of many intermedia experiments undertaken in the mid-1960s by theatre, film, and performance artists. Carolee Schneeman and Robert Whitman, for instance, both staged "Happenings" that juxtaposed live performers with filmed images. For a useful contemporary survey of these activities and other experimental uses of film, video, and live performance, see Youngblood (1970).

If the value of live presence has depreciated in our mediatized culture, it would seem that audiences would be more likely to perceive the live elements of mixed-media performances as the fifty-watt bulbs described by Blossom than as the equal partners of mediatized representations envisioned by Jones. This question is difficult to address in any other than anecdotal terms: when we go to a concert employing a large video screen, for instance, what do we look at? Do we concentrate our attention on the live bodies or are our eyes drawn to the screen, as Benjamin's postulate of our desire for proximity would predict? At an industrial party I attended recently, I found the latter to be the case. There was a live band, dancing, and a video simulcast of the dancers on two screens adjacent to the dance floor. My eye was drawn to the screen, compared to which the live dancers indeed had all the brilliance of fifty-watt bulbs.

Another example, one that carries this discussion into the digital domain, is *Pôles*, by Pps Danse of Montreal, a performance described by its makers as "Dance + Virtual." The piece combines two live dancers with holographic projections of themselves deployed against a shifting background of digital projections. The best moments of *Pôles* are those in which it is difficult to distinguish the living dancers from their holographic counterparts. In one sequence, four figures chase each other through a grotto-like projection; the three-dimensional dancers seem as able to enter into the two-dimensional projected space as the wraith-like holograms. On other occasions, the holograms are projected onto the dancers to produce the effect of dematerializing bodies. The question that such a performance raises for me is: Do we see a piece like *Pôles* as a juxtaposition of the live and the digital, a shifting among realms? My feeling is that the answer is no, that we now experience such work as a fusion, not a con-fusion, of realms, a fusion that we see as taking place within a digital environment that incorporates the live elements as part of its raw material. Rather than a conversation among distinct media, the production presents the assimilation of varied materials to the cultural dominant.[22] In this sense, Dance + Virtual = Virtual.

Against ontology

Live performance thus has become the means by which mediatized representations are naturalized, according to a simple logic that appeals to our nostalgia for what we assumed was the im-mediate: if the mediatized image can be recreated in a live setting, it must have been "real" to

---

22 I am not yet convinced that digitality represents a cultural dominant different from the televisual.

begin with. This schema resolves (or rather, fails to resolve) into an impossible oscillation between the two poles of what once seemed a clear opposition: whereas mediatized performance derives its authority from its reference to the live or the real, the live now derives its authority from its reference to the mediatized, which derives its authority from its reference to the live, etc. The paradigm that best describes the current relationship between the live and the mediatized is the Baudrillardian paradigm of *simulation*: "nothing separates one pole from the other, the initial from the terminal: there is just a sort of contraction into each other, a fantastic telescoping, a collapsing of the two traditional poles into one another: an IMPLOSION." Baudrillard states, with typical insistence, about such implosions: "*this is where simulation begins*" (Baudrillard 1983: 57, original emphasis). In the previous sections of this chapter, I indicated the twin vectors of implosion in the case of live and mediatized performance. As the mediatized replaces the live within cultural economy, the live itself incorporates the mediatized, both technologically and epistemologically. The result of this implosion is that a seemingly secure opposition is now a site of anxiety, the anxiety that underlies many performance theorists' desire to reassert the integrity of the live and the corrupt, co-opted nature of the mediatized. One of the most articulate versions of this position is Peggy Phelan's account of what she understands to be the ontology of performance. For Phelan, the basic ontological fact of performance is that its:

> only life is in the present. Performance cannot be saved, recorded, documented, or otherwise participate in the circulation of representations of representations: once it does so, it becomes something other than performance. To the degree that performance attempts to enter the economy of reproduction, it betrays and lessens the promise of its own ontology.
>
> (Phelan 1993a: 146)

For Phelan, performance's devotion to the "now" and the fact that its only continued existence is in the spectator's memory enable it to sidestep the economy of repetition. "Performance's independence from mass reproduction, technologically, economically, and linguistically, is its greatest strength" (ibid.: 149).[23]

---

23 I realize that I am considering only a portion of Phelan's argument, which ultimately has to do with issues of presence and visibility for a political performance practice. I am concerned here only with her fundamental ontological premises.

Although it may seem that live performance cannot be mass-reproduced, I shall argue otherwise later in this section. I have already suggested that live performance is becoming progressively less independent of media technology. Phelan's claim that performance is linguistically independent from mass reproduction is based on a tautological argument. Phelan posits performance as nonreproductive and writing as a form of reproduction, allowing her to conclude that writing (language) cannot capture performance. To the extent, however, that mediatization, the technology of reproduction, is embedded within the language of live performance itself, performance cannot claim linguistic independence from mass reproduction, either. It interests me that although Phelan discusses performance artist Angelika Festa's *Untitled Dance (with fish and others)* (1987) in the context of her argument concerning the ontology of performance, she does not specifically address the encroachment of technologies of reproduction on this piece, in which Festa made extensive use of video technology to construct the images Phelan analyzes. It is ironic that the video camera, perhaps the *sine qua non* of the pressures that Phelan sees as compromising the ontological integrity of performance, is itself integral to the performance in question.[24]

Much as I admire Phelan's commitment to a rigorous conception of an ontology of liveness, I doubt very strongly that any cultural discourse can actually stand outside the ideologies of capital and reproduction that define a mediatized culture or should be expected to do so, even to assume an oppositional stance.[25] I agree with Sean Cubitt (1994: 283–4) when he says that "in our period of history, and in our Western societies, there is no performance that is not always already a commodity." Furthermore, as Pavis (1992: 134) observes, "'the work of art in the era of technical reproduction' cannot escape the socioeconomic–technological domination which determines its aesthetic dimension." It is not realistic to propose that live performance can remain ontologically pristine or that it operates in a cultural economy separate from that of the mass media.

Despite the recognition by critics such as Pavis (1992: 134) of what he calls the inevitable "technological and aesthetic contamination" of

---

24 I am not suggesting that Phelan presents Festa's performance as an ontologically pure example. Phelan expresses significant doubts about several aspects of the performance.

25 This position is central to my *Presence and Resistance* (Auslander 1992b), where I argue it in detail.

live performance in the economy of repetition, there remains a strong tendency in performance theory to place live performance and media-tized or technologized forms in direct opposition to one another. The terms of this opposition focus around two primary issues: *reproduction* and *distribution*.[26] Herbert Molderings defines the question of reproduction (or recording) by saying that:

> in contrast to traditional art[,] performances do not contain a reproduction element....Whatever survives of a performance in the form of a photograph or videotape is no more than a fragmentary, petrified vestige of a lively process that took place at a different time in a different place.
>
> (Molderings 1984: 172–3)

Or, in Phelan's succinct formulations, performance "can be defined as representation without reproduction" (Phelan 1993a: 3); "Performance's being becomes itself through disappearance" (ibid.: 146). In terms of distribution, Pavis (1992: 101) contrasts the one-to-many model of broadcasting with the "limited range" of theatre: "media easily multiply the number of their spectators, becoming accessible to a potentially infinite audience. If theatre relationships are to take place, however, the performance cannot tolerate more than a limited number of specta-tors." In these formulations, live performance is identified with intimacy and disappearance, media with a mass audience, reproduc-tion, and repetition. Phelan (1993a: 149) offers an apt summary of this view: "Performance honors the idea that a limited number of people in a specific time/space frame can have an experience of value which leaves no visible trace afterward."

Overtly or covertly, the writers I have just cited valorize the live over the mediatized, as is evident in Molderings' contrast between "lively" performance and "petrified" video. Even Pavis, who argues that theatre needs to be seen in relation to other media, nevertheless refers to the influence of other media on theatre as a *contamination*. All too often, such analyses take on the air of a melodrama in which virtuous live performance is threatened, encroached upon, dominated, and

---

26 I have borrowed these categories from Pavis (1992: 104–7). They are two of fifteen vectors identified by Pavis along which live performance and media may be compared. The others are: relationship between production and reception, voice, audience, nature of signifiers, mode of representation, conditions of production, dramaturgy, specificity, framing, norms and codes, repertoire, fictional status, and indices of fictional status.

contaminated by its insidious Other, with which it is locked in a life-and-death struggle. From this point of view, once live performance succumbs to mediatization, it loses its ontological integrity.

At one level, the anxiety of critics who champion live performance is understandable, given the way our cultural economy privileges the mediatized and marginalizes the live. In the economy of repetition, live performance is little more than a vestigial remnant of the previous historical order of representation, a hold-over that can claim little in the way of cultural presence or power. Perhaps making a virtue of necessity, Phelan (1993a: 148) claims that live performance's inability to participate in the economy of repetition "gives performance art its distinctive oppositional edge."[27]

These formulations of the relationship between live performance and mediatization as oppositional are not neutrally descriptive; rather, they reflect an ideology central to contemporary performance studies. Molderings (1984: 178–9) describes performance art as a direct counter-response to television's banalization and objectification of the visual image. Phelan picks up this theme in a discussion of Anna Deveare Smith's *Twilight: Los Angeles, 1992*, suggesting that Smith's performance, which incorporates, alludes to, and reinterprets the widely disseminated media images of the 1992 Los Angeles riots, "seeks to preserve and contain the chaotic flood of images the cameras 'mechanically' reproduced" (Phelan 1993b: 6). Phelan observes that this way of seeing the relationship between the live and the mediatized is based on "an old boast – television cameras give you only 'images,' and theatre gives you living truth" and emphasizes the degree to which Smith's performance is indebted to "the camera that precedes and frames and invites" it. She goes on to suggest that Smith's performance "also offers another way to interpret the relation between film and

27 I would like to suggest in passing that in the context of a mediatized, repetitive economy, using the technology of reproduction in ways that defy that economy may be a more significantly oppositional gesture than asserting the value of the live. I am thinking, for instance, of Christine Kozlov's installation, *Information: No Theory* (1970), which consisted of a tape recorder equipped with a tape loop, whose control was fixed in the "record" mode. Therefore, as the artist herself noted, new information continuously replaced existing information on the tape, and "proof of the existence of the information [did] not in fact exist" (in Meyer 1972: 172). The functions of reproduction, storage, and distribution that animate the network of repetition were thus undermined by this way of using the very technology that brought that network into being (see Attali 1985: 32). In this context, reproduction without representation may be more radical than representation without reproduction.

theatrical performance: the camera's own performativity needs to be read as theatre" (ibid.: 7).[28] Even though Phelan describes a subtle interaction between live and mediatized forms that goes beyond simple opposition, her suggestion that the action of the camera be seen as theatre tends to reinscribe the traditional privileging of the live over the mediatized: for her, it is by entering the space of theatre, or being seen as theatre, that media images become subject to critique. I believe that this privileging of live performance as a site of critique is an article of faith for most who analyze performance in political terms. If I were to insist that Smith's performance actually works in the opposite way that Phelan suggests – that Smith's incorporation of mediatized images does not transform them into theatre but, rather, makes her performances metaphorically into television – many commentators would feel I was denying that her performance could function critically.

My purpose here is to destabilize these theoretical oppositions of the live and the mediatized somewhat, first by reference to what might be called the "electronic ontology" of media (these initial observations will not pertain to film, of course, whose ontology is photographic rather than electronic):

> the broadcast flow is...a vanishing, a constant disappearing of what has just been shown. The electron scan builds up two images of each frame shown, the lines interlacing to form a "complete" picture. Yet not only is the sensation of movement on screen an optical illusion brought about by the rapid succession of frames: each frame is itself radically incomplete, the line before always fading away, the first scan of the frame all but gone, even from the retina, before the second interlacing scan is complete....TV's presence to the viewer is subject to constant flux: it is only intermittently "present," as a kind of writing on the glass...caught in a dialectic of constant becoming and constant fading.
>
> (Cubitt 1991: 30–1)

---

28 Phelan (1993b: 6) describes Smith's *Twilight* as signaling a shift in the relationship between television and theatre: "formerly, live theatre hoped to find itself preserved on television, while Smith's performance transforms the 'raw' televised story into stylized, well-rehearsed drama." I tend to see Smith's work as belonging to a general cultural trend in which mediatized events are reconfigured as live ones. In considering the relationship between theatre and television, does Smith's derivation of her performance from televisual documentary sources constitute a new development or the extension of an established cultural trend into a new area?

As this quotation from Cubitt suggests, disappearance may be even more fundamental to television than it is to live performance – the televisual image is always simultaneously coming into being and vanishing; there is no point at which it is fully present.[29] At the electronic level, the televisual image is hardly a petrified remnant of some other event, as Molderings would have it, but exists rather as a lively, and forever unresolved, process. For some theorists, the televisual image's existence only in the present also obviates the notion that television (and video) is a form of reproduction. Contrasting television with film in this regard, Stephen Heath and Gillian Skirrow point out that:

> where film sides towards instantaneous memory ("everything is absent, everything is *recorded* – as a memory trace which is so at once, without having been something else before") television operates much more as an absence of memory, the recorded material it uses – including material recorded on film – instituted as actual in the production of the television image.
>
> (Heath and Skirrow 1977: 54–6)[30]

Regardless of whether the image conveyed by television is live or recorded (and, as Stanley Cavell (1982: 86) reminds us, on television there is "no sensuous distinction between the live and the repeat or replay") its production as a televisual image occurs only in the present moment. "Hence the possibility of *performing* the television image – electronic, it can be modified, altered, transformed in the moment of its transmission, is a production in the present" (Heath and Skirrow 1977: 53). Although Heath and Skirrow are referring here to broadcast television, what they say is as true for video as it is for broadcast: the televisual image is not only a reproduction or repetition of a performance, but a performance in itself.

If we shift our gaze from the electronic writing on the glass to consider, for a moment, the nature of the magnetic writing on a video-

---

29 Kozlov's tape-recorder installation replicates this process of the continuous replacement of electronic information. The difference is that whereas in the normal usage of video this process is the necessary condition for the creation of a perceivable image, it becomes, when applied by Kozlov to sound recording, a way of making an imperceptible sound image that exists only theoretically.

30 The quotation embedded in this quotation is from Christian Metz.

tape, another issue comes to the fore. Cubitt (1991: 169) posits as a crucial feature of the medium "the phenomena [sic] of lost generations" resulting from the various stages of life a video image is likely to pass through, "from master to submaster, to broadcast, to timeshift, where it begins to degenerate with every play." Video shares this characteristic with other means of technical reproduction, including photographic and sound-recording media. Since tapes, films, and other recording media deteriorate over time and with each use, they are, in fact, physically different objects at each playing, even though this process may only become perceptible when it reaches critical mass (e.g., when the film or video develops visible flaws). Each time I watch a videotape is the only time I can watch that tape in that state of being because the very process of playing it alters it. The tape that I initially placed in my VCR or audio player started disappearing the moment I began watching it or listening to it. Disappearance, existence only in the present moment, is not, then, an ontological quality of live performance that distinguishes it from modes of technical reproduction. Both live performance and the performance of mediatization are predicated on disappearance: the televisual image is produced by an ongoing process in which scan lines replace one another, and it is always as absent as it is present; the use of recordings causes them to degenerate. In a very literal, material sense, televisual and other technical reproductions, like live performances, become themselves through disappearance.[31]

I want to worry this question of reproduction in one last context, by considering the related issue of repetition. Writing on the experience of film, Cavell observes that:

> movies...at least some movies, maybe most, used to exist in something that resembles [a] condition of evanescence, viewable only in certain places at certain times, discussable solely as occasions for sociable exchange, and never seen more than once, and then more or less forgotten.
>
> (Cavell 1982: 78)

It is remarkable how closely Cavell's description of the film experience parallels descriptions of the experience of live performance. The fact that Cavell is talking about the past, probably about the heyday of the

---

31 It is worth wondering about the implications of digital reproductions for this position, since at least some digital media ostensibly do not degrade. My present feeling is that it's too soon to tell whether or not that's true.

American film industry in the 1930s and 1940s, and about a way of experiencing film that we no longer believe to be typical, is critical. Film is no longer an unrepeated experience confined to particular places and times; people frequently see their favorite films multiple times, and have opportunities to do so afforded them by the appearances of these movies on cable and broadcast television, and on video cassettes. If we want to, we can own copies of movies and watch them whenever, and as often, as we wish. Whereas film was once experienced as evanescence, it is now experienced as repetition. The crucial point is that this transition was not caused by any substantive change in the film medium itself.[32] As a medium, film can be used to provide an evanescent experience that leaves little behind, in the manner of a live performance, or it can provide an experience based in repetition and the stockpiling of film commodities.[33] Cubitt (1991: 92–3) makes much the same point with respect to video, arguing that repetition is not "an essence in the medium." Rather, "the possibility of repetition is only a possibility"; the actual use of the medium is determined by "the imaginary relation of viewer and tape." Repetition is not an ontological characteristic of either film or video that determines the experiences these media can provide, but an historically contingent effect of their culturally determined uses.

32 One change that deserves mention is the replacement of highly volatile nitrate film stocks with safety stocks, a transition that was not complete until the 1950s. The early nitrate stocks would frequently ignite in the projector; nitrate prints were often discarded after only a few showings because of the stock's dangerous instability. Following Williams's critique of technological determinism, I would insist that how technologies are used should be understood as *effect* rather than *cause* (Williams 1992 [1974]: 3–8). In this case, I would argue that the transition from the evanscent experience of film to the experience of film as repetition was not caused by such technological changes as the development of safety stocks and the advent of video. Rather, the development of those technologies was the intentional result of a social need for cultural forms offering an experience of repetition, a need perhaps related to the desire for reproductions cited by Benjamin and discussed earlier.

33 Sontag makes two points that challenge the distinction between film as repeatable and live performance as nonrepeatable:

> With respect to any *single* experience, it hardly matters that a film is usually identical from one projection of it to another while theatre performances are highly mutable....a movie *may* be altered from one projection to the next. Harry Smith, when he runs off his own films, makes each projection an unrepeatable performance.

> (Sontag 1966: 31, original emphasis)

Just as recording media like film and video can provide an experience of evanescence, so, too, live forms such as theatre have been used in ways that do not respect, or even recognize, the ostensible spatial and temporal characteristics of live performance. I would go so far as to argue that live performances can be mass-produced. One such example would be the WPA Federal Theater's 1936 production of *It Can't Happen Here*, which opened simultaneously in eighteen different American cities. The intention of this experiment is clearly suggested by a contemporary account, which observes that the Federal Theater produced the play "after a motion picture corporation decided not to do it" (Whitman 1937: 6). To take a more current example, producers of the genre known as "interactive plays" envision live performances as franchisable commodities. Interactive plays are environmental performances that incorporate varying degrees of spectator participation.[34] In *Tamara*, for instance, spectators follow the character of their choice through a series of rooms, witnessing various scenes of a narrative. In *Tony 'n' Tina's Wedding* and similar performances, spectators actually interact with the performers by eating with them, dancing with them, gossiping with them, etc. Barrie Wexler, the California producer of *Tamara*, "franchises...*Tamara* worldwide, replicating the product in exact and dependable detail. 'It's like staying in the Hilton,' he explains, 'everything is exactly the same no matter where you are'" (Fuchs 1996: 142). In these cases, live performance takes on the defining characteristics of a mass medium: it makes the same text available simultaneously to a large number of participants distributed widely in space. In fact, Hollywood saw the Federal Theater as a competitor, and opposed it (Whitman 1937: 130–2). It is crucial to observe that the intentions underlying these two examples of this use of the live medium are very different, and each is arguably reflective of its historical moment. The ideological positioning of these productions is determined not by their shared use of live performance as a mass medium, but by the different intentions and contexts of those uses. The Federal Theater's practices may be said to have grown out of a generally left-populist attitude, while interactive plays are the creatures of postmodern consumer capitalism (see Fuchs 1996: 129). Ironically, interactive plays like *Tamara* commodify the very aspects of live performance that are said to resist commodification. Because they are designed to offer a different experience at each visit, they can be

---

34 For a discussion of the interactive theatre phenomenon, see Peter Marks, "When the audience joins the cast," *New York Times*, April 22 1997, sec. B: 1, 7).

merchandised as events that must be purchased over and over again: the ostensible evanescence and nonrepeatability of the live experience ironically become selling points to promote a product that must be fundamentally the same in each of its instantiations. The promise of having a different experience at each attendance at an interactive play is meaningful only if each is clearly recognizable as a different experience of the same, essentially static, object. One of those selling points is, of course, the intimacy of witnessing the narrative from a particular character's perspective or physically interacting with the characters. Again, the alliance of the desire for proximity with that for reproduction suggested by Benjamin is apparent.

My contention that theatre can function as a mass medium leads me to disagree with Noël Carroll, who defines "mass art" in a way that excludes theatre and all live performance from that category. Carroll asserts that:

> X is a mass artwork if and only if 1. x is a multiple instance or type artwork, 2. produced and distributed by a mass technology, 3. which artwork is intentionally designed to gravitate in its structural choices (for example, its narrative forms, symbolism, intended affect, and even its content) toward those choices that promise accessibility with minimum effort, virtually on first contact, for the largest number of untutored (or relatively untutored) audiences.
>
> (Carroll 1998: 196)

Although there clearly is much theatre and live performance that meets the third condition, Carroll would place such work into the category of "popular art" rather than mass art because he believes it cannot meet his first two criteria. But it seems to me that live performance events like *Tamara* pose difficulties for those parts of Carroll's theory. If all productions are functionally identical, as Wexler describes, then we have a case of theatre as a multiple instance or type artwork. If multiple productions of the play are staged simultaneously all over the world, then theatre fulfills Carroll's definition of a mass technolgy as "capable of delivering multiple instances...of mass artworks to widely disparate reception points" (ibid.: 188).

Carroll argues that performances of live theatre differ from those of films by saying that whereas the performance of a film is generated directly from a template (a print of the film), a theatrical performance is generated from an interpretation of the play text. He goes on to generalize from this basis that the generation of performances from

templates, rather than interpretations, is a crucial ontological characteristic of mass art forms. While it takes no particular artistic or
interpretive skill to be a projectionist, "it takes artistry and imagination
to embody an interpretation" (ibid.: 213–14). It is for this reason that
we recognize theatrical performances as works of art in themselves but
do not accord that status to film showings.

The distinction Carroll draws between template and interpretation
is provocative. I am not persuaded, however, that they are mutually
exclusive categories. If we take the producer of *Tamara* at his word and
assume that he does succeed in mounting numerous productions of the
play that are functionally identical, would it not be fair to say that the
interpretation used in all cases functions as a template? (When I refer
to the various productions as functionally identical, I am not
suggesting that there would not be differences among them, only that
such differences would be trivial – differences, but not distinctions that
would differentiate one production of *Tamara* from any other in
aesthetically significant ways.[35]) While the actors would have to
possess a certain amount of craft and skill to replicate the performances
established in the template (just as it takes a certain amount of craft
and skill to be a good projectionist), individual artistry and imagination would be negative qualities in such a performance, since they
would tend to work against the success of *Tamara* as a standardized
product. (Similarly, we would not want a projectionist to be "creative"
in showing a conventional film.)

If this argument seems a bit far-fetched in the context of theatre
(though I do not believe it is), we can switch for a moment to another
kind of franchised performance. Consider the various live performances of the trademark clown character Ronald McDonald that may

---

35 Carroll (1998: 201) describes the different reception instances of the same mass
artwork as "identical in the same sense that two dimes of the same minting are identical." If Carroll means this analogy to indicate a strong criterion for identity, that
criterion problematizes another area of his own analysis. In discussing broadcast
media, Carroll (ibid.: 216) identifies the broadcast signal as the template that generates distinct reception instances. Because the perceptual and affective character and
qualities of each reception instance depend so much on the particular equipment
used to receive the signal, there can be very sharp variations among them. Arguably,
a television program seen on a small, old, black and white set is not identical in
perceptual and affective terms to the same program seen on a brand new, big-screen,
high definition set. It may well be that the producer of *Tamara* could create standardized productions of the play that would be more similar to each other than the
same television program seen on radically different sets.

be undertaken simultaneously at McDonald's restaurants all over the world. It is precisely the point of these performances that they all represent a single, standardized Ronald. All performances of Ronald McDonald are generated from a single interpretation of the character, which functions as a template. I have chosen this example in part to make the point that a template is not the same as a script: improvisational performances, too, can be generated from a template. (It is significant in the context of this chapter that our familiarity with this template derives mostly from seeing Ronald on television commercials. The live presentations of Ronald McDonald are further instances of live performance's recreation of the televisual.) If a child were led to make judgments concerning the interpretive quality of the various Ronald McDonalds he/she had seen – such as: "I liked the Ronald at that restaurant in Cleveland better" or "This guy did Ronald better when we were here yesterday" – then the performances would have been dismal failures precisely because they, like *Tamara*, are instances where live performance aspires to the condition of mass art. These instances also suggest how live performance may participate in the economy of repetition, not just by being recorded and replicated, but through the mass production of the live event itself.

I return now to Benjamin's observation on what he called "contemporary perception" and its hunger for reproductions. "To pry an object from its shell," he writes, "to destroy its aura, is the mark of a perception whose 'sense of the universal equality of all things' has increased to such a degree that it extracts it even from a unique object by means of reproduction" (Benjamin 1986 [1936]: 32). I have tried to suggest here that this is exactly the state in which live performance now finds itself: its traditional status as auratic and unique has been wrested from it by an ever-accelerating incursion of reproduction into the live event. Following Benjamin, I might argue that live performance has indeed been pried from its shell and that all performance modes, live or mediatized, are now equal: none is perceived as auratic or authentic; the live performance is just one more reproduction of a given text or one more reproducible text. (To say that no performance in any medium can be perceived as auratic is not to say that all such performances are experienced in the same way – just that no one of them is experienced as the auratic, authentic original.) Live performance could now be said to partake of the ontology that Benjamin ascribes to photography: "From a photographic negative…one can make any number of prints; to ask for the 'authentic' print makes no sense" (ibid.: 33). Similarly, it makes little sense to ask which of the many identical productions of *Tamara* or Disney's *Beauty and the Beast* is the "authentic" one. It does not even make much sense to ask which of the many iterations of that *Beauty and the Beast* – as animated film, video cassette, CD, book, or theatrical performance – is the "authentic" iteration. This situation represents the historical triumph of mechanical (and electronic) reproduction (what I am calling mediatization) that Benjamin implies: aura, authenticity, and cult value have been definitively routed, even in live performance, the site that once seemed the last refuge of the auratic.

I am suggesting further that thinking about the relationship between live and mediatized forms in terms of ontological oppositions is not especially productive, because there are few grounds on which to make significant ontological distinctions. Like live performance, electronic and photographic media can be described meaningfully as partaking of the ontology of disappearance ascribed to live performance, and they can also be used to provide an experience of evanescence. Like film and television, theatre can be used as a mass medium. Half jokingly, I might cite Pavis's observation that "theatre repeated too often deteriorates" (Pavis 1992: 101) as evidence that the theatrical object degenerates with repeated use in a manner akin to a recorded object! I am not proposing, however, that live performance and mediatization partake of a shared ontology. As the historical allegory I presented in the first section of this chapter suggests, that claim is the basis for mediatization's displacement of the live within cultural economy. I am suggesting, rather, that how live and mediatized forms are used is determined not by their ostensibly intrinsic characteristics but by their positions within cultural economy. To understand the relationship between live and mediatized forms, it is necessary to investigate that relationship as historical and contingent, not as ontologically given or technologically determined.

As a starting point for this exploration, I propose that, historically, the live is actually an effect of mediatization, not the other way around. It was the development of recording technologies that made it possible to perceive existing representations as "live." Prior to the advent of those technologies (e.g., sound recording and motion pictures), there was no such thing as "live" performance, for that category has meaning only in relation to an opposing possibility. The ancient Greek theatre, for example, was not live because there was no possibility of recording it. In a special case of Baudrillard's well-known dictum that "the very definition of the real is *that of which it is possible to give an equivalent reproduction*" (Baudrillard 1983: 146), the "live" can only be defined as "*that which can be recorded.*" Most dictionary definitions of this usage of the word "live" reflect the necessity of defining it in terms of its opposite: "Of a performance, heard or watched at the time of its occurrence, as distinguished from one recorded on film, tape, etc." (*Oxford English Dictionary*, 2nd edn).

I want to emphasize that *reproduction* (recording) is the key issue. The Greek theatre may have been technologically mediated, if one subscribes to the theory that the masks acted as megaphones. What concerns me here, however, is technological reproduction, not just technological mediation. Greek theatrical masks may have amplified the actors' voices, but they did not reproduce them, in the manner of electric amplification. Throughout history, performance has employed available technologies and has been mediated in one sense or another. It is only since the advent of mechanical and electric technologies of recording and reproduction, however, that performance has been mediatized.

Although I realize this is a contentious point, I will stipulate that I do not consider writing to be a form of recording in this context, for several reasons. Scripts are blueprints for performances, not recordings of them, even though they may contain some information based on performance practice. Written descriptions and drawings or paintings of performances are not direct transcriptions through which we can access the performance itself, as aural and visual recording media are. I would draw the same distinction here that Roland Barthes (1977: 44) makes between drawing and photography: whereas drawings, like writing, transforms performance, audio-visual technologies, like photography, record it.[36] In everyday usage, we refer to "live" or "recorded" performances but not to "written" performances or "painted" performances, perhaps for this reason. This means that the history of live performance is bound up with the history of recording media; it extends over no more than the past 100 to 150 years. To declare retroactively that all performance before, say, the mid-19th century was "live" would be an anachronistic imposition of a modern concept on a pre-modern phenomenon. In fact, the *Oxford English Dictionary*'s earliest examples of the use of the word "live" in reference

---

36 I am not suggesting that recording media do not transform live performance in the process of capturing it, only that they provide a kind of access to the live event that writing and static visual media do not. This is in part because recording media may be used to capture performance in real time: the duration of the recording can be identical with that of the performance itself. The question of temporality places still photography in an ambiguous position, since photography does record performance but only as a series of individual moments divorced from their temporal procession. The question of whether or not a static visual medium can be said to reproduce the temporality of performance will return in a legal context in Chapter 4.

to performance come from the mid-1930s, well after the advent of recording technologies and the development of broadcasting systems. If this word history is complete, then the concept of live performance came into being not at the appearance of the basic recording technologies that made the concept possible but only with the maturation of mediatized society itself.

On this basis, the historical relationship of liveness and mediatization must be seen as a relation of dependence and imbrication rather than opposition. That the mediated is engrained in the live is apparent in the structure of the English word *immediate*. The root form is the word *mediate* of which *immediate* is, of course, the negation. Mediation is thus embedded within the *im-mediate*; the relation of mediation and the im-mediate is one of mutual dependence, not precession. Far from being encroached upon, contaminated, or threatened by mediation, live performance is always already inscribed with traces of the possibility of technical mediation (i.e., mediatization) that defines it as live. Although the anxiety of critics who champion live performance is understandable, theorizations that privilege liveness as a pristine state uncontaminated by mediatization misconstrue the relation between the two terms.

Connor summarizes the relationship between the live and the mediatized in related terms:

> In the case of "live" performance, the desire for originality is a secondary effect of various forms of reproduction. The intense "reality" of the performance is not something that lies behind the particulars of the setting, the technology and the audience; its reality consists in all of that apparatus of representation.
>
> (Connor 1989: 153)

Connor's frame of reference is the performance of popular music, my subject in the next chapter. A good example of the inscription of the apparatus of representation within live performance in that realm is the status of the microphone in popular music performance: consider its central role in Elvis Presley's performance style, the microphonic acrobatics of James Brown, or the way the Supremes' and Temptations' choreography is centered around the positioning of their microphones. As Connor implies, the very presence of the microphone and the performers' manipulation of it are paradoxical markers of the performance's status as live and im-mediate. Far from suppressing the apparatus of reproduction, as a performer such as Madonna may be said to be attempting when she uses a headset mike not clearly visible to the audience (with the effect of naturalizing mediatized representations, as I discussed earlier in this chapter), these performers emphasize that the apparatus of reproduction is a constitutive element of their liveness. In short, they *perform* the inscription of mediatization within the im-mediate.

The im-mediate is not prior to mediation but derives precisely from the mutually defining relationship between the im-mediate and the mediated. Similarly, live performance cannot be said to have ontological or historical priority over mediatization, since liveness was made visible only by the possibility of technical reproduction. This problematizes Phelan's claim that "to the degree that live performance attempts to enter into the economy of reproduction it betrays and lessens the promise of its own ontology" (Phelan 1993a: 146), not just because it is not at all clear that live performance has a distinctive ontology, but also because it is not a question of performance's *entering into* the economy of reproduction, since it has always been there. My argument is that the very concept of live performance presupposes that of reproduction – that the live can exist only *within* an economy of reproduction.

In challenging the traditional opposition of the live and the mediatized, I am not suggesting that we cannot make phenomenological distinctions between the respective experiences of live and mediatized representations, distinctions concerning their respective positions within cultural economy, and ideological distinctions among performed representations in all media. What I am suggesting is that any distinctions need to derive from careful consideration of how the relationship between the live and the mediatized is articulated in particular cases, not from a set of assumptions that constructs the relation between live and mediatized representations *a priori* as a relation of essential opposition. I attempted to do something of the kind in the first section of this chapter by examining the way that television came to be positioned discursively first as a replication of theatrical discourse, then as a replacement for live theatre. That theatre and television came to be competitors within cultural economy resulted from this particular discursive history, not from some intrinsic opposition between them. In Chapter 3, I will analyze the changing status of live performance within rock music culture to make a related point: that the relation of live performance to mediatized forms needs to be understood historically and locally, in particular cultural contexts.

Got live if you want it

My claim that live performance recapitulates mediatized representations has sometimes been challenged by the demand to know why people still want to see live performances if that is the case. This is an important question usually addressed by recourse to clichés and mystifications concerning aura, presence, the "magic of live theatre," etc. Although any attempt at a general response is bound to be flawed, the single most important point to make with respect to the continued attractiveness of live performance in a mediatized culture is that, like liveness itself, the desire for live experiences is a product of mediatization. "[I]t is possible to see how the proliferation of reproductions actually intensifies the desire for origin, even if that origin is increasingly sensed as an erotic lack rather than a tangible and satisfying presence" (Connor 1989: 151). Ultimately, however, a question like this is best answered from the perspective of particular cultural contexts: what does live performance mean, and why is it demanded, within particular groups defined by shared cultural identity and/or tastes? Before undertaking that kind of contextual analysis in the next chapter, I will address two of the conventional explanations for the continued interest in live performance – that it appeals broadly to the senses and that it creates community – then comment on the value of live performance as symbolic capital.

One of the main conventional explanations advanced for the continued appeal of live performance is that it offers a fuller sensory experience than mediatized performances. Whereas mediatized representations appeal primarily to the visual and auditory senses, live performances engage all the senses, including the olfactory, tactile, somatic, and kinesthetic. I would argue that this is not the case, that these other senses *are* engaged by mediatized performances. It certainly can be the case that live performance engages the senses *differently* than mediatized representations, but a difference in kind is not the same thing as a difference in magnitude of sensory experience.

Another conventional argument is that the experience of live performance builds community. It is surely the case that a sense of community may emanate from being part of an audience that clearly values something you value, though the reality of our cultural economy is that the communal bond unifying such an audience is most likely to be little more than the common consumption of a particular performance commodity. Leaving that issue aside, I would argue against the idea that live performance itself somehow generates whatever sense of community one may experience. For one thing, mediatized performance makes just as effective a focal point for the gathering of a social group as live performance. Theodore Gracyk, who discusses this issue as it pertains to popular music, observes that:

> One does not need a live performance to create such a [social] space or its attendant sense of being part of a community engaged with the music: discos, Jamaican "sound system" trucks, bars and pubs and pool halls with juke boxes, and the British rave scene have created diverse public sites for recorded music.
>
> (Gracyk 1997: 147)

Gracyk's point can be generalized across performance genres. A parallel example from a different cultural realm would be that of the crowd that gathered in the town square of a small city adjacent to Atlanta to watch a big-screen simulcast of the opening ceremonies of the 1996 Olympic Games. The people gathered around the giant television screen constituted a community in all the same senses as the audience attending the live event a few miles away. Since most of the people gathered in the town square were neighbors, not merely people drawn together to attend an event, their experience was arguably more genuinely communal than that of the audience attending the live performance. My point is simply that communality is not a function of liveness. The sense of community arises from being part of an audience, and the quality of the experience of community derives from the specific audience situation, not from the spectacle for which that audience has gathered.

Another version of this account of the appeal of live performance proposes that live performance brings performers and spectators together in a community. This view misunderstands the dynamic of performance, which is predicated on the distinction between performers and spectators. Indeed, the effort to eliminate that distinction destroys the very possibility of performance: "The more you approach a performer, the more you inhibit the very performance you are there to see. No matter how much a performer gives, no matter how intensively you attend to her, the gap remains between" (Cubitt 1994: 283). Those like Jerzy Grotowski and Augusto Boal, for whom bridging this gap has become the primary purpose of their work, albeit for very different reasons, have found themselves constrained to abandon performance as such altogether (see Auslander 1997: 26–7, 99–101). Blau addresses these issues of performance and communality in his discussion of the theatre audience:

> Desire has always been…for the audience as community, similarly enlightened, unified in belief, all the disparities in some way healed by the experience of theater. The very nature of theater reminds us somehow of the original unity even as it implicates us in the common experience of fracture, which produces both what is time-serving and divisive in theater and

what is self-serving and subversive in desire....as there is no
theater without *separation*, there is no appeasing of desire.

(Blau 1990: 10)

As Blau suggests in this extraordinary passage, the experience of theatre
(of live performance generally, I would say) provokes our desire for
community but cannot satisfy that desire because performance is
founded on difference, on separation and fragmentation, not unity. Live
performance places us in the living presence of the performers, other
human beings with whom we desire unity and can imagine achieving it,
because they are there, in front of us. Yet live performance also inevitably
frustrates that desire since its very occurrence presupposes a gap between
performer and spectator. Whereas mediatized performance can provide
the occasion for a satisfactory experience of community *within* the audience, live performance inevitably yields a sense of the failure to achieve
community *between* the audience and the performer. By reasserting the
unbridgeable distinction between audience and performance, live
performance foregrounds its own fractious nature and the unlikelihood
of community in a way that mediatized representations, which never
hold out the promise of unity, do not.

Another dimension to the question of why people continue to
attend live events in our mediatized culture is that live events have
cultural value: being able to say that you were physically present at a
particular event constitutes valuable symbolic capital – certainly, it is
possible to dine out on the cachet of having been at Woodstock, for
example.[37] One remarkable aspect of performance's position within
cultural economy is that our ability to convert attendance at a live
event into symbolic capital is completely independent of the experien-

37 I agree with Simon Frith (1996: 9) that Pierre Bourdieu's concepts of cultural capital
and symbolic capital can and should be extended beyond his original usage.
Bourdieu's "interest...is in the creation of a taste hierarchy in terms of high and low:
the possession of cultural capital, he suggests, is what defines high culture in the first
place." Frith's rejoinder "is that a similar use of accumulated knowledge and discrim-
inatory skill is apparent in low cultural forms, and has the same hierarchical effect"
of differentiating those who are truly adept in a particular cultural arena from those
who are not (see also Shuker 1994: 247–50). Cultural capital and symbolic capital,
in this extended sense, must be understood as determined contextually. Particular
subcultural and taste groups attribute symbolic capital to experiences that other
groups do not recognize as valuable. That kind of discrimination is at the heart of
my analysis of rock music culture in the next chapter: to an adept of "rock," "pop"
music carries no symbolic capital. (More accurately, an enthusiasm for pop carries
negative symbolic capital within the context of rock culture!)

tial quality of the event itself. Attending Woodstock might have meant spending three days hungry, sick, covered with mud, and unable to hear any music whatsoever. Seeing the Beatles at New York's Shea Stadium in 1965 almost undoubtedly did mean hearing no music and might have meant suffering hearing loss as a result of screaming fans. None of this matters, however; merely being able to say you were there, live, translates into symbolic capital in the appropriate cultural contexts.

This aspect of liveness has a complex relation to cultural economy. Despite the claim, discussed earlier, that performance's evanescence allows it to escape commodification, it is performance's very evanescence that gives it value in terms of cultural prestige.[38] The less an event leaves behind in the way of artifacts and documentation, the more symbolic capital accrues to those who were in attendance, at least

---

38 Considering the concept of symbolic capital in the context of taste or fan cultures, as I am implicitly doing here, makes certain aspects of the nature of symbolic capital visible. Randal Johnson argues that Bourdieu's various "capitals" (e.g., cultural capital, symbolic capital, linguistic capital, economic capital) "are not reducible to each other" (Johnson 1993: 7). Within fan cultures, however, cultural capital does translate into symbolic capital: the more you know about a particular rock group, for example, the more prestige you will have among fans of that group. Among collectors, the symbolic value of an object is generally a function of its rarity and inaccessibility, which also determine its economic value. It is roughly true, then, that the greater the economic value of a collectible, the greater its symbolic value. (One class of exceptions would be those in which an object that is worth very little economically carries great symbolic value because it attests to the rarefaction of the owner's taste. There are, for instance, rare but not particularly valuable psychedelic rock albums. Owning these records is a sign of expert knowledge and an indication that your taste for the music extends well beyond what is known to most fans, even though the records have little actual economic value.) Even taking into consideration Johnson's admonishment that "Bourdieu's use of economic terminology does not imply any sort of economism" (Bourdieu 1993: 8), it becomes apparent that symbolic capital can be quantified, relatively even if not absolutely. In considering the symbolic value of attendance at live performances, rarity, distance in time, and proximity to an imagined originary moment are determining factors. It is clear, for example, that having seen a Rolling Stones concert in 1964 is worth more symbolic capital within rock culture than having seen the Stones in 1997, for all the reasons I just mentioned. It may even be that having seen the Beatles live is worth more than having seen the Stones, even in 1964, precisely because the Beatles' performing career was relatively short. Whereas one may still see the Stones, one will never again be able to see the Beatles. Although such comparisons probably can be made, it is unlikely that symbolic capital can be quantified to the point of determining the exchange values that would justify a statement such as: having seen the Rolling Stones ten times between 1964 and 1997 is of equivalent symbolic value to having seen the Beatles live once.

in some cases (see Cubitt 1994: 289). In other cases, however, the symbolic value of having attended an event may be a function of that event's notoriety, which, in turn, may result from the extent to which the event has been circulated as reproductions. Arguably, having been at the Isle of Wight Festival carries less symbolic capital than having been at Woodstock precisely because Woodstock has been so widely reproduced as multiple sound recordings, books, and a film, and thus has become culturally iconic in a way the other festival has not (at least in the American context).

However one may assess the relative symbolic values of live events, it is important to observe that even within our hyper-mediatized culture, far more symbolic capital is attached to live events than to mediatized ones, at least for the moment. In the cultural contexts in which Laurie Anderson matters, for example, I bank far more symbolic capital from having seen her perform *The Nerve Bible* live than I would from being able to say that I had heard it on CD or that I had read the book. The irony of the fact that live performances are still worth more symbolic capital within our culture than mediatized performances, even as live performance becomes more and more like mediatized performance, is clearly illustrated by *The Nerve Bible*, almost all of which was prerecorded and run by computers. During the second half, Anderson wandered on- and off-stage, as if to suggest that the computerized, audiovisual machine she had set into motion could run itself, that *it* was the show, with her or without her. Even though Anderson's performance is barely live at all, it still commands greater symbolic capital than fully mediatized forms.

I suspect that this is a very temporary condition, however, and that we can begin to imagine a culture in which more prestige would accrue to someone who said she had seen Anderson on videotape or listened to her on CD than to the person who had seen her live. It is actually not at all difficult to imagine cases in which owning the mediatized version of a performance is worth the same, if not more, symbolic capital as having attended the live event. I would derive substantial symbolic capital from having seen the Beatles at the Cavern Club in Liverpool in 1960, for instance. But it is open to question whether I would garner more cultural capital than someone who owns a bootleg recording of the same performance. The bootleg would surely be worth at least as much symbolic capital as attendance at the live event; as a tangible artifact of the performance that would make it accessible to others, it might even be worth more.

The question of whether mediatized performance will come to be valued over live performance in the culture at large will be answered by the next few generations. In an essay on internet romance, Meghan Daum offers the following confession: "[I] have a constant low-grade fear of the telephone, and I often call people with the intention of getting their answering machines. There is something about the live voice that I have come to find unnervingly organic, as volatile as live television" (Daum 1997: 80). Many of us have made calls hoping to get an answering machine, but it is important to take note of the terms in which Daum describes her anxiety. Daum represents a generation already come of age, brought up in a world dominated by communications technologies, for whom *television* represents immediate, live experience (notice that she cites television rather than, say, theatre as her model for the live), and live experience of any kind is undesirable and actually distressing. In thinking about the generation after Daum's, I wonder whether having seen the live stage presentation of Disney's *Beauty and the Beast*, for instance, counts for more among children today than owning a copy of the movie on video cassette. What value will be attached to live performance when these generations attain cultural power?

3

TRYIN' TO MAKE IT REAL

Live performance, simulation, and the
discourse of authenticity in rock culture

In the spring of 1990, the Franco-German pop singing and dancing
duo Milli Vanilli was awarded the Best New Artist Grammy for 1989.
The award prompted a spate of newspaper articles with titles like
"That Syncing[1] Feeling" (*Detroit News*, July 31 1990) and other media
commentary concerning various performers, including Milli Vanilli,
who allegedly lip-synched to pre-recorded vocals in concert (Madonna,
Michael Jackson, Paula Abdul, and many others were similarly
accused).[2] Most of the commentary was adamantly opposed to the
practice, though virtually all of it also admitted that the main audiences for the performers in question, mostly young teenagers, did not
seem to care whether their idols actually sang or not.[3] In November,
Milli Vanilli's producer created fresh controversy when he admitted
that not only had the duo lip-synched their concerts, they had not
even sung on the recording for which they were awarded the Grammy,
which was then rescinded, much to the embarrassment of the National
Academy of Recording Arts and Sciences (NARAS), the Grammys'
institutional sponsor. In response to these waves of scandal, legislators
in many American states followed the lead of those in New York and
New Jersey by introducing bills mandating that tickets and posters
promoting concerts during which performers lip-synch state that fact;

---

1 There is no consensus as to whether "lip-synch" or "lip-sync" is the proper spelling. I
  prefer the former but retain the latter in quoted materials.
2 I have been asked whether race was a factor in the singling out of Milli Vanilli. My
  own feeling is that their status as Europeans is probably more significant than their
  African heritage. The fact of their being German places them outside the American
  music establishment in a way that their being Black does not, and may account for
  why they rather than, say, Michael Jackson, were challenged. Christopher Martin
  (1993: 71, 73) implies that since the two members of Milli Vanilli were rumored to
  be gay, homophobia may have played a role in their stigmatization.
3 My own younger students, polled in the Fall of 1990, felt precisely that way.

stiff fines were to be levied against violators.[4] These legislators claimed to see the lip-synching issue as a question of consumer fraud.[5]

My purpose in this chapter is to analyze the changing meaning and status of live performance within a particular cultural context, that of rock music. The Milli Vanilli scandal is central to this analysis and to an understanding of how liveness has come to be devalued in that cultural realm. Before discussing the devaluation of liveness, however, it is necessary to establish the nature of the value that live performance once had within rock culture. To that end, the first part of this chapter offers a description of what live performance meant in the rock culture of the 1960s and 1970s. Because rock culture is specifically organized around recordings, it is a particularly interesting arena in which to examine the question of liveness. The early sections of this chapter, therefore, focus on the relationship between the two main forms in which rock music is consumed: as live performances and as recordings. I then take up the question of what happened to the status of live performance of rock with the rise of music television and digital technologies. The last portion of the chapter offers a Baudrillardian reading of Milli Vanilli in relation to the institutional discourses of the Grammys and the law.

Rock culture and the discourse of authenticity

In *Rhythm and Noise: An Aesthetics of Rock* (1996), Theodore Gracyk argues persuasively that the primary object of rock music as an aesthetic form is the recording, not live musical performance. Arguing

4 The same issue has arisen, belatedly, in newly capitalistic Russia, and the response has been the same: a revision to consumer law forcing lip-synching artists to say so in their publicity (see Bronwyn McLaren, "Lip-synch proposal could drive stars off stage," *Moscow Times*, 10 June 1997: 3).
5 A class action suit against Milli Vanilli's record company was settled in favor of consumers: anyone who had purchased their recordings was entitled to a refund. However, the judge who oversaw the settlement, and other judges in the Cook County (Illinois) Circuit where the case was filed, considered the use of the courts to address such a matter an abuse of process. In its decision in *Ippolito v. Lennon* (542 N.Y.S.2d 3 [1989]), a New York case involving some similar issues, the court had written: "In the realm of entertainment media, where the use of stand-ins, stunt doubles, voice overs and lip-syncing is commonplace, there is some reluctance to create a cause of action out of such activity" (quoted in Clarida 1993: 191).

that musical instruments are not the primary materials of rock, as they are of many other genres of music, Gracyk offers the following analysis:

> The vast majority of the time, the audience for rock music listens to *speakers* delivering *recordings*. Exploring the limitations and possibilities of the recording process, crafting music in those terms, rock's primary materials are often the available recording and playback equipment. Guitars, pianos, voices, and so on became secondary materials. Consequently, rock music is not essentially a performing art, no matter how much time rock musicians spend practicing on their instruments or playing live.
>
> (Gracyk 1996: 74–5)

Therefore, "studio recordings have become the standard for judging live performances,"[6] and "musicians are usually re-creating music [in live performances], not making it" (ibid.: 84, 77).

Gracyk is clearly correct: there is no question that rock exists primarily as recorded music and that rock culture is organized around recordings.[7] Indeed, rock culture as such can be said to have come into existence partly as a result of the development of the 45 rpm record in 1948, which made popular music cheaper to produce and easier to

---

6 Note that Gracyk's comment exactly parallels Steve Wurtzler's observation about the relationship of live and televised sports cited in Chapter 2 and supports my general point there that live performance now tends to recapitulate mediatized representations. Wurtzler (1992: 94) extends his analysis into the realm of music by arguing that live albums are judged not according to the accuracy with which they represent the concerts they document, but by comparison with the "original," *recorded* versions of the music. "Again the live is conceived as a degraded version of the recorded."

7 By "rock culture," I mean the cultural formation that includes and surrounds rock music itself, a culture whose main adherents are: on the production side, musicians, their producers, and those peopling the apparatus of the music industry; on the reception side, rock music fans and critics. I have in mind something similar to what Lawrence Grossberg (1994: 41) calls "the rock formation," a term he uses to suggest that "the identity and effect of rock always depends on more than its sonorial dimension....We always locate musical practices in the context of a complex...set of relations with other cultural and social practices...." With Grossberg, I acknowledge that there is diversity within rock culture but justify the use of a seemingly monolithic concept by pointing out that "there is some unified sense to 'rock'...the overemphasis on locality and specificity often leads us away from important generalities, as well as from the fact that such generalities are part of the reality of the local articulations." It is in terms of these generalities that I am speaking here.

integrate into social life than the more cumbersome and fragile 78 rpm discs (Curtis 1987: 44–5; Shuker 1994: 42–3). It is equally the case, however, that rock music *is* performed live and that, within rock culture, live performance is important and demanded. If we accept Gracyk's characterization of rock music as primarily a recorded form, how do we account for the importance of live performance in rock culture? Looking at the production side of rock, this question appears to be easy to answer: the primary function of live performance is to promote the sale of recordings. But even this self-evident proposition becomes less plausible in light of Gracyk's analysis, for if rock is primarily a recorded music, why shouldn't the presence of the recordings on the radio and television suffice as a means of promoting them? And how exactly could live performances, which Gracyk insists belong to a different aesthetic order than recordings, serve to promote them? These questions intertwine with a basic question framed from the point of view of reception: if rock fans are primarily engaged with recordings, what need does live performance fulfill for them?

Gracyk's own handling of the question of live performance is not altogether consistent. Initially, he describes the pleasures of live performance as deriving from interaction with others: the individual listener has the opportunity to commune with fellow fans and to experience an illusory bond with the performer (Gracyk 1996: 78). He goes on, however, to lump live performance together with other visual representations of rock, including coffee-table books, magazine spreads, album covers, and television, saying "A major trap is to buy into the imagery of rock promotion" (ibid: 75). According to Gracyk, since all of these media tend to represent rock musicians primarily as live performers and not as the studio artists they truly are, they are all guilty of a pernicious misrepresentation. The problem with Gracyk's argument is that most rock *recordings* are guilty of the same misrepresentation. Only a few rock records foreground the artifice of their studio construction; most are made to sound like performances that could have taken place, even if they really didn't (and couldn't).[8]

Simon Frith's description of his own listening experience can probably stand as typical for that of a sophisticated rock fan: "I listen to

---

8 The idea that recordings represent musical performances that never took place is not specific to rock music. An oft-cited early example comes from the realm of classical music performance: on a 1951 recording, Wagnerian soprano Kristen Flagstad's high notes as Isolde were sung by Elizabeth Schwarzkopf to produce a perfect vocal performance. See Eisenberg (1987: 116) and Attali (1985: 106).

records in the full knowledge that what I hear is something that never existed, that never could exist, as a 'performance,' something happening in a single time and space; nevertheless, it is now happening, in a single time and space: it is thus a performance and I hear it as one" (Frith 1996: 211). In a general discussion of the ontological status of musical recordings, Gracyk argues that recordings "offer either a reproduction or a representationof the music's *performance*….Undoctored recordings of live performances reproduce a performance. Les Paul's 'Lady of Spain' [in which Paul plays several overdubbed guitars] is a representation of a performance" (Gracyk 1997: 142, original emphasis). Frith suggests that the rock fan knows that recordings are representations, but hears them as reproductions nevertheless. If Frith is right when he says that rock recordings create the impression of being performances taking place in a single space and time, even for a listener who is fully aware that the performance exists only on the recording, then they should be just as deceptive and pernicious for Gracyk as visual representations of rock that depict musicians as performing live rather than at work in the studio. The grounds on which Gracyk wants to dismiss live performance of rock, together with its representations, as promoting a false view of the music's origins would seem to be grounds on which to dismiss the music itself. If rock music can be seen as a form worthy of aesthetic appreciation, despite (or because of?) its industrial origins and commercial character, the visual culture that surrounds the music and its live performance must be seen as contributing to that aesthetic experience, not merely as a systematic misrepresentation of the music whose sole purpose is the cynical promotion of an attractive illusion. The visual culture of rock is neither more nor less cynical than the music itself: like rock records, live performances, photographs, and so on, are products of the commercial apparatus of the music industry that contribute to the impression that rock music is a performing art. However inaccurate that impression may be, it defines the experience of rock for its listeners.

I want to suggest that the visual artifacts of rock serve a particular function within rock culture and that live performance plays a pivotal role in this regard. The function to which I am alluding is that of establishing the *authenticity* of the music for the rock fan. Before proceeding, some definitional discussion is in order.

> First, *authenticity*. This clearly relates to questions of production but not to a thought-through theory; "inauthentic," that is to say, is a term that can be applied evaluatively within genres which are, in production terms, "inauthentic" by definition – fans can distinguish between authentic and inauthentic

Eurodisco, and what is being described by implication is not how something was actually produced but a more inchoate feature of the music itself, a perceived quality of sincerity and commitment....What is it about a record that makes us say, "I just don't believe it!" (my reaction to Paul Simon's *Graceland*, for example)?...This is obviously related somehow to the ways in which we judge people's sincerity generally; it is a human as well as a musical judgment. And it also reflects our extra-musical beliefs – what I already knew about Paul Simon obviously had an effect on how I heard his music (and new knowledge – new music – might mean I changed my mind).

(Frith 1996: 71)

Frith makes two important points here: that authenticity can be heard in the music, yet is an effect not just of the music itself but also of prior musical and extra-musical knowledge and beliefs; that what counts as authentic varies among musical genres and subgenres. Because I am focusing here on the genre called "rock," I will consider the concept of authenticity as it is understood within that cultural context. Following a conventional usage, I employ the word "rock" to denote a kind of popular music that originated in the mid-1960s, as distinct from its 1950s predecessor, rock and roll. Friedlander (1996) offers a good summary history of rock and its predecessor. The first generation of rock and roll musicians consisted primarily of Black artists (e.g., Chuck Berry, Little Richard, Fats Domino). The one important White artist was Bill Haley. The roster of the second generation of rock and roll artists, which emerged around 1956, contained only White artists: Elvis Presley, Jerry Lee Lewis, Buddy Holly, etc.[9] By the end of the 1950s, this music had:

---

9 Robert Palmer (1995: 8) elucidates this distinction, though he uses the term "rock and roll" where I use "rock": "[T]he term 'rock and roll' came to designate guitar-based music with a 'black' beat, primarily played by and for whites. By the sixties, 'rock and roll' carried such 'white' connotations that writers began referring to the new, rhythm-oriented styles first as 'soul,' then 'funk.'" Friedlander (1996: 12) also describes soul and Motown, musical styles that evolved contemporaneously with rock, as "African–American genres" distinct from rock. Indeed, one of the more disappointing aspects of rock culture is its exclusion of Black musicians, who have had great difficulty in being accepted as rock artists. Producers and record companies have typically wanted to market African–American musicians as soul or rhythm and blues artists, rather than rock acts.

all but faded from view. In its place records from female vocal groups (who became known as the "girl groups") and clean-cut young men (teen idols), a budding California "surf" sound, and a developing folk revival all became popular....In 1964, the United States awakened to the sound of the Beatles, with their variety of classic rock styles combined with touches of pop and rockabilly. This British invasion, which included music from the Rolling Stones, the Dave Clark Five, the Who, and others, reawakened America's rock and roll urges.

(Friedlander 1996: 11–12)

Rock contains multiple subgenres, including acid rock, hard rock, folk rock, and many others. Lawrence Grossberg (1993: 202) suggests that there have always been "many forms of rock authenticity": what is considered authentic in the context of one subgenre is not necessarily seen that way in another. While rock culture can accommodate multiple definitions of authenticity, the concept of authenticity has also always been exclusionary: "At every moment in its history, rock fans have always identified some music which, along with their [sic] associated cultural apparatuses and audiences, are dismissed, not merely as bad or inferior rock but somehow as not really rock at all."[10] The

A case in point is that of the Chambers Brothers, best known for the psychedelic anthem "Time Has Come Today" (1968). An African–American family group from Mississippi that had moved to Los Angeles in the mid-1950s, the Chambers Brothers began as gospel singers, becoming active on the coffee-house and folk-festival circuit by the early 1960s. Their controversial performance of "Time Has Come Today," which they had written, at the 1965 Newport Folk Festival (the same festival at which Bob Dylan created even more controversy by using electric instru-mentation; see note 49) reflected their identification with rock and hippie culture. Even so, the record companies interested in signing them wanted to treat them as an "R&B act with uniforms and choreography." Columbia Records, with whom the Chambers Brothers did sign, did not place that demand on them but said that "Time Has Come Today" could only be recorded by a White rock group. Only after the Chambers Brothers had a successful record with another song did Columbia permit them to record "Time Has Come Today." In the 1970s, the Chambers were remanded by Columbia to the R&B producers Gamble and Huff, who attempted to make them over into a "Black" act (Jud Cost, "Liner notes," *Time Has Come: The Best of the Chambers Brothers*, Columbia Records 1996). Needless to say, the Chambers Brothers were far more successful as a rock group in the 1960s than as an R&B act in the 1970s.

10 Frith (1996: 40) points out that the discourses surrounding other forms of popular music also define them in terms of this kind of distinction. The discourse of folk music, for instance, emphasizes its difference from "commercial pop."

name most frequently used for rock's Other is "pop."[11] Rock and pop can be distinguished on a more-or-less objective basis: whereas rock derives historically from African–American roots in 1950s rock and roll, pop derives historically from the White popular music of the 1950s: Perry Como, Patti Page, and their ilk. In most cases, this historical difference is quite evident in the music itself: no one would ever mistake the Lettermen or Barry Manilow for rock musicians.

In rock culture, however, the distinction between rock and pop is not primarily historical or stylistic. As Grossberg (1992: 131) puts it, "rock cannot be defined in musical terms," for "there are, for all practical purposes, no musical limits on what can or cannot be rock....There is nothing that cannot become a rock song or, perhaps more accurately, there is no sound that cannot become rock."[12] Richard Meltzer (1987 [1970]: 270) had made a similar observation much earlier: "everything...is contextualizable as rock." Indeed, if the substitution of the string quartet for rock instrumentation on the Beatles' recordings of "Yesterday" and "Eleanor Rigby" can be heard as rock, it is hard to imagine what musical sound could not be so contextualized. Keith Negus (1997: 162) objects to this way of thinking about rock on the grounds that it tends simultaneously to privilege rock as the central category of popular music and to define it far too broadly: "This is an approach to studying popular music that ignores the vast numbers of generic distinctions made by musicians and audiences across the world and which reduces popular music to the category of rock." As my own insistence on distinguishing "rock" from "rock and roll" should suggest, I sympathize with Negus's view that rock needs to be defined specifically. I doubt, however, that such a definition can be constructed by identifying rock's "stylistic practices," as Negus would

---

11 There is some terminological confusion in the use of the expressions "popular music" and "pop music." The distinction between rock and pop I just cited derives from American parlance; British music commentators frequently use the term pop in a way that includes rock in that category, though the same commentators may also distinguish rock from pop in other contexts. I use "pop" to refer to rock's ideological Other and "popular music" to refer to the broader sphere that encompasses both, as well as many other genres.

12 At least, this is the case when rock is defined broadly. It may be that particular subgenres of rock do have identifiable musical and stylistic characteristics, and canons of acceptable and unacceptable sounds. Sheila Whiteley (1992) does an admirable job of analyzing the stylistic and structural features of psychedelic rock. It is noteworthy, however, that Whiteley supports her case with extensive analysis of the lyrics of songs as well as their purely musical features.

wish, since Grossberg and Meltzer are surely correct in asserting that any musical style can be assimilated to the category "rock." Ultimately, "the designation of rock music is more of a sociological than a musical one" (Shuker 1994: 247).[13] The question of generic distinctions that Negus raises is nevertheless central to understanding that the way rock fans define the music is principally *ideological*, not stylistic.

The ideological distinction between rock and pop is precisely the distinction between the authentic and the inauthentic, the sincere and the cynical, the genuinely popular and the slickly commercial, the potentially resistant and the necessarily co-opted, art and entertainment.[14] Susan Douglas offers the following succinct definition of rock ideology and the expectations it imposes on the music: "Real rock and roll must be 'authentic' – meaning it features instrumental virtuosity, original songwriting, social criticism, a stance of anger and/or alienation" (Douglas 1997: 22; see also Negus 1997: 149–50). From the point of view of rock ideology, there can be no such thing as "authentic Eurodisco," for example, all Eurodisco is condemned as intrinsically inauthentic pop music, precisely because it does not meet the requirements Douglas identifies.[15] The interesting cases, then, are not those like disco or Barry Manilow, where identification as pop is obvious, but those in which the artist has a suspect claim to being an authentic rock musician (I shall discuss the Monkees in this connection later in this chapter). The fact that there is even a rock subgenre called "pop-rock" itself suggests that this distinction is not always clear-cut, and is open to negotiation. These are the cases that are subject to extensive debate by rock fans. By not taking this aspect of rock culture into account, Gracyk commits the error of defining rock too broadly. While it is fair to say that rock is a diverse stylistic category with fuzzy borders, it is

---

13 In a related vein, Nicholas Cook (1995–6: 39) argues that the basic compositional unit of rock music is not best understood on the model employed in classical musicology of an *Urtext* (the composition) which gives rise to "a variety of subordinate and derivative texts" when performed. A piece of rock music exists primarily as "a cultural entity," not a formal composition, and that entity is "the sum total" of the "multiplicity of texts" (e.g., recordings, live performances) in which it is embodied.

14 See Grossberg's similar list of oppositions (1992: 206) and Shuker's discussion of the pop/rock dichotomy (1994: 7–8).

15 The distinction between rock and pop has been the subject of parliamentary debate in Great Britain. A consortium bidding to broadcast over a radio frequency that had been designated for music "other than pop" argued that their plan to broadcast rock music was consistent with this requirement. For accounts of the ensuing debate, see Frith (1996: 81–4) and Shuker (1994: 9–10).

nevertheless true that, within rock culture, the music is often defined in terms of an exclusionary concept of authenticity (and Gracyk (1996: 222) certainly goes too far when he identifies Whitney Houston as a rock musician!). The concept of rock authenticity is linked with the romantic bent of rock culture, in which rock music is imagined to be truly expressive of the artists' souls and psyches, and as necessarily politically and culturally oppositional. The romantic ideals of rock music are nicely expressed in Neil Young's song "Tonight's the Night (Part 1)" in which he sings of a deceased roadie: "Late at night when the people were gone/He used to pick up my guitar/And sing a song in a shaky voice/That was real as the day was long." These few lines summarize the mythology of self-expression central to rock in terms of authenticity, anti-commodification (the "real" singer takes the stage after the paying customers have left), and populism (since the roadie is described as "a working man" who also makes music). Gracyk (1996: 175–206) points out the untenability of rock romanticism, which wants to treat industrial products as individual expression and cultural resistance. Gracyk's analysis notwithstanding, the fact that the criteria for rock authenticity are imaginary has never prevented them from functioning in a very real way for rock fans.

I want to be very clear on one point. Taken on its own terms, rock authenticity is an essentialist concept, in the sense that rock fans treat authenticity as an essence that is either present or absent in the music itself, and they may well debate particular musical works in those terms. It is my intention to recognize this usage and to explore its implications. In my own discourse, however, I treat rock authenticity as an *ideological* concept and as a discursive effect. My approving cita-tion of Frith's definition notwithstanding, I will argue that authenticity is not simply present in the music itself and will also emphasize its cultural, rather than ethical, dimension. In other words, I posit that the creation of the effect of authenticity in rock is a matter of cultur-ally determined convention, not an expression of essence. It is also a result of industrial practice: the music industry specifically sets out to endow its products with the necessary signs of authenticity.

The specific semiotic markers of authenticity vary by musical genre and subgenre. Tightly choreographed unison dance steps may be neces-sary for a soul vocal group to establish itself as authentic but would be a sign of inauthenticity in a rock group because they belie the effect of spontaneity rock audiences value. Whereas acoustic playing is a sign of authenticity for the blues rock and folk rock of the 1960s and 1970s, it does not function that way for the more recent rock subgenre of Industrial Noise, which employs only highly-amplified sounds not always produced by conventional rock instruments. In order to appear authentic, many British rockers sing in American accents, thus acknowledging the historical origins of their musical genre (Durant 1985: 112). Female hardrockers frequently employ the aggressive vocal inflections and macho physical gestures and postures associated with male musicians, because that vocabulary is the established iconography of authenticity for that particular rock subgenre.

Not only do the signs of rock authenticity differ among its subgenres, they also change over time.

> Rock must constantly change to survive; it must seek to repro-
> duce its authenticity in new forms, in new places, in new
> alliances. It must constantly move from one center to another,
> transforming what had been authentic into the inauthentic in
> order to constantly project its claim to authenticity.
>
> (Grossberg 1992: 209)

Rock's authenticity effects are thus dependent on the nomination of something to serve as the inauthentic Other, whether that thing is current pop music or other rock. Alternative rock, for example, first presented itself in the 1980s as more authentic than the bloated art-rock left over from the 1970s, and still beloved to the baby-boomers. In this respect, rock ideology is conservative: authenticity is often located in current music's relationship to an earlier, "purer" moment in a mythic history of the music. In the 1970s, some rock groups (Queen, for instance) wrote in the liner notes to their albums that they did not use synthesizers, thus stressing their connection to the traditional instrumentation of roots rock ("real" electric guitars, drums, etc.).[16] The advent of digital musical instruments, however, changed the historical status of the synthesizer relative to authenticity:

> Playing analogue synthesizers is now a mark of authenticity,
> where it was once a sign of alienation – to pop iconography

---

16 The two rock subgenres I mention here can be defined as follows: art-rock, or progressive rock, which originated in the late 1960s and emphasizes compositional complexity and instrumental virtuosity, is rock with pretensions to status as classical music or jazz. Groups such as Yes, Emerson, Lake and Palmer, and Jethro Tull belong in this category. Roots rock, on the other hand, which looks back to rock's origins in folk, country, and rock and roll, emphasizes straightforward compositions on tradi-tional themes. Both self-conscious revivalists like the Stray Cats and more sophisticated groups like Creedence Clearwater Revival and the Band make up this category.

the image of musicians standing immobile behind synths
signified coldness....Now it is the image of a technician
hunched over a computer terminal that is problematic – but
that, like the image of the synth player, can and will change.

(Goodwin 1990: 269)

Synthesizers, once seen not as musical instruments but as machines that
had no place in rock, have come to be seen as just another form of
keyboard instrument. The computer keyboard has yet to be assimilated
in quite the same way, though that process has begun. In a 1997 appearance on US television, the British pop group Duran Duran foregrounded
their use of a computer by having the camera cut to the keyboard player
at moments when he was typing commands on a laptop.

Rock authenticity is performative, in Judith Butler's sense of that
term[17]: rock musicians achieve and maintain their effect of authenticity by continuously citing in their music and performance styles the
norms of authenticity for their particular rock subgenre and historical
moment, and these norms change along with changes in the prevailing
discourse of authenticity. The interplay of these factors is complex,
however. In her analysis of *Their Satanic Majesties Request* (1967), the
album on which the Rolling Stones attempt psychedelic rock, Sheila
Whiteley (1992: 90–9) points out that because the Stones' authenticity derives from their roots in American rhythm and blues, their
switch to psychedelic rock came off as forced and inauthentic. In this
case, the group's own musical history was at odds with their attempt to
cite the stylistic norm of that moment in rock history.

Grossberg locates rock authenticity in the music's sound, not the
visual aspects of its performance: [18]

The authenticity of rock has always been measured by its
sound, and most commonly, by its voice. Obviously, given the
contexts in which rock was made available to the majority of
its fans, it is not surprising that its ideology would focus on

17 See Butler (1993: 12–16) for a succinct discussion of her notion of performativity.
18 Grossberg (1993: 204) makes the curious observation that "rock's appeal to its black
    roots further secured the primacy of sound" as opposed to visual elements. This
    seems not to take into account the rather troubling history of the discourse of
    authenticity in the blues and soul music, in which, at various places and times, the
    question of authenticity has hinged on the pigmentation of the performer's skin. It
    also ignores the importance of visual elements in the performance of
    African–American popular music.

sound....The eye has always been suspect in rock culture; after all, visually, rock often borders on the inauthentic....It was here – in its visual presentation – that rock often most explicitly manifested its resistance to the dominant culture, but also its sympathies with the business of entertainment.

Grossberg (1993: 204)

Like Gracyk, Grossberg suggests that only the music itself as it is experienced on records can be treated seriously, that the visual culture of rock reflects its imbrication with a venal entertainment industry. All aspects of rock culture are products of this industry, however: the music, the visual artifacts that surround it (including live performances), even rock ideology and the effect of authenticity itself are manufactured to a very large extent. It makes little sense to separate the music from these other discourses, as if it transcends its origins in ways that they cannot.

Seeing is believing

Historically, one consequence of the reification of music in recordings is the century-old separation of the musical experience from live performance, and, particularly, the aural experience of music from its visual experience. The critical impact of the gramophone when it became widely available in the 1890s was "a vital shift in the experience of listening to music: the replacement of an audio-visual event with a primarily audio one, sound without vision" and it is from this originary point that the culture of popular music, and its emphasis on the aural aspects of music performance, has evolved (Laing 1991: 7–8). Nevertheless, sound recording certainly did not render the visual aspects of music irrelevant; indeed, listening to recordings may always be a visual as well as aural experience. Evan Eisenberg distinguishes the experience of monophonic and stereophonic recordings by saying that: "Stereo...arrays the musicians before you in empty space....The introduction of stereo...changed the phenomenology of the phonograph by adding a spatial, and hence a *visual* aspect" (Eisenberg 1987: 64–5, my emphasis).[19] Eisenberg's point is an important one: when sound is

---

19 Although I agree with Eisenberg that recorded sound evokes a visual image, I question this historical point. I doubt that monophonic sounds completely lacks a spatial aspect – even when a recording is designed to be played through a single speaker, the arrangement of sounds still evokes spatial concepts like foreground and background.

divorced from sight by virtue of technological mediation, the aural experience nevertheless evokes a visual one: "every mode of record listening leaves us with a need for something, if not someone, to see and touch" (ibid.: 65).

This visual experience of recorded music is generically specific: Eisenberg argues that "rock listeners, who have no preconception as to how live musicians should be deployed" tend to prefer to listen through headphones, which give the impression that the music is inside them rather than emanating from an exterior space (ibid.). Although Eisenberg does not say so explicitly, I assume he is contrasting rock with classical music and jazz, each of which uses well-known spatial configurations of musicians (the arrangement of symphony musicians is the most highly conventionalized). While it is true that rock recordings frequently contain "exaggerated stereo effects," I think that Eisenberg is wrong – rock listeners *do* visualize the musicians while listening to recordings: "to hear music is to see it performed, on stage, with all the trappings" (Frith 1996: 211). Meltzer suggests that listening to rock on records engages the visual imagination in a highly developed way: "Required [when 'listening to a standard guitarist on record'] is a mental picture of the guy facing you and occasionally moving around; in conjunction with this you visually change the situation and sit behind him or turn the stage around, or you put yourself right in his shoes" (Meltzer (1987 [1970]: 229). Precisely because there are fewer conventions for the arrangement of rock musicians on stage than there are for a symphony orchestra (though there are some: drums upstage center, for example) and because rock recordings frequently generate an irrational stereo field (that is, an imaginary aural space with no possible physical analogue),[20] our ability to visualize the performance of rock music as we listen to it is dependent on the availability of visual artifacts that show us what the musicians look like in performance.

Rock "has always stressed the visual as a necessary part of its apparatus – in performance, on record covers, in magazine and press photographs, and in advertising" (Goodwin 1993: 8), and it is from such sources that these images derive. "[S]ince," as Meltzer (1987

---

20 On many of Jimi Hendrix's recordings, for example, his guitar sound pans back and forth from right to left, rather than remaining on one side of the field or at its center. This movement of the sound may be somewhat reflective of rock guitarists' penchant for stalking back and forth across the concert stage. The irony is that, in live performance, the sound does not move with the guitarist, as the amplifiers and speakers from which it actually emanates remain stationary.

[1970]: 152–3) puts it, "a black circular piece of plastic is just a drag" the listening experience must be supplemented by additional artifacts: posters, booklets that come with the recordings, and the paraphernalia of fan-dom (trading cards, souvenirs, etc.). It is clear that such images help to define, but also must conform to, the visual standards of rock authenticity prevalent at a given historical moment. Whereas it was possible at the moment of rock's emergence in 1964 for the Beatles to be a credible rock group while wearing identical "mop-top" haircuts, tailored suits, and "Beatle boots" in photographs, including those on their record covers, that was no longer possible by the psychedelic era. Hence, the inclusion of pictures of the long-haired and bearded Beatles packaged with the so-called White Album (1968). Similarly, the members of the Jefferson Airplane would not have had much credibility as a psychedelic group had they appeared on their album covers dressed in business suits.

It is the case, however, that this kind of visual evidence is not enough to assure the authenticity of a rock group. In photographs, members of the Ohio Express, a late sixties bubblegum rock group, were appropriately hirsute and displayed Carnaby Street fashions, yet the group never actually existed; it was the studio creation of its producers.[21] Grossberg's claim that "the authenticity of rock has always been measured by its sound" is nevertheless misleading. Sound alone cannot establish rock authenticity (or inauthenticity) any more than visuals alone. It is not self-evident from listening to a Monkees album such as *Pisces, Aquarius, Capricorn and Jones, Ltd.* (1968) that their music is inauthentic. In terms of style, sound, and lyrical content, songs on this album compare favorably with the work of the Beatles, Crosby, Stills, and Nash, and the Jefferson Airplane.[22] (It may be tempting

21 For a useful overview of the bubblegum rock phenomenon, including the Monkees' relationship to it, see Cafarelli (1997), who reproduces a photograph of the Ohio Express. From the point of view of rock ideology, bubblegum is necessarily inauthentic because it was made mostly by groups that did not exist outside the studio. Yet, one of Cafarelli's sources goes so far as to suggest that only nonexistent groups can make authentic bubblegum rock!

22 In comparing the Monkees' music with that of other groups, Cafarelli (1997: 17) observes that "each [song] sounds like a stirring sample of AM-friendly pop-rock, with the Monkees' (inaudible) artificial origin the sole, negligible difference between these records and contemporary records by the Raiders,...Turtles, Dave Clark Five, Hollies, etc., etc." Each of these groups was commercially oriented but all had followed the conventional rock career path described below. My own list is intended to force a comparison between the Monkees and groups considered less overtly commercial in outlook who nevertheless had hit records, even on AM radio.

to argue that this plurality of styles is itself evidence of inauthenticity, but a certain musical eclecticism was in fact a hallmark of the psychedelic era, nowhere more evident than on the Beatles' *Sergeant Pepper's Lonely Hearts Club Band* (1967). Meltzer (1987 [1970]: 92–9) argues that eclecticism is in fact a hallmark of rock.) The Monkees' inauthenticity is not directly audible on their records but is a function of other knowledges that the rock fan brings to the record (e.g., that the Monkees were created for television, that they did not play their own instruments, etc.). Whiteley's examination of *Their Satanic Majesties Request* cited earlier is one of the best close analyses of rock sound in terms of authenticity. On the basis of its lyrics and musical structures, she concludes that the album is a calculated attempt at imitating the psychedelic style established by the Beatles on *Sergeant Pepper* and, therefore, inauthentic. Whiteley (1992: 99) ends her discussion by saying that "there is a mismatch between the expectations generated by the [album's psychedelic] cover, [and] the content, style and presentation [of the music itself]" thus acknowledging that the album's visual aspects play a role in the creation of expectation and the determination of (in)authenticity. Would Whiteley have heard the music on the album differently if it had had a different cover? I am suggesting that the determination of rock authenticity cannot be made on the basis of either visual or aural evidence alone, but only by considering both, and the relationship of one to the other in light of other knowledge the listener brings to bear.[23]

While recordings and the visual artifacts of rock culture proffer evidence of authenticity, only live performance can certify it for rock ideology. Live performance contributes to the process of authentication in two crucial ways. First, to be considered an authentic rocker, a musician must have a history as a live performer, as someone who has paid those dues and whose current visibility is the result of earlier popularity with a local following. Pursuing rock's traditional career path, musicians must first establish themselves and find an audience through live

---

23 It is significant in this context that Meltzer (1987 [1970]: 30) asserts that "the Beatles do not have to be seen or heard to produce an audience reaction of awesome magnitude." (He is referring to the frenzy of the crowd at a concert before the Beatles took the stage.) "This represents the growth of true 'inauthentic experience.'" Meltzer seems to be arguing that in a case in which neither the group's music nor their presence really matters, in which audience desire is projected entirely onto an inchoate image or idea of the group, then the group has been reduced to inauthenticity. The implication of his argument is that authenticity derives from the musicians' sound and presence.

performance; musicians are chosen to record by industry scouts on the basis of live performances. Subsequent moves from live performance at the local level to live performance at the national and international levels serve as indices of the musicians' popularity with audiences and status within the industry (Frith 1988b: 111–12). Even in the case of an act like the Beatles, who opted out of live performance to become exclusively a studio group very shortly after ascending to international fame, the fact that they had once been a performing band (and, conceivably, might be again) and that they had made their original reputation through live performance lent authority and authenticity to their recordings.[24] In an essay of 1968, for example, rock critic Albert Goldman refers to the Beatles as "the *best costumed*, best produced, most versatile, and technically resourceful of rock bands" (Goldman 1992: 60, my emphasis). Goldman's reference to costuming implies a perception of the Beatles as a performing unit even though they had abandoned live performance several years earlier. Similarly, continual rumors in the mid-1970s that Steely Dan, a group known to exist primarily in the studio, would be embarking on a tour helped the group maintain credibility with the rock audience even though the tour never materialized.[25] On the other hand, groups lacking a history of live performance and, like the Monkees or the Ohio Express, known (or suspected) to have been created only as studio aggregations, were dismissed by rock critics and fans as mere pop even when they did perform live.[26] Whereas the Beatles retained their authenticity even

---

24 For a decade before the death of John Lennon, rumors that a reformed version of the Beatles would soon be on tour continued to circulate. Even after Lennon's death, rumors persisted that the Beatles would reform with his elder son, Julian Lennon, in his place.

25 In fact, Steely Dan stopped touring in 1974, two years after the formation of the group, and did not play live again until a reunion tour in 1993. Steely Dan is a particularly difficult case to assess in terms of rock ideology. While rock fans held it against the group that they did not play live, "to the true afficianado, Steely Dan's unwillingness to waste time touring in order to focus on the bigger rewards of record-making was just the ultimate measure of their ornery integrity" (Chris Willman, Liner Notes *Citizen's Steely Dan*, MCA Records 1993). Willman argues that their refusal to tour "allowed them a sort of infamous anonymity on a scale more in line with their bebop heroes than with rock and roll's cult of personality." As the anthology of critical responses to their music reprinted in the booklet accompanying the *Citizen Steely Dan* box set (MCA 1993) suggests, critics had a hard time deciding whether they were best understood as a rock group, a pop group, or even a jazz group.

26 Jim Curtis (1987: 218) dismisses this disdain of the Monkees as elitism on the part of the critics (and, by extension, the rock culture generally). He points out that,

after they stopped performing live because they possessed a history as live performers, and Steely Dan was given the benefit of doubt, the Monkees could never be considered authentic, no matter how many live concerts they played, because they were known to have originated as a synthetic, televisual group, not as musicians with an "organically" developed history of live performance. It is for this reason that the producer of Radish, a recent group, "wanted Radish to build up a local following around Dallas prior to the release of the band's first album....He felt that Radish should be from Texas – from somewhere real, and not just from the music industry, like a nineties version of the Monkees" (Seabrook 1997: 80–1). The fact that the evidence of authenticity results from a calculated effort of the promotional apparatus does not prevent it from counting for rock fans. Nor should it, given the commodity context in which all aspects of rock culture are produced.

The second, and most critical, reason that live performance enables the determination of authenticity is that it is only in live performance that the listener can ascertain that a group that looks authentic in photographs, and sounds authentic on records, really *is* authentic in terms of rock ideology. In the context of his argument that the locus of rock authenticity is in sound, not sight, Grossberg claims that:

> the importance of live performance lies precisely in the fact that it is only here that one can see the actual production of the sound, and the emotional work carried in the voice. It is not the visual appearance of rock that is offered in live performance but the concrete production of the music as sound. The demand for live performance has always expressed the desire for the visual mark (and proof) of authenticity.
>
> (Grossberg 1993: 204)

Although I believe that Grossberg has put his finger on a matter of

authentic or not, the Monkees were extremely popular and states that "there must have been something in the grooves which made those records sell." Indeed there was: the Monkees' records stand up quite well more than thirty years later as examples of well-crafted pop-rock. The point, however, is that popularity is not an index to authenticity. Paradoxically, even though some authentic rock groups are enormously successful financially, their authenticity hinges on the counter-cultural aura that derives from a putative *lack* of mass market appeal or from the accretion of a coterie audience, however large (e.g., the Deadheads). It is also possible that some of the Monkees' records might have sold to rock fans who would never admit to a fondness for their music. The inauthentic has its (guilty?) pleasures.

vital importance in understanding the function of live performance in rock culture, his insistence that live performance is not visual but auditory in nature again reflects the anti-visual bias I have identified in his and Gracyk's work, the insistence that the visual is necessarily inauthentic in a way that the auditory is not.[27] I agree emphatically that live rock performance is precisely about establishing the authenticity of the recorded sound, but surely this must involve not just the "concrete production" of that sound, but also visual evidence of the sound's production by musicians whose appearance suggests that they are its legitimate makers. It is for this reason that producers of rock recordings will not hire a group on the basis of a demonstration tape alone, but always insist on seeing the group perform live.

Because it is well known within rock culture that the sound is manufactured in the recording studio, the visual aspects of rock music performance do not work merely as a secondary confirmation of an authenticity established primarily in the rock sound. Prior to *seeing* a band perform live, the rock fan cannot be sure that their music really is *their* music. The visual evidence of live performance, the fact that those sounds can be produced live by the appropriate musicians, serves to authenticate music as legitimate rock and not synthetic pop in a way that cannot occur on the basis of the recording alone; only live performance can resolve the tension between rock's romantic ideology and the listener's knowledge that the music is produced in the studio. A provocative statement by Neil Tennant of the Pet Shop Boys underlines the association of musical ability and live performance with rock and studio artifice with pop: "It's kinda macho nowadays to prove you can *cut it* live. I quite like proving we *can't* cut it live. We're a pop group, not a rock and roll group" (quoted in Goodwin 1990: 268, original emphasis). A case in point is that of the Beach Boys' well-known recording of "Good Vibrations" (1966), a performance pieced together with extreme care over numerous recording sessions and one of the most elegant and complex examples in popular music of "phonography," the art of recorded – as distinct from live – music (Eisenberg 1987). The assertion of rock authenticity was particularly problematic

27 Gracyk and Grossberg typify, in this respect, what Martin (1993: 67) has identified as the "demonization of the visual" in music criticism underwritten by the ideology of rock. It is noteworthy that rock critics are not the only ones who reject visual spectacle as part of rock. Some musicians, particularly "progressive" rockers who want their music to be perceived as "serious" (i.e., art) music, and not as popular entertainment, specifically refuse to engage in spectacular live performance, preferring that the focus be exclusively on the sound.

for the Beach Boys, as their music, which derives as much from the pop tradition of vocal groups like The Four Freshmen as from the proto-rock and roll of Chuck Berry (see Curtis 1987: 105–7), has always been regarded somewhat suspiciously within rock culture, especially since it is associated with a reactionary cultural politics. The passage from Friedlander (1996) quoted earlier indicates that surf music, of which the Beach Boys are a principal representative, is a pre-rock form. The prosperous, suburban Southern California lifestyle of which it is an expression was not valued by the rock counterculture of the late 1960s. As Jim Curtis (1987: 117) puts it, the Beach Boys, like President Lyndon Johnson, seemed to embody "an implicit belief in the frontier as the unending hegemony of white Protestant democracy." He points out that the Beach Boys' popularity waxed and waned with that of the war in Vietnam, and indicates that their failure to appear at "the one brief, shining moment of the counterculture," the Monterey Pop festival in 1967, was damaging to their credibility as a rock act. In the mid-1960s, the word on "Good Vibrations" was that it was purely a studio product that could not possibly be performed live. Yet, a live recording of 1966 reveals the group struggling through the song before the single had even been released. A later live recording, of 1969, shows that by that point, the group had mastered the ability to repro-duce the sound of the recording – including some of its special effects – in a live setting, thus enhancing their credibility with rock audiences at the height of the psychedelic era, a time when their style seemed hopelessly out of touch.[28] It is noteworthy that the group's visual style had changed considerably: in the late 1960s, the Beach Boys sported hippie garb, long hair, and beards in place of their previous uniform of striped shirts and clean-cut hair styles.

An anecdote that circulated in the late 1960s summarizes much of what I'm saying here. According to this story, Jimi Hendrix toured with the Monkees as one of their backing musicians. Because the Monkees could not play their own instruments and wanted to disguise that fact, they placed Hendrix behind a curtain, hiding him from the audience and making it seem as if the Monkees were responsible for his guitar sound. At one fateful concert, the curtain fell away, revealing Hendrix and unmasking the Monkees as frauds. Though the story is

---

28 The 1966 live version of "Good Vibrations" is available on the CD box set *Good Vibrations: Thirty Years of the Beach Boys* (Capitol Records, 1993), which also includes some of the session tapes from the studio recording of the song, making it possible to hear just how it was constructed. The 1969 recording is on *Live in London* (Capitol Records, c. 1972).

false (Hendrix did tour the United States with the Monkees briefly in 1967, but only as their opening act),[29] it is very revealing of rock ideology and the premium it places on the ability to perform one's music live. From the perspective of rock ideology, the juxtaposition of Hendrix and the Monkees, artists placed at opposite ends of the spectrum of authenticity, is delicious, as is the way the revelation of the fraudulent results in the glorification of the authentic.[30]

The idea that live performance establishes the authenticity of the rock recording suggests a particular relationship between live and recorded music in that cultural context. In jazz and classical music, recorded and live performances are considered separate artforms. No concertgoer, for example, would expect the flutes in Khatchaturian's Second Symphony to be louder than the brass, as they are on Stokowski's recording (Eisenberg 1987: 153), and jazz fans expect the music they hear live to feature spontaneous inventions and improvisations different from those on recordings. (Improvisation plays an important role in certain kinds of rock music [progressive rock, for instance] but it is not an essential characteristic of rock the way it is of jazz. Nonimprovisational jazz is arguably an oxymoron; nonimprovisational rock is not (Gracyk 1996: 170).) The relationship between the live and the recorded in rock music is different, however, precisely

---

29 There is no reference to this event in the discussions of Hendrix's tour with the Monkees in either Jerry Hopkins' or Harry Shapiro's and Caesar Glebbeek's respective Hendrix biographies, for example (see Hopkins 1983: 122–4 and Shapiro and Glebbeek 1990: 196–201). Monkee Michael Nesmith confirmed in a personal communication that Hendrix had served only as an opening act. Both Hopkins and Shapiro and Glebbeek emphasize that Hendrix did not go down well with the Monkees' audience and opted out of the tour after less than two weeks. His management chose to circulate a false story that Hendrix had been kicked off the tour because his performance style was too raw and sexual for the teenie boppers in the Monkees' audience. This fabrication, too, enhanced Hendrix's authenticity effect by playing on ideological distinctions between rock and pop.

30 Hopkins (1983: 123) points out the irony of the ideological view that posits Hendrix as more authentic than the Monkees by underlining the fact that the Jimi Hendrix Experience was a manufactured British group constructed around an American guitarist by Hendrix's English manager, Chas Chandler. Meltzer (1987 [1970]: 277) makes the same point, somewhat obscurely: "Jimi Hendrix, who left the U. S. and r&b for England and 'acid' and would have become the Monkees but instead became the Monkees." The fact that Hendrix took the United States by storm only upon returning from England contributed to his mythology and made him seem that much more authentic. When he left the United States, Hendrix was a talented journeyman rhythm and blues musician. Chandler transformed him into an exotic and iconic incarnation of Carnaby Street psychedelia.

because live performances and recordings are *not* treated as fully sepa-
rable artworks in rock culture. Gracyk argues that live performance and
recordings are "two different media," and goes on to claim that
"recording facilitates a certain indifference as to whether the music can
be re-created in live performance" (Gracyk 1996: 80, 84). His differen-
tiation of live and recorded performances is valid in terms of his
ontological argument but not when considered in the context of rock
culture. I have been arguing that rock fans and critics are not at all
indifferent to whether the music can be recreated in live performance,
that the ability to do precisely that is a hallmark ideological distinction
between authentic rock and contrived pop.[31] Listeners steeped in rock
ideology are tolerant of studio manipulation only to the extent that
they know or believe that the resulting sound can be reproduced on
stage by the same performers.[32] When that belief is substantiated, the
music is authenticated. When it is shown (or even strongly suspected)
to be false, the music is condemned to inauthenticity. While live and
recorded performance are indeed different media, they are linked
symbiotically in rock culture. Rather than existing as an autonomous
artwork, the rock recording calls up the desire for a live performance

31 In the elided section of the last passage I quoted from Gracyk (1996), he quotes
    Rolling Stone Keith Richards to support his contention that "recording facilitates a
    certain indifference as to whether the music can be re-created in live performance."
    Therefore, it is not clear whether Gracyk intends this statement to apply to rock
    musicians, listeners, or both. I contend that whether or not it applies to rock musi-
    cians, it does not apply to fans of their music.
32 The question of *who* performs the studio manipulation can be important, as well.
    Gracyk (1996: 77; see also p. 82) quotes both Eddie Kramer, who engineered many
    recordings by Jimi Hendrix, and Jerry Garcia, of the Grateful Dead, to the effect
    that the mixing of a recording constitutes "a performance at a console." In terms of
    rock ideology, it is preferable that this technological performance be carried out by
    the musical artist. If it is performed only by a producer or engineer, the taint of inau-
    thenticity creeps in. Hence, the controversy surrounding the posthumous release of
    studio recordings by Hendrix, many of which featured overdubs recorded after his
    death. The problem with these recordings was not that they were manipulated in
    the studio, as were all of the albums Hendrix made when alive, but that these
    manipulations occurred after the death of the artist. The resulting recordings were
    suspected, therefore, of being inauthentic Hendrix. (Gracyk (1996: 86) sees them as
    wholly unproblematic in this regard.) The producers of the live album *Band of
    Gypsys 2* (Capitol Records), which came out in 1986 after a large amount of
    Hendrix's remaining studio material had been issued on albums, sought to capitalize
    on the questions raised about those albums by emphasizing in the cover copy that
    the record contains "no studio tricks, just Jimi live."

that will serve to authenticate the sounds on the recording.[33] It is this relationship that makes live performance a better way of marketing a recording than simply exposing the recording itself on the radio. In live performance, the rock audience is exposed to the music in a context that endorses it as authentic in the terms of rock ideology.[34] The concert answers the question raised implicitly by the recording.

As a cultural form based in mass production, rock music both illus-trates and complicates Walter Benjamin's account of authenticity and the disappearance of aura in the age of mechanical reproduction. Benjamin's postulate that "the whole sphere of authenticity is outside technical...reproducibility" (Benjamin 1986 [1936]: 30; see also p. 47) is certainly borne out in rock culture, for the mass-produced rock recording in and of itself cannot be authentic: its authenticity must be ratified by live performance. This process is at once a challenge to and a symptom of what Benjamin (ibid.: 31) describes as the "decay of the aura," which he defines as an aspect of the "contemporary perception" conditioned by mechanical reproducibility, as discussed in Chapter 2. It is a challenge in the sense that rock ideology, itself a product of the age of mechanical reproduction, is a form of contemporary perception that allows its adherents to experience mass-produced objects as auratic through the process of authentication. Rock ideology also attempts to arrest the process described by Benjamin (ibid.: 29–30) in which the mass-produced object loses its historical specificity: authen-tication requires that the recording be positioned within historical discourses (e.g., the story of the musicians that produced it, its relation

---

33 There is no one way in which authentication by live performance occurs, however. In some cases, such as that of the Beach Boys, it is necessary for the group to repli-cate its recordings in concert to demonstrate authenticity. In other instances (the Grateful Dead comes to mind), authenticity resides in the fact that live versions of songs are different from the recorded versions. These differences in the triangulation of live performance, recordings, and the establishment of authenticity depend in part on which rock subgenre is involved and which ideological issues are engaged. Because the Beach Boys were suspected of being a pop group, it was crucial that they demonstrate their ability to perform their music live. Somewhat like a jazz audience, the audience for the Grateful Dead expected the group to demonstrate its authen-ticity by showing they could recreate their recorded sound, then go beyond it improvisationally.

34 Rock ideology has always been exploited for marketing purposes: see Frith (1988b) and Gross (1986: 105). Without endorsing the manipulative tactics of marketeers, I will say that I find Gracyk's emphasis on the fact that rock music has always been produced in a commercial context salutary as a warning against slipping into a simplistic, romanticized opposition of "commodified" and "non-commodified" music. It is fair to say that rock, by definition, is always already commodified.

to the history of rock, etc.). Certification as authentic is also historically contingent: a recording can lose its certification as those histories
are revised (e.g., as groups thought to be authentic are discovered not
to be and vice-versa), and the authentic music of the past becomes the
inauthentic music of the present. Arguably, the desire to reestablish
the aura expressed in both these aspects of rock authentication is itself
symptomatic of the aura's decay (see Crimp 1993 [1980]: 174).

By positing mass-produced recordings as being authentic, rock
ideology paradoxically recreates the conditions that governed the
perception of works of art prior to mechanical reproduction within the
terms of a cultural formation based on mass production. In doing so, it
complicates Benjamin's concepts of the authentic and auratic. For
Benjamin (1986 [1936]: 29), "the presence of the original is the prereq-
uisite to the concept of authenticity." He derives this argument from
the fact that a work of plastic art must be physically present to have its
authenticity tested. At first glance, this schema seems to map fairly
well onto rock's ideology of authenticity, in which a mass-produced
recording must be authenticated through the presence of a unique
object, a live performance. To leave the question at that would be to
forget, however, that in rock, the live performance is a recreation of
the recording, which is, in fact, the original performance. Rock
ideology is in perfect accord with Benjamin in stipulating that because
the original artifact is mass-produced, its presence does not imply its
authenticity. But it does not follow for rock ideology as it does for
Benjamin that this recognition entails relinquishing the idea of
authenticity.

But where does rock ideology locate the aura? Live performance of
rock is not in itself any more authentic than recordings. It makes little
sense, in fact, to speak of live performance of rock apart from
recording, since rock is music made to be recorded: it is constructed
along principles derived from recording practices, inspired by earlier
music heard primarily on recordings, etc. Even if a group is unlucky
enough not to have recorded, epistemologically their music is still
recorded music. In Benjaminian terms, rock music is "designed for
reproduciblity" (ibid.: 33) and is therefore always already inauthentic,
even when played live. Rock authentication is not a process by which
an aura located in the live performance spreads to the record, nor is it a
case in which the aura is displaced onto a reproducible object in the
absence of a unique object, as Douglas Crimp suggests of postmodern
photographic practices (Crimp 1993 [1980]: 177). In the case of rock
ideology, the aura must be seen as existing *between* the recording and
the live performance. The aura is located in a dialectical relation

between two cultural objects – the recording and the live performance – rather than perceived as a property inherent in a single object,[35] and it is from this relation of mutuality that both objects derive their authenticity.

I want my MTV

Up to this point, I have been treating rock culture and ideology as discourses that retain their currency after more than thirty years. There is reason to question whether this is actually the case, however, for changes in rock culture over the last ten or more years suggest that the values championed by rock ideology may have lost their hold. The Milli Vanilli episode may be seen as a watershed in this regard. Milli Vanilli's young audience was not upset at their lip-synching. This is perfectly understandable in terms of the ideological distinction between rock and pop. Milli Vanilli was not a rock group; it was a pop dance group whose audience would not be expected to be concerned about authenticity. Rather, it was the fans' parents and parental surrogates (such as the representatives who called for legislation and the attorneys who filed consumer fraud suits) who were disturbed. Jon Pareles, a *New York Times* popular music journalist, inveighing against the use of lip-synching, computer-programmed musical instruments, and other forms of automation in concert, and, upholding the value of traditional live performance, referred to the entrance of these techniques into live performance as a paradigm shift. "I'm not ready for the new paradigm," he wrote. "The spontaneity, uncertainty and ensemble coordination that automation eliminates are exactly what I go to concerts to see" (Jon Pareles, "The midi menace: machine perfection is far from perfect," *New York Times*, May 13 1990, sec. H: 25). Like Pareles, most commentators were adamantly opposed to the incursion of automation into live music performance.

---

35 I want to emphasize that I am talking here about how rock fans would locate the aura were they to speak in those terms. I am not suggesting that Benjamin himself locates the aura in objects. For Benjamin, aura is a function of perception, not a property inherent in objects. As I suggested at the end of Chapter 2, the withering of the aura in the age of mechanical reproduction is a withering of the ability to perceive objects as auratic due to changes in the social conditions that shape perception, not an objective change in the objects themselves. (Of course, I also argued there that live performances themselves have changed in response to cultural and economic changes.)

The intriguing aspect of the Milli Vanilli scandal is that those commentators did not simply dismiss it as the logical outcome of the pop audience's indifference to authenticity. It was seen, rather, as signifying a crisis in the ideology of authenticity with implications well beyond the specific case:

> the Milli Vanilli lip-synching scandal of 1990 must be seen as the culmination of nearly a decade of concern over the status and legitimacy of live performance in an era of sequencers, samplers, and backing tapes. For critics the problem was not simply that musicians were trying to sound like their recordings when performing on stage (a longtime preoccupation among pop musicians) but that concerts had indeed *become* recordings.
>
> (Théberge 1997: 231)

It is clear, then, why Milli Vanilli was scandalous from the point of view of the rock ideology endorsed by these older commentators, even if not to the group's young listeners. It suggested the arrival of a new era of music performance in which the visual evidence of performance would have no relation to the production of the sound. The dialectic of recordings and live performances central to rock ideology was threatened. Were it to break down, live performance would be deprived of its traditional authenticating function. Live concerts would become what recordings had always been: *simulations* – recreations of performances that never took place, representations without referents in the real.

This change in music culture was anticipated by alterations in the structure of the music industry, and its relation to other entertainment industries, in the 1980s. Frith (1988b: 113–14) argues that the traditional rock career path – in which musicians worked their way up a career ladder from live performances at the local and regional levels, to ever more prominent recordings, perhaps to eventual stardom – had given way to an "irrational" system in which music is packaged by entertainment conglomerates and sold to a public that has evinced no previous demand for that music. Grossberg (1988: 318) notes the same shift in industry patterns: "The new star does not need a history. The old model of a star building an ever-expanding audience while 'paying their dues' is being replaced by the immediate insertion of a figure into a position of stardom already waiting for them." A history of live performance is no longer meaningful as a source of rock authentication; while some artists come up the traditional way, many do not, and the distinction seems not to matter to the audience.[36]

The crisis in the ideology of rock authenticity[37] is also reflected in the changing relationship of rock to television.[38] Rock music and television are traditionally opposed within rock ideology: "For many fans, television has often been seen as part of the dominant culture against which the rock culture is defined" (Grossberg 1993: 189).[39] Indeed, the aforementioned antagonism of the rock culture toward the Monkees derived precisely from the fact that not only were the Monkees a manufactured group, they were manufactured *for television*.[40] This antagonism toward television was fueled by an association of television with pop, rather than rock, and even extended to MTV: "MTV became the target of hostility from the established rock audience....It seemed to mean the replacement of rock values (sincerity, musical dexterity, live communion) with old pop conceits (visual style, gimmickry, hype)" (Frith 1988a: 210).

Although the mutual distrust of television and rock culture was

36 Robert Burnett (1996) points out that the concentration of the music industry in the hands of a few, multinational corporations has meant that the new way of building a performer's career is practiced on an increasingly international scale. Artists from anywhere can be promoted anywhere else.

37 Gracyk (1996: 222) disagrees that there is a crisis. He states that "the ideology of authenticity is not on the wane in the rock community," arguing that although some artists may represent the trends I describe above, many do not. He justifies his position, however, by reference to what I have already described as his over-broad definition of rock music: "As long as rock is catholic enough to embrace both Whitney Houston and Courtney Love, we should not assume that either is a truer indication of the current state of rock." That Gracyk does not recognize a crisis of authenticity is directly related to his lack of interest in the distinction between rock and pop that I, along with Grossberg and Frith, take to be one of the defining elements of rock culture.

38 For an overview of rock music's relationship to television prior to MTV, see Banks (1996: 23–9). Curtis (1987: 43–4, 219) also makes some useful observations.

39 For Grossberg (1993), the defining change in rock culture has been a shift in the balance of the relative importance of visual and aural media. Whereas traditional rock culture, in his view, privileged aural media as sites of authenticity and suspected the visual of inauthenticity, the new rock culture privileges the visual and no longer values authenticity. I concur with Grossberg that there has been a reconfiguration of the relationships between cultural texts in rock. But since I do not agree that the visual aspects of rock culture are less authentic than the aural, I do not see the same realignment he does.

40 It is noteworthy that one of the Monkees, Michael Nesmith, became the first producer of music videos for MTV and has been described as "the father of the [American] music video" (Nance 1993: 15).

clearly manifest in the counter-cultural 1960s, it has a longer history. Until the advent of MTV in 1981, rock had no home on American television (see Goldman 1992: 51), partly because of sociological factors that differentiate television's relationship with its audience from rock's.

> TV entertainment works on what audiences have in common across class/gender/race/generational divides, it rests on an ideology of the *family* as ideal and real TV viewer. Rock, by contrast, is about difference and what distinguishes us from people with other tastes. It rests on an ideology of the *peer group* as both the ideal and reality of rock community.
>
> (Frith 1988a: 213, original emphasis)

Even the popular and long-lived *American Bandstand* was a somewhat marginal affair, for "television could accommodate innovative music only when it was not in prime time, and when television itself was a secondary medium: *American Bandstand*" (Curtis 1987: 44). The mid-1960s saw a flurry of rock programming in the wake of Beatlemania (*Shindig*, *Hullabaloo*, etc.) but, again, these were nonprime time shows and the trend came to a halt in 1967. "The limitations of network television, demographic as well as technical, doomed all attempts to make music shows viable" (ibid.: 219). In any case, the widespread practice of lip-synching on all of these programs (and on many prime time variety shows that sometimes featured rock groups) marked them indelibly as inauthentic in terms of rock ideology.[41]

Curtis proposes that the turn toward theatricalism in rock music performance of the 1970s indicated that rock was competing with television by offering in live settings experiences that could not be obtained from recordings or television (his examples are Elton John, Alice Cooper, and David Bowie) (ibid.: 252). Goldman sees the same development as a transition from authentic to inauthentic rock performance. Whereas in 1968 Goldman saw in performances by the Doors and others "a nascent theater that is already squalling with vigor" (Goldman 1992: 57), in 1974 he saw performances by John, Cooper,

---

41 In the 1970s, *Saturday Night Live*, which regularly featured performances by rock artists, was a partial exception. Musical artists did not lip-synch on the show, which also had a certain counter-cultural appeal because it was not in prime time and had been banned in some American cities. That appeal was further enhanced by the association of some writers and cast members with counter-cultural humor outlets like *The National Lampoon*. For a brief discussion of some of the connections between rock and comedy, see Auslander (1992b: 132–4).

and Bowie as a "new rock show business" reflecting values of commercialism and professionalism (the same "pop" values that prompted the early anxiety over MTV) spurned by the rock performers of the 1960s (ibid.: 86). Ironically, it is probable that, rather than establishing live music performance as an alternative to television, these spectacular concerts paved the way for music video by associating specific, highly cinematic images with particular songs. Curtis's and Goldman's respective descriptions of the theatricality of performances in the 1970s by John, Cooper, and Bowie sound, from the vantage point of today, like descriptions of music videos. Paradoxically, then, the performances Curtis sees as designed to provide a quintessential experience of liveness actually constituted a decisive step toward the incorporation of rock into television, the crisis of the ideology of authenticity in rock, and the breakdown of the dialectical relationship between the live and the mediatized manifest in the Milli Vanilli effect.

It is significant in this context that the performers in question were more concerned to create spectacular stage personae than images of authenticity.[42] This is particularly true for Bowie, whose systematic and self-conscious metamorphoses of persona (including his sexuality) and musical style represent a significant departure from the ideology of authenticity (see Curtis 1987: 259). I have already suggested that rock musicians need to transform themselves periodically in order to keep up with the multiple and ever-changing definitions of rock authenticity: the photographs of the longhaired and bearded Beatles that accompanied the White Album were crucial in this regard. Bowie's distinctiveness lies not only in the frequency and extremity of his transformations but more importantly in his assertion of the conventionality and artificiality of all of his performance personae. His summary statement of this point is the album *Pin Ups* (1973), on which he performs songs by groups he admired during the mid-1960s. The photographs accompanying the record feature Bowie in a number of personae, including the spaced-out Ziggy Stardust and a much cooler musician wearing a suit and holding a saxophone. The cover shows Bowie (and

---

42 Vincent Furnier (Alice Cooper) has gone on record as saying that he intentionally sought to keep his performing and private identities completely separate: "Alice had a life of his own that existed only on stage....But then my other life was my own, and it had a lot more aspects to it than Alice's did" (quoted in Hall 1997: 15). No rocker who wished to be thought of as authentic would refer to his performance persona as a separate entity existing only in a theatrical context. Rock ideology demands parity between the performer's stage and private personae, even if that parity is wholly illusory.

Twiggy, herself an icon of swinging, mid-60s London) in highly stylized make-up, which suggests that their faces are masks. On the recording itself, Bowie sings songs in a number of styles in different voices, including different accents, another variant of masking that suggests that, *contra* rock's romantic ideology of self-expression, the singer's "self" is determined by the song, not vice-versa. Bowie's strategy of mutating identities anticipates the devaluation of rock authenticity that is a hallmark of popular music culture in the age of the music video. The valorization of authenticity has given way to "a logic of authentic inauthenticity" in which "the only possible claim to authenticity is derived from the knowledge and admission of your inauthenticity" (Grossberg 1993: 205–6), knowledge that Bowie had foregrounded ten years before MTV.[43] (The statement by Tennant quoted earlier marks the Pet Shop Boys as a more recent example of authentic inauthenticity.) Bowie's deconstruction of rock authenticity also anticipates Frith's video-era identification of "the rock version of the postmodern condition: a media complex in which music has meaning only as long as it keeps circulating, 'authentic' sounds are recognized by their place in a system of signs, and rock history only matters as a resource for recurrent pastiche" (Frith 1988b: 91).

Although it is tempting to describe music video as *causing* the devaluation of the live event as a marker of authenticity in rock music, that temptation should be resisted. As Andrew Goodwin (1993: 35–6) has shown, music video and lip-synched concerts are not causally linked; rather, both are *symptoms* of changes in the culture and production of rock music after punk that were driven by the developments in the music industry already discussed, changes in musical style (British New Pop, the resurgence of dance music), and changes in musical technology (see Beadle 1993 and Théberge 1997). Increased access to recording technology contributed to the devaluation of live performance as an essential part of the rock career path:

---

43 Grossberg (1992: 234–5) notes that "rock has always, at least implicitly, played with the idea of authentic inauthenticity" but argues that it became dominant in rock only in the late 1970s: "The logic of authentic inauthenticity is foregrounded most visibly in the contradiction and conjunction of punk and disco." I am suggesting here that Bowie anticipated this development by several years. He is a pioneer of what Grossberg (1992: 227–9) calls "ironic inauthenticity," which posits that any given identity is a construction to be occupied only temporarily. Meltzer (1987 [1970]: 185) deserves credit for having raised the issue of "the authenticity of inauthenticity" in the context of rock well before Grossberg.

Suddenly..."paying your dues" in the music business took on a new meaning...instead of struggling with a band year after year, performing in bars and night clubs, the purchase of suitable recording equipment seemed a more viable route to a successful career in pop music. "Paying your dues" now meant making payments on your gear.

(Théberge 1997: 221)

The year 1981 – the debut of the MTV Music Television cable network – also saw the refinement of the digital sampler and other high-tech, computerized musical instruments. Greater access to automated musical instruments accompanied by a decrease in the number of venues for – and the profitability of – live music (Théberge 1997: 221, 265, n. 4) resulted in "the displacement of the musician" in both the studio and the live concert (Goodwin 1993: 32). "[T]his argument suggests that the later development of acts such as Milli Vanilli was *not* a 'result' of MTV and music television. Rather, both Milli Vanilli and MTV were effects of the uses to which the new pop technologies were put" (ibid.: 33).

Goodwin takes issue with those who claim that live music performance now generally replicates the images and effects of music video (my argument in Chapter 2) by pointing out that those effects derive originally from the conventions of rock music performance rather than from television:

The argument is constructed around a chronological sleight of hand. The problem...is that [the argument] conflate[s] those artists who present live music based on representations from music videos (Madonna, for instance) with a more common phenomenon: artists whose live performances look like their videos because the video clips are closely based on their stage acts. My point is that visual spectacles (dancing, gesture, the display of virtuosity, lighting, smoke bombs, dry ice, back projection, etc.) have always worked in tandem with the music itself. Performance videos on music television mirror many of these codes and conventions (established in more than thirty years of rock and pop concerts).

(Goodwin 1993: 18)

While Goodwin's historical point is provocative, it implies that the conventions of rock performance have not changed significantly over its thirty-year development. If, as I have suggested, the theatricalization of live performance of rock music in the 1970s was an important

91

innovation that proved to be a condition of possibility for music video, then live performance now imitates music video imitating live performance, and is thus another example of live performance's recapitulation of mediatized representations based originally on live performances, as discussed in the previous chapter.

The simulationist logic that now binds together live performance, recordings, and music video recapitulates the discourse of authenticity in another register. Goodwin (1993: 47) insists that the live performance and the video do not mirror each other; rather, the referent of each is the commodity both promote: the sound recording. While it is important to emphasize the promotional function of both concert and video in the economics of rock music, from the point of view of affect, the middle term to which the other two refer is the video, not the sound recording. Richard Dienst spells out how "the performative distinction between video clip transmission and the commodity object [the recording]" enables the video to carry out its promotional function without sacrificing its own ability "to occupy the primary sites of music consumption":

> The video clip must somehow fail to be that other thing, the recording itself, even while giving every appearance of improving on it, expanding it, or giving it away free. Adding images turns out to be a form of subtraction: not only in the realm of sensory plenitude, but also in the mobilization of desire as a temporal vector leading (perhaps) to a moment of exchange at which value is at last realized for capitalist and consumer alike.
>
> (Dienst 1994: 81)

Video is the primary experience of music in a mediatized culture.[44] Because that experience is constructed to lack plenitude, the consumer seeks out the sound recording – not because it contains the musical experience to which the video refers but in order to complete the experience initiated by the video. This, of course, recapitulates the previous relationship between rock recordings and live performances, in which the listener needed recorded music to be completed and authenticated by live performance. The crucial difference is that now one recording (the video) creates desire for another recording (the album), not for a live performance of the music.

---

44 See, for example, Csaba Toth (1997), who analyzes the meanings and cultural significance of Industrial Gothic rock by discussing the imagery of its videos.

Goodwin notes that music videos frequently expose the apparatus of music-making. The particular iconography he cites is "the all-pervasive mise-en-scène of the rehearsal room/warehouse space in music video clips," arguing that representation of the sites on which the music is made serves as "a *guarantor of authenticity*" (Goodwin 1993: 77, original emphasis). Jody Berland (1993: 37) suggests that "with the emergence of rock video, the 'authenticity' of the performer is assured (if not that of the performance whose sound is still frequently dubbed)." Taken together, these two observations suggest that music video works to authenticate sound recordings in much the same way – and that authentication is necessary for much the same reason – as when live performance was the main guarantor of authenticity. Now as then, the fan needs to witness the production of the music on the appropriate site by the appropriate people in order to be assured of its authenticity. The difference, of course, is that both site and people are now simulated in televisual space rather than witnessed live, yet count for the audience in the way only live performance counted previously.[45] In terms of rock ideology, and its previous rejection of television as necessarily inauthentic, this change represents a major cultural shift.

Under the traditional schema, live performance authenticated the record, and (usually lip-synched) performance on television was deemed intrinsically inauthentic and, therefore, simply irrelevant to that process. Now, the music video occupies the place formerly held by the sound recording as the primary musical text *and* has usurped live performance's authenticating function. The function of live performance under this new arrangement is to authenticate the *video* by showing that the same images and events that occur in the video can be reproduced onstage, thus making the video the standard for what is "real" in this performative realm. "For an increasing number of rock fans the meaning of 'live' performance, the look of music 'in reality'…comes from its ubiquitous simulation. This is an example of what we might call the Baudrillard effect: a concert feels real only to the extent that it matches its TV reproduction" (Frith 1988b: 124–5). While the video authenticates the sound recording by replicating the live production of the sound, live performance authenticates the video by replicating its images in real space. Live performance retains a

---

45 Cf. E. Ann Kaplan (1987: 53): "Earlier [i.e., pre-music video] promoters at least manipulated live bodies, who could resist in certain ways; but now the 'materials' that are manipulated, positioned, circulated in a certain fashion are *simulations* which begin to *replace* the 'real'" (original emphasis).

certain value in this reconfigured schema, but its value is subordinate to that of the televisual image. MTV is more than the *Shindig* of the 1980s and 1990s: rather than constituting a way of presenting music *on* television, music video is symptomatic of music's having been made *into* television, even in live performance.

Panic Clapton

The Grammy awarded to Milli Vanilli can be read as the institutional acknowledgment of the centrality of simulation to the music industry. Rumors that Milli Vanilli did not sing live and had not sung on their album were in circulation as long as a year before the Grammy vote. In fact, one member of NARAS voted for Milli Vanilli even though he had specific knowledge that they had not sung on the record (Bruce Britt, "Milli Vanilli's pact with the Devil," *Los Angeles Daily News*, 21 November 1990, *NewsBank Review of the Arts, Performing Arts*, 1990, fiche 173, grids G4–5). He knew this because he was their vocal coach (though exactly what he coached is not clear). There was nothing particularly novel about what Milli Vanilli had done – the possibility of passing off one voice as another was implicit from the moment music was first recorded. Substitutions of this kind have been quite typical in recordings of popular music for several decades, and there are many well-known cases of groups having been formed by producers specifically to exploit recordings made using other voices.[46] The practice of lip-synching itself was nothing new, either, especially when music groups appeared on television, including the Grammy award show. What *was* significantly different about Milli Vanilli was that they were discovered to be transporting these techniques from the studio and the television screen onto the concert stage.

As I noted earlier in this chapter, it is easy to understand why Milli Vanilli would have been scandalous from the perspective of rock's ideology of authenticity, since their actions deprived live performance of its authenticating function. Rock ideology, however, is not the institutional ideology of NARAS. The premise of the Grammy awards, that

---

46 One particularly convoluted case is that of the early 1960s "girl group" the Crystals, whose producer, Phil Spector, had another group, the Blossoms, record as the Crystals while the Crystals were out on tour. Before and after this episode, the Crystals also sang on their own records, with the result that recordings by "The Crystals" are actually by two completely different groups (Gaar 1992: 44–6). See also note 8.

it is not the music itself that should be acknowledged but the *recording* of the music, accords with the realities of how rock music is primarily consumed, but also privileges the recording in a way that does not altogether accord with the relationship between live and recorded performances in rock culture. As I have argued, rock authenticity resides in a dialectical relationship between recording and live performance. The recording cannot be severed from this relationship without losing its authenticity as rock. This is not the case for pop music and, not surprisingly, the popular music Grammys have consistently been awarded to pop, rather than rock, recordings.

Historically, NARAS has been overtly hostile to rock music and rock culture. NARAS was founded in 1957 precisely as a counter-response to the emergence of rock and roll, which its founders "regarded…as a kind of antimusic – lyrically inane, shoddily produced, a mockery of any reasonable set of musical standards" and as antithetical to postwar conformist culture (Schipper 1992: 1). Quincy Jones, whom Grammy historian Henry Schipper describes as "a low-profile, background industry figure…excellent in his own limited arena but mediocre when held up against the musical giants of the last thirty-three years" (Schipper 1992: 92–3), has won more Grammys than anyone else – second place belongs to pop film composer Henry Mancini. By contrast, neither the pioneers of rock and roll (Chuck Berry, Little Richard, etc.) nor most of the important figures of rock (the Rolling Stones, the Doors, etc.) have been awarded Grammys, except posthumously or in the Lifetime Achievement category, an award generally granted well after the artist has ceased making vital contributions to music.[47] From this perspective, the awarding of the Grammy to Milli Vanilli, a pop group *par excellence* that existed musically only on its recordings, was hardly aberrant. Rather, it seems to have been the logical expression of NARAS's values. Milli Vanilli was scandalous only from the perspective of rock ideology, and NARAS is

---

47 "The list of sixties artists who never won a Grammy seems all-encompassing: the Doors, Janis Joplin, Jimi Hendrix, Jefferson Airplane, the Grateful Dead, Cream, the Who, Credence Clearwater, Santana, Van Morrison, the Byrds, The Rolling Stones, Rod Stewart, Led Zeppelin, and many more" (Schipper 1992: 43). Schipper also points to the Grammys':

> practice – perhaps the strategy – of giving Lifetime Achievement Grammys…to artists whose records and careers Grammy voters have largely or completely ignored. The Rolling Stones, Chuck Berry, Jimi Hendrix, James Brown, Paul McCartney, John Lennon, Motown Records founder Berry Gordy (whose legendary label won just one Grammy during the entire sixties)…and Bob Dylan.

no champion of that ideology. How, then, do we explain *l'affaire Milli Vanilli?*

I propose that we begin by recognizing, as Baudrillard (1983: 26–7) says of Watergate, that the Milli Vanilli "scandal" was not a *real* scandal at all but rather a *scandal effect* used by agencies of power and capital to "regenerate a reality principle in distress." Power requires for its working a matrix of significant oppositions and "capital, which is immoral and unscrupulous, can only function behind a moral super-structure" (ibid.: 27). Simulation threatens the structures on which power and capital depend by implying that moral, political, and other distinctions are no longer meaningful: the Right *is* the Left; the Mediatized *is* the Live. "When it is threatened today by simulation (the threat of vanishing in the play of signs), power risks the real, risks crisis" (Baudrillard 1983: 44).

Baudrillard also points out that:

> When the real is no longer what it used to be, nostalgia assumes its full meaning. There is a proliferation of myths of origin and signs of reality; of second-hand truth, objectivity and authenticity. There is an escalation of the true, of the lived experience....And there is a panic-stricken reproduction of the real and the referential.
>
> (Baudrillard 1983: 12–13)

I believe we witnessed these very phenomena in the wake of Milli Vanilli. I am thinking primarily of two developments: the renewed emphasis within rock music on acoustic performance, of which the television program MTV *Unplugged* is the apotheosis, and the multiple awards given to Eric Clapton at the 1993 Grammy ceremony.[48] These two phenomena overlap significantly, since the recording for which Clapton won his awards was the live album derived from his acoustic performance on MTV *Unplugged*. The lauds heaped on Clapton in the Spring of 1993 signaled a complex confluence of institutional and cultural discourses (NARAS, rock ideology, television), some of which previously had been mutually antagonistic. The result of this conflu-

---

48 Like other rock artists, Clapton previously had been neglected by the Grammys. Active in blues and rock since 1965 and a member of such seminal groups as the Yardbirds, the Bluesbreakers, Cream, and Blind Faith, Clapton received his first Grammy only in 1990.

ence was the recuperation of rock's ideology of authenticity for a simulationist cultural economy.

Lest I be accused of a "chronological sleight of hand" because I juxta-
pose Milli Vanilli's 1989 Grammy with Clapton's wins in 1993, I shall
comment briefly on the awards made at the two Grammy ceremonies
that took place in between. One thing that is immediately apparent is
that the awards for 1990 and 1991 were entirely conventional, given
primarily to the kind of mainstream pop artists NARAS was founded
to support. Phil Collins won Record of the Year for 1990, while the
ubiquitous Quincy Jones won Album of the Year. In 1991, Natalie
Cole swept the Grammys, including both of those categories, with her
recording of "Unforgettable," a simulated duet with her deceased
father, Nat King Cole, who had been on the steering committee that
originally set up the NARAS (Schipper 1992: 4). In both years, the
choices for the New Artist Grammy, the category in which Milli
Vanilli had won in 1989, were, like Milli Vanilli, pop artists whose
careers conform to the new pattern identified by Grossberg and Frith:
both Mariah Carey and Marc Cohn appeared on the charts with no
previous history and without having built an audience through live
performance. In neither case, however, was there any doubt about the
winning artist's musicianship. The extravagance of Carey's vocal
ability, in fact, could almost be seen as a direct rejoinder to the Milli
Vanilli debacle. Other awards anticipated Grammy's colonization of
rock ideology in 1992: in 1990, Clapton himself won for Rock Vocal
Performance, while the group award went to the almost equally venerable Aerosmith. A year later, Bonnie Raitt, whose career reflects a
commitment to roots rock and the blues that parallels Clapton's own,
won the same award he had in 1990. All three of these awards suggest
a displacement of NARAS's practice of recognizing important rock
acts only very late in their careers from the the Lifetime Achievement
category to other categories. In both years, younger artists whose style
reflects a commitment to rock history and ideology, such as Living
Colour and R.E.M., won Grammys as well. Between 1989 and 1992, in
the wake of the Milli Vanilli debacle, NARAS retrenched by awarding
Grammys to the kind of pop artist it has always endorsed, and it also
looked ahead by making room on its lists for artists committed to the
ideology of rock.

Given NARAS's historical disdain for rock music, it is noteworthy
that the values it implicitly endorsed by giving awards to Clapton after
Milli Vanilli correspond to the standards of authenticity in rock
ideology. MTV Unplugged, from which Clapton's Grammy-winning
work derived, takes acoustic performance and liveness as its twin

imperatives and is a veritable cornucopia of signs of the real as that category is articulated in the context of the rock and folk-rock music of the 1960s, the historical discourse with which Clapton is associated. Since at least the early 1960s, acoustic playing has stood, within that discourse, for authenticity, sincerity, and rootsiness; hence the dismay that greeted Bob Dylan's use of an electric guitar at the 1965 Newport Folk Festival.[49]

Many commentators on music television agree with E. Ann Kaplan (1987: 29) that MTV's continuous rotation of music videos "simply takes over the history of rock and roll, flattening out all the distinct types into one continuous present." Goodwin (1993: 145) disagrees, drawing attention to the fact that MTV's schedule is not, in fact, made up of homogeneous units and that some materials within the flow, such as "Woodstock Minutes," are presented from a specifically "*historicizing* perspective" (original emphasis). *MTV Unplugged* also might be seen as standing out from the MTV flow because it is implicitly historicizing – as I have already indicated, the discourse of authenticity invoked on *MTV Unplugged* is at root a discourse based in the historical meaning of live performance and acoustic musicianship in rock culture.

My own argument is that *MTV Unplugged's* celebration of authenticity and historicity is only apparent and that the program is in itself symptomatic of the crisis state of the distinction between authenticity and inauthenticity in rock culture. The apparent restoration of the imploded polarity of authenticity and inauthenticity central to rock ideology on *MTV Unplugged* is, in fact, a simulation of restoration. That this artificial resuscitation of rock ideology occurred under the sign of the simulacrum is apparent from the way an appearance on *MTV Unplugged* became a rite of passage for all kinds of popular musicians, even those who work in musical genres for which the liveness and acoustic musicianship valorized in rock ideology are not traditional signs of authenticity. Most of the artists who have appeared on *MTV Unplugged* are either historical figures whose association with rock ideology is obvious (e.g., Neil Young, Rod Stewart, Paul McCartney), artists of the next musical generation who have carried on the rock

49 This tale of Dylan's "going electric" may be as false as the story of Hendrix and the Monkees. According to Al Kooper, Dylan's organist at Newport, the crowd there consisted mostly of Dylan fans who booed because he played only three songs, not because they abhorred his use of electric instrumentation (Palmer 1995: 105–6). The story nevertheless has achieved the status of myth in rock culture, and it is for that reason that I cite it here.

legacy (e.g., Bruce Springsteen, Elvis Costello), or still younger artists with an allegiance to rock ideology (e.g. Nirvana, R.E.M., 10,000 Maniacs). Pop singers Mariah Carey and Tony Bennett[50] have both appeared, however, as have rap and hip-hop artists whose musical idioms are directly linked with such simulationist technologies as digital sampling. Arrested Development, the hip-hop group chosen as the Best New Artist at the 1993 Grammy awards ceremony, lost no time in making an appearance on *MTV Unplugged*. By imposing the ideology of rock authenticity on performers from other musical genres in which authenticity is defined differently than in rock or is not ideologically important at all, *MTV Unplugged* actually negates the kinds of distinctions the polarity of authenticity and inauthenticity in rock ideology, and its attendant historicism, is meant to support even as it appears to reaffirm that very polarity.[51]

In addition to seeming to resurrect rock ideology, *MTV Unplugged* apparently recapitulates the traditional relationship between live performance and the live recording. Just as in the past, the live event precedes its recorded version: there is a whole series of albums derived from the television broadcasts.[52] The irony is that the "live" event recorded on the album was itself produced as a recording – a television program shown repeatedly on MTV. *MTV Unplugged* thus simulates the polarities that define rock ideology, even as the program is itself

---

50 The popularity of Tony Bennett with the MTV generation is an intriguing phenomenon in need of analysis. The enthusiasm for him is undoubtedly part of the same wave of retro-chic that has seen renewed interest in cocktail jazz, "bachelor pad" mood music, atomic age decor, cigars, steakhouses, and martinis. Bennett's popularity is not due, however, to camp appeal: if that were the desired affect, crooners like Wayne Newton, Tom Jones (whose career also has seen a recent resurgence), and Englebert Humperdinck would have been more likely candidates. Aside from his genuine talent, I think that Bennett's appeal lies in the possibility of seeing him on the model of an authentic rocker. According to this mythology, he could be seen as a saloon singer who has been faithful to his roots by never having sold out to become a megastar (i.e., he's not Frank Sinatra [or Elvis]) and who has protected his music's jazzy integrity by not succumbing to Las Vegas glitz (i.e., he's not Wayne Newton [or Elvis]).

51 My argument here is of the same form as Kaplan's, except that I see a version of the "flattening out" she describes within *MTV Unplugged* itself, not as a characteristic of MTV's flow.

52 An unfortunate side-effect of the Unplugged phenomenon has been the resurrection of racial segregation in music programming. It is well known that, in its early years, MTV was accused of racial bias because Black artists were poorly represented in its video rotation. One outcome of this debate was the development in 1988 of *Yo! MTV Raps*, a show devoted to Black music (see Nance 1993: 46–51). Although this

symptomatic of the crisis in that same ideology. Bob Dylan's appearance on *MTV Unplugged* in 1995 was, therefore, an ironic historical counterpoint to his having plugged in at Newport thirty years earlier. Dylan, who had precipitated a defining moment in the development of rock ideology, was also there to usher it into the age of simulation.

The fact that Clapton's *Unplugged* album is given over largely to performances of venerable blues numbers is another bid for authenticity and also an evocation of myths of origin. "[T]he image of authenticity in rock culture derives from a particular, historical imagination of black culture, and of the relationship between the blues and its black performers and fans" (Grossberg 1993: 208, n. 5). This myth is frequently invoked in music videos by the inclusion of "black musicians and audiences to 'authenticate' white rock music" (Goodwin 1993: 116). Even rock music that is stylistically considerably removed from the blues retains its aura of authenticity if it seems to have developed organically from its creator's earlier experience playing blues (see Whiteley 1992: 36). Clapton has always portrayed himself in these terms, as in this excerpt from an interview with *Rolling Stone*:

> Because he was so readily available, I dug Big Bill Broonzy; then I heard a lot of cats I had never heard of before: Robert Johnson and Skip James and Blind Boy Fuller. I just finally got completely overwhelmed and listened to it and went right down in it and came back up in it. I was about seventeen or eighteen. When I came back up in it, turned on to B. B. King and it's been that way ever since.
>
> (quoted in Cook 1973: 178–9)

Both rock music's ancestry in the blues and Clapton's own personal history as a rock music legend who launched his career in the mid-1960s as a faithful dévoté of American blues guitar styles, and whose own musical style, which has changed considerably over time, remains traceable to that original commitment to the bedrock of the music, are invoked as indices of authenticity. These two strands intertwine in one

may have meant that MTV was more active in presenting current Black music, it also meant that few videos by Black artists were included in other parts of the rotation. This segregation has been replicated in the recordings deriving from *MTV Unplugged*. The anthology *The Unplugged Collection Volume One* contains only one song by a Black artist (Lenny Kravitz). Instead, Black artists appear on a separate album called *MTV Uptown Unplugged*.

of the most popular selections from the recording, Clapton's acoustic revision of his own song "Layla." Thus, both the myth of the blues as rock's progenitor (and rock's consequent mythological claim to authenticity as folk expression) and Clapton's own authenticity as a blues-educated rock legend are brought into play.

It is worth referring again to David Bowie's *Pin Ups* album to contrast Clapton's claim to authenticity with Bowie's authentic inauthenticity. Whereas on the *MTV Unplugged* album (and, even more strongly, on his subsequent album *From the Cradle* and its accompanying video documentary) Clapton identifies his musical origins as residing in American blues, Bowie identifies his musical origins as residing in the performances of American blues and rock (among other material) by British bands such as the Yardbirds (of which Clapton was a member). These bands, active on the London club scene of the mid-1960s, where Bowie saw them, themselves made the kind of claim to authenticity through their relationship to the blues that Clapton continues to make. It is significant that, in the mid-1960s, Bowie himself, then still known as Davy Jones,[53] had been in similar blues-rock groups, such as The Manish Boys, named with a phrase derived from blues parlance. On *Pin Ups*, however, Bowie elides that part of his own musical history, preferring to construct his musical "roots" as self-consciously second-hand. His claim to authentic inauthenticity lies in his highly mannered pastiche of the British blues-rock that was already at (at least) one remove from the origins it cited to establish its own authenticity. Authentic inauthenticity is not, however, the same thing as the pop ideology represented by Milli Vanilli. Authentic inauthenticity, which demands that performers acknowledge and assert their own inauthenticity, defines itself against traditional rock authenticity. It thus reasserts the original meaning of authenticity in rock even while critiquing it. Although it revels in its own inauthenticity, authentically inauthentic music such as Bowie's nevertheless takes rock's ideology of authenticity as its point of reference and is therefore allied with that ideology in a way that pop, for which the whole concept of authenticity articulated in rock culture is simply irrelevant, does not.

The excessive proliferation of signs for the real and the authentic

---

53 One of the trivial but wonderful wrinkles in the history of rock is that Bowie changed his name from Davy Jones to avoid confusion with the Monkee of the same name. The manufacture of the Monkees as a group thus had as its consequence the manufacture of the identity Bowie has made a career of redefining.

manifest in *MTV Unplugged* and, particularly, in Clapton's performance on the program, constitutes the panic to which Baudrillard refers, the music industry's urgent program of damage-control designed to rescue the reality principle and, hence, its own power, from the exposure of simulation. In place of Milli Vanilli we are given what Arthur Kroker (Kroker *et al.* 1989) might choose to call "Panic MTV" and "Panic Clapton" that apparently reinstate the signs that signify the real in the cultural context of rock music. A Baudrillardian reading of the Grammy awards to Clapton would suggest that NARAS sought to tap into rock's ideology of authenticity in order to preserve its own power. Contraposing Clapton to Milli Vanilli, NARAS was able to "regenerate a reality principle in distress" by appearing to recreate a matrix of oppositions that are significant in the cultural context of rock music (e.g., authentic vs. inauthentic, rock vs. pop, real vs. simulated). NARAS thus produced the real-effect necessary to reaffirm its position as the arbiter among such distinctions. Rescinding the award also gave NARAS the appearance of morality necessary to the operation of capital: "whoever regenerates this public morality (by indignation, denunciation, etc.) spontaneously furthers the order of capital" (Baudrillard 1983: 27). (Although the legislators who proposed consumer regulations following the Milli Vanilli revelation represented themselves as challenging a dishonest music industry, their indignation, too, was actually complicit with capital.) The end result was that rock's ideology of authenticity which, as we have seen, was already in crisis, was brought back to life to serve the interests of capital.

I am arguing that a scandal effect had to be created around Milli Vanilli because the music industry and the concentric rings of power that attend it (including music critics) could not afford to admit that it is an industry devoted to simulation. If the distinction between live and mediatized performance were to be revealed as empty, then the ability to sell the same material over and over again – as a studio recording, as a music video, as a live performance, as a video of the live performance, as a live album – would disappear. The Grammys' ideological procedure of awarding the prize to performers, as though they are the authors of their recordings and not merely "the tip of an elaborate commercial network of investors, managers, agents, and publishers" (Sudjic 1990: 143), would be exposed. And what of rock critics? On what basis would they discriminate among recordings and performances once it is acknowledged that all are simply different articulations of the same code, recombinant variations on the same genetic material?

More is at stake here than simply the survival of the music industry in its current form or even the interests of capital generally. Law, as well as capital, depends on the maintenance of a system of polarities and is therefore threatened by simulation. "Simulation neutralizes the poles that organize the perspectival space of the real and the Law" (Baudrillard 1990: 155). NARAS's reinscription of binary oppositions, effected by rescinding Milli Vanilli's Grammy and subsequently granting Clapton multiple awards, generated a real-effect that worked not only in the interest of capital but in the interest of law as well, for "the denunciation of scandal always pays homage to the law" (Baudrillard 1983: 27). To understand how this scenario played out in this particular instance, it is necessary to examine more closely the landscape of technological change against which the drama of Milli Vanilli unfolded and the challenges to the reign of law, copyright law in particular, implied by those changes.

The historical progression of technologies of musical reproduction exactly recapitulates the three orders of simulacra and the three stages of the image Baudrillard identifies in the general movement from the dominance of reproduction to that of simulation.[54] First-order simulacra are *counterfeits* that "never abolished difference" but suppose "an always detectable alteration between semblance and reality" (Baudrillard 1983: 94–5). Baudrillard's example is that of the automaton, which counterfeits the human figure, but imperfectly, and thus defers to the human being as the referent of the real. In terms of musical technologies, I would suggest that the player piano is a first-order simulacrum, a device that counterfeits a human performance but clearly is not human. The second order is associated with an industrial economy in which the serial production of objects ultimately obliterates the unique object from which they were generated, Attali's economy of repetition. "In a series, objects become undefined simulacra one of the other" (ibid.: 97). The phonograph record is a second-order simulacrum, a mass-produced object whose reference back to an original artifact has been rendered irrelevant. In rock culture, as we have seen, live

---

54 Wurtzler's description of three phases in the development of music recording practices follows a similar:

> trajectory: firstly, recording conceived as the documentation of a pre-existing event; secondly, recording conceived as the construction of an event; and thirdly, recording conceived as the dismantling of any sense of an original event and the creation instead of a copy for which no original exists.

> (Wurtzler 1992: 93)

performance serves to authenticate the recording but does not function explicitly as its originary referent; live performance can and does authenticate the recording in the absence of any claim that the recording is of that particular performance.

The third stage of the image is what Baudrillard (ibid.: 83) refers to as simulation proper, "the reigning scheme of the current phase that is controlled by the code":

> And here it is a question of a reversal of origin and finality, for all the forms change once they are not so much mechanically reproduced but even *conceived from the point-of-view of their very reproducibility,* diffracted from a generating nucleus we call the model....Here are the models from which proceed all forms according to the modulation of their differences.
>
> (ibid.: 100–1; original emphasis)

In terms of technologies of musical reproduction, the age of digital music technologies such as the compact disc is the age of simulation proper. The code and model is the binary code that defines all products of digital technology, products that differ from one another only according to different modulations of the common code from which they are all diffracted. There is no intrinsic difference between the binary code on a music disc and the code in the software that controls the launching of missiles: regardless of its purpose or destination, all digital information is generated from the same model and is, in that sense, of the same genetic stuff and, therefore, perfectly exchangeable with all other digital information. And since digital code is reproduced through a process of "cloning," the information on all compact discs and their sources is identical: all are "originals"; there is neither an originary referent nor a first in the series. (In a *reproductive* process, one can speak of a "parent." A clone, however, is a *simulation,* the replication of a model, not the offspring of a parent.) As simulated on *MTV Unplugged,* live performance, too, becomes the replication of a model rather than an originary event on which reproductions are (imagined to be) based. In a way, the historical relationship of live performance to recorded music in rock culture anticipated the logic of simulation, since live performances always derived from the very recordings they served to authenticate.

Since the early 1980s, digital technologies have been increasingly implicated not just in the reproduction of music (on CDs) but in its production as well, especially through the extensive use of digital sampling instruments both in the studio and in concert.

Digital samplers allow one to encode a fragment of sound, from one to several seconds in duration, in a digitised binary form which can then be stored in computer memory. This stored sound may be played back through a keyboard, with its pitch and tonal qualities accurately reproduced or, as is often the case, manipulated through electronic editing. Because of its unsurpassed mimetic capabilities, one common use of the sampler has been to store in computer memory a note or set of notes played by an individual who has a unique playing style. When played back through a keyboard, one could construct an entire solo line which would potentially sound as if that person were playing it. Another common use of the sampler is to extract a fragment of sound from one context and place it in a new one.

(Porcello 1991: 69)

As this description suggests, digital musical technologies imply both an enhanced ability to incorporate parts of existing musical texts into new ones and to simulate the playing style of particular musicians themselves. These technologies therefore "place authenticity and creativity in crisis, not just because of the issue of theft [of musical texts], but through the increasingly *automated* nature of their mechanisms" (Goodwin 1990: 262).

Because it transforms music into transportable bits of information, digital technology also holds out the promise of enabling music consumers to construct the music itself.

When digital recording is the norm, the "listener" will have as much opportunity to unfix and refix a piece of music at home as the "producer" in the studio....The music consumer of the future will thus be "active" in new ways – editing out the bass, feeding in a drum line from another package altogether, adding their own voice.

(Frith 1988b: 123)

Although digital technologies are based on binary logic, they have had the ironic effect of dismantling cultural binaries, including distinctions between original and copy, producer and consumer, music and nonmusic (since the digitization of music renders it exchangeable and interchangeable with any other digital information), human being and machine. For this reason, digital technologies, including those specifically associated with music production, offer a profound challenge to "the print-oriented model of the creative process" that underlies copy-right law (Katsh 1989: 175). Copyright, which controls the ownership of and the right to disseminate cultural texts, has meaning only within a cultural economy in which the very binary oppositions challenged by digital technologies are in force.

Despite Ethan Katsh's claim that "the redefinition of copyright is inevitable" (Katsh 1989: 176) in the face of these new technologies, the legal response thus far has been to try to bring simulationist practices under the authority of existing legal structures by characterizing the issues they raise as moral ones. This is what legislators did when they defined lip-synching in concert as a question in consumer law and also what Judge Kevin Thomas Duffy did when he decided, late in 1991, that sampling from a recording without obtaining prior permission of those who hold the copyright on the song and its recording is simply theft.[55] In a highly unusual disposition of a civil copyright infringement claim, Duffy referred the case to the District Attorney for possible criminal prosecution (*Grand Upright Music Ltd.* v. *Warner Brothers Records, Inc.*, 182, 185). Because such contentions prior to 1991 were settled out of court, sampling had not been brought under the rule of law (Beadle 1993: 199). The decision in *Upright Music* v. *Warner Brothers* brought sampling definitively within the domain of law and therefore had a chilling effect on the music industry both in the United States and the United Kingdom (Beadle 1993: 201–2, 208).

It is in the context of the growing dominance of digital technologies in music production, their implicit ability to redefine the traditional roles of musician and consumer, and the resulting challenge to copy-right that the Milli Vanilli scandal must be seen. These developments must themselves be seen, in turn, as part of a larger picture in which the authority of law generally is threatened by the evolution of simula-tionist technologies that break down the polarities on which that authority depends. It is for this reason that Baudrillard uses the word "Digitality" to describe the cultural logic of simulation. The word "Polarity" describes the logic replaced by Digitality; whereas "the *polar relation*, or the dialectical or contradictory relation, organizes the universe of the Law, the social and meaning[,] the *digital relation* (but it is no longer a 'relation' – let us speak instead of the digital connection) allocates the space of Norms and Models" (Baudrillard 1990: 156). By

55 The facts of the case concerned rapper Biz Markie's appropriation of a sample from Gilbert O'Sullivan's recording of his "Alone Again (Naturally)" and Markie's apparent lack of interest in securing permission to do so.

scapegoating Milli Vanilli, then seemingly endorsing rock's ideology of authenticity, the music industry, through NARAS and MTV *Unplugged*, recreated "the poles that organize the perspectival space of the real and the Law" within the culture of rock music and, thus, paid homage to the law at a crucial moment when the legality of some musical practices was being questioned. That the music industry acted in its own interest is clear: even as it implicitly endorsed the bringing of simulationist musical practices under the rule of law, the music industry placed itself outside the law by subverting the need for legislation and establishing the appearance of a moral superstructure behind which to conduct business as usual. The chronology of events is important here: notice that it was only *after* anti-lip-synching legislation was proposed that the award to Milli Vanilli was rescinded and that the subsequent awards to Clapton were made immediately following Judge Duffy's decision in *Upright Music* v. *Warner Brothers*. In each case, the music industry responded to a challenge to its simulationist practices by reasserting the polar discourse of rock authenticity. The 1991 awards to Natalie Cole take on a new significance in this light: they stand, in fact, for the whole development I have described. In this allegory, the exposure of Milli Vanilli represents simulation as a rogue element threatening NARAS (power), the music industry (capital), and the law. The awards to Natalie Cole for her technologically simulated duet with her father enact the forced accommodation of simulation to the interests of all three agencies. An acknowledged simulation, Cole's bizarre but fundamentally sentimental reunion with her deceased father transformed the scene of simulation from one entailing the victimization of child music consumers to one supportive of family values: safe simulation.

At the risk of seeming cynical, I will also suggest that the song singled out for particular Grammy recognition from Clapton's *Unplugged* album, "Tears in Heaven," itself contributed greatly to the real-effect sought by the music industry in the wake of Milli Vanilli. Like Cole's duet with her late father, the song – a memorial to Clapton's young son, who died in a freak accident – imagines the field of recorded sound as the space for a posthumous reunion of parent and child. Clearly, this corresponds to what Baudrillard calls "an escalation of the true, of the lived experience." As opposed to Milli Vanilli, who won an award for a song they neither composed nor sang, Clapton was rewarded for a song that he not only wrote and actually performed but that also alludes to a well-known personal tragedy. Does it get any "realer" than this? The song's regret at the death of an individual seems to reinstate the value of the unique that has lost ground within the current cultural conformation. Under the economy of repetition, the single representation cannot be stockpiled and, therefore, has no value. In the age of digital cloning, the model is infinitely replicable – death is no longer the ultimate limit, as can be seen from the posthumous performances by musicians and, now, actors digitally cloned from their existing recordings and films.[56] Through the specificity of the personal experience it describes and the personal relationship of singer to song, Clapton's performance seems to return us to an economy of representation in which the singular event is valorized. By poignantly reinstating death as an unmitigable absence and, thus, apparently recovering the life/death opposition from implosion, the song valorizes living presence and underscores MTV Unplugged's assertion of its own liveness and authenticity. All of this, however, is merely another diversionary tactic designed to mask the fact that the music industry is fully given over to simulation. The challenge Clapton's song and performance seem to offer to the regime of simulation took place on television and was designed from the start to occupy a position in the economy of repetition through its many lives as cable television show, compact disc, and video cassette, all of which are replications of the model. The small audience that participated in the taping and for whom Clapton's Unplugged concert was a "real" live event was similarly packaged for repetition and becomes another exploitable sign of the event's liveness and authenticity. The experience of the audience present at a live musical event that has been designed for repetition is "to be totally reduced to the role of an extra in the record or film [or, in this case, television show] that finances it," to become part of a simulated, commodified audience (Attali 1985: 137). If Milli Vanilli provided capital with the opportunity to stage a scandal-effect, Clapton's meditation on living presence and the abundance of signs insisting on MTV Unplugged's status as live event contribute to the simulation of liveness, the creation of a live-effect that appears to denounce simulation while actually furthering its dominance.

As must be apparent from the foregoing analysis, the psychic trope of Baudrillardian cultural analysis is paranoia. I will push my paranoid

---

56 For a discussion of performance in the age of digital technology that includes reference to the practice of posthumous cloning, see Auslander (1992a). Many television commercials now feature actor-cloning: long-dead celebrities pitch various products. Actor Brandon Lee, who was killed during the making of the film The Crow (1994), appears in scenes he never had the opportunity to shoot through the intervention of digital technology.

interpretation one step further to show that it ultimately rebounds on Baudrillard's own assertion that simulation is symptomatic of the undoing of the power structure on which capital depends. Surely it is important that MTV has been an active agent at almost every crucial point in the story I have been telling. It is largely through MTV that music videos have become the "reality" that live performance of music seeks to recreate. It was during an MTV-sponsored tour in 1988 that rumors about Milli Vanilli's inability to sing live first appeared. And, of course, the whole "unplugged" phenomenon that was so powerfully implicated in restoring the reality principle post-Milli Vanilli was institutionalized, if not actually created, by MTV.

Coincidence? I think not. Power requires a matrix of clearly defined oppositions in which to operate and will create the appearance of oppositions in response to the implosion of a previously operational system. "[P]ower is absolute only if it is capable of diffraction into various equivalents, if it knows how to take off so as to put more on. This goes for brands of soap-suds as well as peaceful coexistence" (Baudrillard 1983: 134). Baudrillard suggests here that governments must appear to have different interests even though they may all be part of a single, global system of power, just as products with different brand names must appear to be different from one another even though the same company manufactures them all. This diffraction of power is clearly visible in the operation of MTV. MTV's establishment of the music video as a cultural form was symptomatic of musical performance's entrance into the age of simulation. Through *MTV Unplugged*, MTV also proposes itself as the antidote to the regime of simulation. A truly paranoid reading of the fact that Milli Vanilli first came under suspicion during an MTV-sponsored tour would suggest that MTV actually engineered the whole scenario as a way of solidifying its own power, first by problematizing the reality principle through the promotion of simulation, then by creating a scandal-effect around Milli Vanilli, and finally by establishing itself as the champion of the reality principle through a seemingly panicked reassertion of reality and authenticity in popular music that was, in fact, merely the creation of a liveness-effect through a cynical merchandizing of Eric Clapton's personal loss. In the context of MTV's regime of simulated liveness, Clapton's touching memorial becomes a means of bringing the one realm that might seem to evade simulation under its thrall. It may be that, in a mediatized culture, live performance inevitably brings death into the economy of repetition. The live asserts itself not as a triumph over death (it is *simulation* that represents such a triumph, as in Nat King Cole's return to sing with his daughter or the reunification of the late John Lennon

with the other Beatles in the space of digital recording) but as a celebration of the unique, nonrepeatable event, of which death is the
ultimate example.[57] Ironically, the effect of this attempt to recuperate
death as a sign of the live results in the commodification of death
itself, for the live finally cannot evade the economy of repetition.
"[R]epetition makes death exchangeable, in other words, it represents
it, puts it on stage, and sells it as a spectacle" (Attali 1985: 126).

To put the matter more generally, it may be that the implosion of
the opposition between live and mediatized performance in popular
music posited earlier in this chapter was actually a *simulation* of implosion created by an agency of capital to consolidate and extend its
power by *recuperating simulation itself as one of its strategies*. It seems to
be just as possible to see simulation as the latest weapon in the arsenal
of capital (or at least as a phenomenon co-opted by capital, as my analysis of Natalie Cole's Grammys suggests) as to insist that it means the
end of the entire system of real power within which capital operates.
At the end of a passage I quoted earlier, Baudrillard (1983: 44) claims
that when power "is threatened today by simulation...[it] risks the
real....This is a question of life and death for it. But it is too late." But
is it, in fact, too late? Or is it possible that simulation can be brought
into the system of power to be used by capital to maintain its dominance, as I have suggested in my paranoid interpretation of the
machinations of MTV?

At the very least, it would seem that the development that
Baudrillard treats as a *fait accompli* is actually in the process of occur-
ring. At the start of this chapter, I alluded to the fact that the young
audiences for Milli Vanilli and other acts are not concerned with their
idols' liveness: simulation does not create anxiety for them in the way
it does for the first (and second?) generations of Clapton's fans and for
the performance theorists discussed in Chapter 2. In giving us both
Clapton and Milli Vanilli, MTV may be working both sides of the

---

57 A sad but pertinent example is the suicide of Kurt Cobain. According to published
accounts, Cobain's self-murder was motivated by his sense that as his band, Nirvana,
became more successful, their music was losing its spontaneity and authenticity.
Rather than face the prospect of endlessly repeating his performances, Cobain
sought refuge in what he seems to have thought of as the only authentic gesture left
to him. It was, of course, a gesture that was instantly recuperated by the very
economy that drove Cobain to self-destruction, as has been the case with all famous
"rock and roll suicides" (David Bowie). Witness the marketing of Elvis Presely, Jimi
Hendrix, and Jim Morrison, in particular, since (and because of) their respective
demises.

generational street by placating rock's older fans with simulations of authenticity while simultaneously ushering in the new paradigm for the children of those fans. When this latter generation assumes "power," the regime of simulation may be in full force, its expansion into and voiding of the realms of the social and the political may be complete.

4

LEGALLY LIVE

Law, performance, memory

Herbert Blau (1996: 274) has noted the strong desire in current theory for "a language of 'performativity' that will outwit, baffle, or abolish the regulatory functions that work in the name of the law." This desire is certainly reflected in contemporary performance theory. Peggy Phelan (1993a: 148), for instance, argues that "without a copy, live performance plunges into visibility – in a maniacally charged present – and disappears into memory, into the realm of invisibility and the unconscious where it eludes regulation and control." Despite the overheated rhetoric of this passage, Phelan makes an influential claim. Her suggestion that a performance cannot be copied and still remain a performance derives from her view that performance's most crucial ontological characteristic is its disappearance, discussed in Chapter 2. In Phelan's view, if performance cannot be copied, it cannot participate in a cultural economy based in repetition and is therefore exempt from control by the forces that govern that economy, including the law. She invokes another ostensibly ontological quality of performance when she refers to its continued existence only as spectatorial memory. Patrice Pavis (1992: 67) explains the relationship between performance's evanescence and its storage in memory: "The work, once performed, disappears for ever. The only memory which one can preserve is that of the spectator's more or less distracted perception." Phelan extends this analysis of performance into the political realm by arguing that performance's disappearance and subsequent persistence only in memory makes performance a privileged site of resistance to forces of regulation and control. Her position depends on two premises: that performance resists reproduction and that memory is a safe haven from the law.

In this chapter, I hope to problematize this way of thinking about the relationship of performance and the law by showing that the law attributes to performance the same ontological qualities – existence only in the moment and persistence only as memory – as those who see performance as resisting the law. Although those qualities enable performance to escape regulation in one very limited sense, they also make performance available and useful to the law in other, more comprehensive, ways. Live performance is, in fact, essential to legal procedure. I will explore this issue in terms of two different areas of jurisprudence: I discuss evidence law in the first section of this chapter and intellectual property law in the second. To show that the assumption that a trial is an ontologically live event is fundamental to the discourse of American law, I will examine the phenomenon of the prerecorded videotape trial and pose the question of why it never achieved the popularity predicted for it. To demonstrate the centrality of live performance to legal procedure, I will discuss the system's strong preference for live testimony and the ways in which testimony is defined as a live performance of memory-retrieval. This discussion focuses primarily on evidence law. In the next section, I take up the question of live performance's status under intellectual property law. It is here that performance evades regulation to an extent, since performance as such is not regulated as a cultural commodity under copyright. The third section of this chapter, however, problematizes the claim that performance's continued existence in spectatorial memory places it outside the reach of regulation by showing that memory is both policed by law and pressed into service as a mechanism for the enforcement of law.

Whereas evidence law regulates "the proof used to persuade on fact questions at the trial of a lawsuit" (Rothstein 1981: 1) and therefore sets conditions that regulate the conduct of trials as performances *of* the law, copyright governs the ownership and circulation of cultural objects, and therefore determines the conditions under which performance participates in a commodity economy. As such, it is the branch of jurisprudence that deals most directly with the status of performance *in* the law. I want here to survey statutes and decisions that shed light on both performance's status in the law and the nature of legal proceedings as performance. Although copyright and evidence are separate areas of law, considering them in relation to performance reveals that memory is a thematic common to both – perhaps the central thematic of law generally. Using the thematic of memory as a pivot point, this chapter's discussion of law and performance will re-examine many of the issues raised in Chapters 1 and 2 from a specifically legal angle. The discussions of testimony and copyright reassert the dual focus of this study on liveness in both ontological and cultural-economic terms.

Teevee's courthouse, or the resistible rise of the videotape trial

The American courtroom has undergone the same incursion of media-tization as other cultural sites formerly devoted to live performance. Video and digital information technologies are now used in many phases of trials. A suspect may be arraigned from jail by means of a remote video hook-up. In some cases, such as the use of home videos of births as evidence in medical malpractice trials, the event at issue itself may be shown on video, as a form of eyewitness testimony.[1] Other types of testimony – the depositions of expert and even substantive witnesses – also may be presented on video. So-called "day-in-the-life" videos are used to show the impact of an injury on its victim. Demonstrative evidence, such as reenactments of crimes, may be staged on video or animated on the computer screen. Even closing arguments may incorporate video. *Standard Chartered PLC* v. *Price Waterhouse* (88–34414 [Super. Ct., Maricopa Co., Ariz.]) gained noto-riety in legal circles because the plaintiff's attorneys incorporated into their closing argument a screening of a production entitled "The Titanic" to present an analogy they would otherwise have made verbally. "In this $17,000 video, scenes from *A Night to Remember*, a 1958 British movie about the sinking of the Titanic, are alternated with information and graphics about how Price Waterhouse's faulty audit financially sunk an investment by the British bank Standard Chartered PLC" (Sherman 1993: 1). In order to accommodate the many possible forms of mediatized testimony and evidence,[2] the well-equipped, contemporary courtroom may include such devices and systems as the following, excerpted from a much longer list:

---

1 In such cases, the cross-examining attorney must employ a variation on a classic strategy. Rather than trying to persuade the jury that the witness did not see what she claimed to have seen, the attorney must persuade the jury that the video does not show what the plaintiff claims it shows. The jurors become eyewitnesses who must be persuaded of the unreliability of the video representation rather than of their own perceptual unreliability.

2 Ronald K. L. Collins and David M. Skover (1992) refer to video and other nonprint media used as legal documents as "paratexts." They make the interesting argument that as law becomes more and more dependent on paratexts and less bound to the written word, the performative aspects of legal proceedings (such as gesture, facial expression, and so on) will become part of the record in the way that only words are at present. In some respects, the law will then be practiced in a manner reminiscent of pre-literate societies. Bernard J. Hibbitts (1992, 1995) has elaborated this posi-tion through his analyses of legal performativity.

- Recorded or real-time televised evidence display with analog optical disk storage using the…Litigation Sciences videodisc system, which features bar code indexing and light pen control;
- Built-in video deposition playback facilities;
- Automatic Court Technologies microchip-controlled, multi-camera, multi-frame, video recording of proceedings using ceiling-mounted cameras and Shure Microphone voice-initiated switching;…
- Text, graphics, and TV-capable jury computers and monitors;…
- The A.D.A.M. simulation and display of the human body.

(Lederer 1994: 1099–1100)

Given the potentially extensive presence of media technology in the courtroom, it is possible for a jury to find itself in much the same position as a concert audience or sports crowd attending an ostensibly live event and watching most of it on video displays.[3] Nevertheless, I shall argue that the courtroom has proved far more resistant to the incursion of mediatization than the other cultural sites discussed here.

A proposition for fully mediatized trials was put forth in the early 1970s, when the simplification of videotape technology made it accessible to users outside the television industry. Sparing no fanfare, jurist Alan Morrill made the following proclamation in a law journal article of 1970:

One day very soon now, a courtroom somewhere in this illustrious land will introduce a sweeping change in the present system of trial by jury.…A jury will have decided the issues of a law suit by merely viewing and hearing the entire proceedings of a trial on a television screen.…The lawyers who conducted the trial probably will have been in the presence of the jury only during the jury selection.…Regardless of the domain, this destined event will take place – be it in one of the large cities or in a remote county seat – that location will be recorded in history as the place where it all began. This unique modification in the resolving of law suits will spread

3 This is not even to mention the further mediatization of the trial as it is presented by means of video on the nightly news or Court TV, which is to the American legal system what MTV is to the music industry. For a useful historical overview, and a skeptical evaluation, of this kind of mediatization, see Thaler (1994). Important as it is, external mediatization of the trial as news event is not my concern here; I am focusing on the internal mediatization of the courtroom event itself.

rapidly over the length and breadth of our nation, notwithstanding entrenched attitudes of a portion of the trial bar.

(Morrill 1970: 237–8)

Morrill was a true prophet – most of what he prognosticated came to
pass, with the major exception of the sweeping reform he describes in
his last sentence. The kind of trial he predicted, which came to be
known as the "prerecorded videotape trial," usually abbreviated
PRVTT or PRVT (I will use the latter abbreviation), took place
numerous times in several jurisdictions and acquired staunch advocates
within the judiciary.

History records where the first PRVT took place without, alas,
enshrining that city as the birthplace of a legal paradigm shift in the
manner Morrill anticipated. The experiment took place on May 23,
1971 in Sandusky, Ohio, and was overseen by the Hon. James L.
McCrystal, Judge in the Erie County Common Pleas Court, who intentionally chose a simple case so as to incur a minimum of technical
problems. In *McCall v. Clemens* (Civil No. 39301 [Erie County Court
of Common Pleas, Ohio]), the plaintiff had been injured when the
elderly defendant lost control of her car. "Liability was admitted and
the only fact questions for the jury were the nature and extent of
McCall's injuries and the amount due him as damages" (Murray 1972a:
268). McCrystal considered the experiment an unqualified success; the
two participating attorneys also reported satisfaction with the procedure (McCrystal 1972, Murray 1972b, Watts 1972).[4] The Supreme
Court of Ohio was sufficiently impressed with the outcome to change
the state's Rules of Civil Procedure and its Superintendence Rules to
make the PRVT a regular possibility in its jurisdiction.[5]

It is worth quoting at length a description of the procedures used in
McCall v. Clemens and subsequent PRVTs to establish a clear sense of
just what a prerecorded videotape trial was:

> All witnesses testified under oath in mutually agreed upon
> settings in the presence of the lawyers and a court officer
> other than the trial judge. The order of taping the testimony

---

4 It may be, of course, that the two attorneys, who were presumably likely to appear
before McCrystal again, were loath to disagree with the judge's assessment!
5 See McCrystal and Young (1973: 561–3) for a discussion of this change in Ohio's
procedural rules. For the complete, annotated text of these rules and others relevant
to the PRVT, see McCrystal (1983: 109–25).

was not stipulated, nor was it binding on the subsequent order of presentation. All objections were formally noted, but questioning was not curtailed. The master tape, containing the entirety of the testimony, was reviewed subsequently in chambers in the presence of the attorneys. At this time, the trial judge passed and ruled on all objections.[6] Both the formal objections and the objectionable statements were deleted on a second tape.[7] Thus, the edited version of the trial tape was prepared without destroying the continuity of the admissible testimony. The trial tape was then further spliced so that the witnesses could be presented in the agreed upon order. The master tape remained intact for appeal purposes.

The jurors were not impaneled until the completion of the trial tapes. After the attorneys delivered their opening statements in the courtroom, the trial tape was shown to the jurors on monitors. Neither lawyers nor trial judge remained in the courtroom throughout the presentation, although an officer of the court was in attendance at all times. In all cases, lawyers gave their closing statements live, but judges rendered instructions to the jurors on tape.

[P]robable appelate [sic] procedures have been discussed.... If a new trial were ordered, it would be accomplished by re-

6 In a later, streamlined version of this procedure, the attorneys would note their objections on a chart keyed to particular points on the unedited tape. The judge would make rulings on these objections alone in chambers, often by watching only those moments of the tape at which objections occurred. The trial tape would be edited from the master tape according to the judge's rulings (McCrystal 1983: 114–18).

7 There were actually two different editing procedures used. Sometimes, objectionable material was simply excluded from the edited trial tape. On other occasions, a technician would black out portions of the audio and visual tracks during playback. (An automated version of this system, in which the selections shown are controlled by a computer, was proposed by a later PRVT advocate; see Perritt 1994: 1083). By these means, the jury would know that something had been excluded at that point. Two communications scholars who studied prerecorded trials during the 1970s note that this latter method, which involves no actual editing of the tape, was particularly appropriate to "this post-Watergate era when suspicions of tampering and subversion are relatively commonplace." They nevertheless recommend the first editing procedure as less distracting to jurors and because they found that "when jurors knew material was edited, they speculated about its content, an activity that might be even more biasing than knowing what the excerpt contained and being instructed to disregard it" (Miller and Fontes 1979: 23, 137).

editing the trial tape according to the findings of the higher court, and presenting this new tape to another jury.

(Shutkin 1973: 365–6; original footnotes excluded)

As this description indicates, PRVTs were simulations, in the strict, Baudrillardian sense: the trial tape is a reproduction of an event that never took place. It reflects the "inversion of the structural dependence of copies upon originals" (Connor 1989: 153) characteristic of simulations. As one commentator observes, the trial tape is "a transcript of the trial [made] before the trial occurs" (Perritt 1994: 1071).

After presiding over *McCall* v. *Clemens*, Judge McCrystal became the PRVT's strongest advocate. With missionary zeal, he barnstormed law journals, conferences, and seminars, preaching the virtues of the PRVT to anyone in the legal community who would listen (see McCrystal 1972, 1983; McCrystal and Maschari 1983 [1981], 1983, 1984 [1983]; McCrystal and Young 1973). The benefits he and other advocates pointed to were largely administrative and procedural (see Marshall 1984, McCrystal and Young 1973: 563–4, Morrill 1970: 239–47). The PRVT was said to be more efficient than live trials: neither judges nor attorneys had to spend much time in the courtroom and could attend to other cases, even participate in other trials, while the jury was watching a completed trial tape. Additionally, judges could make more considered replies to objections since they did not have to be delivered in the heat of trial. Trials would never have to be delayed to await a witness's arrival, and witness testimony could be presented in the best possible sequence. Witnesses could be deposed at their leisure and would not feel inconvenienced by having to spend time in the courtroom. Jurors' time was used more efficiently, as well, since they did not have to be present for conferences between attorneys and clients or the judge, and the trial was never interrupted for any reason, resulting in a much shorter running time. As a result of these efficiencies, the PRVT was seen as a way of clearing crowded dockets.[8] Because the jurors would never see or hear inadmissible testimony or prejudicial comments and would not be influenced by the demeanor of the judge, the chances of a mistrial and the likelihood of

8 McCrystal bragged of having been "assigned by the presiding Ohio chief justice to a nearby metropolitan county to hear over 100 highway-appropriation and eminent domain cases. Over 50 of these cases were terminated by PRVT in less than a year, and the pre-recorded testimony of nearly 25 cases was edited...and forwarded on to the nearby county where local judges presided at the trials" (McCrystal and Maschari 1984 [1983]: 246).

appeal were smaller. The fact that the whole trial could be seen before it was presented to the jury meant that directed verdict motions – in which one or both of the parties request that the judge, not the jury, rule on the case – could be resolved prior to impaneling the jury, and that attorneys could show their clients exactly what the jury would see and discuss settlements or plea bargains on that basis. Attorneys would also have a much clearer idea of what to ask when interviewing prospective jurors in the *voir dire* phase of the trial. PRVTs were also touted as more cost effective than live trials, supposedly reducing the costs of discovery depositions taken as part of the pre-trial information-gathering process and those of conducting the trial itself by more than half (Marshall 1984: 855, McCrystal and Maschari 1983).[9]

By 1983, over 200 PRVTs had occurred in Ohio, with McCrystal presiding over many of them (McCrystal and Maschari 1983: 70). Although the vast majority of these cases were civil suits, there were also criminal PRVTs; McCrystal presided over the first prerecorded murder trial in 1982 (Croyder 1982). The PRVT experiment spread to other states. Michigan inaugurated Project T.A.P.E. (an acronym for "total application of prerecorded evidence"; Brennan 1972: 6–7); and, by 1984, Indiana and Texas had joined the PRVT family (see Marshall 1984, McCrystal and Maschari 1983 [1981]).

Several social scientific studies of the PRVT were undertaken, including one by communications scholars at Michigan State University (Miller and Fontes 1979) and another by the National Bureau of Standards (Robertson 1979). The Michigan State study was reported at book length; McCrystal quoted its generally favorable conclusions on every possible occasion. Comparing jurors' responses to the same trial performed live and on videotape, the authors found that neither the verdicts nor the awards differed significantly from one form of presentation to the other. They also found that jurors' perception of the witnesses' truthfulness did not differ significantly, that the deletion of inadmissible testimony did not effect the jurors' perception of the

9 These were among what might be called the "official" benefits PRVT advocates cited, but there were probably other reasons for its appeal, especially to judges, to whom it promised an unprecedented degree of control over what happens in the courtroom. The historical context of the early 1970s is important here. Morrill (1970: 245) refers to "the recent political trials," such as the Chicago Seven trial, and notes that the videotape process makes it impossible for a defendant to throw the trial into chaos or to use the courtroom as a political platform. Although other advocates of the PRVT do not broach this issue as bluntly as Morrill, it crops up as a motif in several discussions.

attorneys' veracity, and that jurors remembered the facts of the case better when the trial was presented on videotape than when they saw it live (Miller and Fontes 1979: 211–12).

The PRVT concept seemingly had a lot going for it. As I indicated at the beginning of this chapter, the courtroom has shown itself to be amenable to the incorporation of new technologies. The PRVT enjoyed the staunch support of several jurists. Even those skeptical of the PRVT's virtues acknowledged that it might be a way of conducting a trial more in tune with contemporary, mediatized perception than the traditional live event.[10] Yet, the PRVT never became an accepted practice. Far from the paradigm shift envisioned by its proponents, the PRVT has languished as a fairly obscure footnote to American legal history. The clearest indication of its failure to take root is that the author of a 1994 law journal article describes the PRVT as "a concept that is gaining support" and advocates it in exactly the same terms as Morrill had a quarter-century earlier (Perritt 1994). The standard explanation proposed by PRVT advocates for this failure is that the PRVT would be opposed by trial attorneys because it deprived them of the opportunity to grandstand in front of the jury. To the extent that this position seeks an explanation for the failure of the PRVT in a consideration of performance, it charts the course I will follow. At stake, however, is much more than the desire of attorneys to show off. The PRVT challenged some of the most basic assumptions underlying American jurisprudence, assumptions that have shaped debates on constitutional and procedural rights, and underlie the important question of just what sort of performance testimony is understood to be. It is always easier to explain why something happened than why something failed to happen, but this inquiry may permit at least a speculative understanding of why the PRVT never caught on.

Of the PRVT's various advocates, Morrill acknowledged most directly the procedural obstacle confronting it (see also McCrystal and Young 1973: 564–5). After citing various decisions to demonstrate that films, sound recordings, and videotapes had all been accepted as evidence, he identifies what he considers a paradox:

---

10 In his critical analysis of the PRVT, David M. Doret (1974: 249) states that the novelty of the concept may be only temporary: "The communications revolution of our time may ultimately acclimate people to accept interpersonal interaction through television screens *as the norm*" (original emphasis). The connections between this statement and Walter Benjamin's notion that "contemporary perception" is shaped, in part, by technology are self-evident.

in spite of the court's complete stamp of approval upon the reliability of these mechanical devices to accurately reproduce sound and sight, their use is severely restricted. There is complete agreement among the jurisdictions that an evidence deposition...cannot be admitted in evidence if the witness himself is available....There is, therefore, a complete road-block set up in the path of a pressing need for change.

(Morrill 1970: 256–7)

Morrill refers here to a doctrine enshrined in the Confrontation Clause of the Sixth Amendment to the US Constitution, which states that "in all criminal prosecutions, the accused shall enjoy the right...to be confronted with the witnesses against him." Although this clause is far more ambiguous than it may first appear and has a long and contentious history of Supreme Court interpretation,[11] it has always been taken to mean that the testimony of live witnesses who are physically present in the courtroom is preferable to any form of deposition.[12]

---

11 For an excellent summary of the contentious history of Confrontation Clause inter-pretation, see Nichols (1996), who argues persuasively that confrontation has proved such a sticky issue because of the Supreme Court's desire to balance the Constitution with public policy. In many instances, it has seemed in the public interest to allow the admission of types of testimony that a strict reading of the Clause would deem hearsay: the spate of child abuse cases in the 1980s, and the various policies crafted by the states to permit child victims to testify outside the presence of the accused, are one large category of examples. "At the same time, the Court has been reluctant to let go of the notion that the Clause connotes 'a prefer-ence for face-to-face confrontation at trial'" (Nichols 1996: 395). These conflicting imperatives have proved impossible to reconcile. There is general agreement that the historical trend in Supreme Court decisions has been away from protecting the Sixth Amendment rights of the accused and toward allowing more and more kinds of formerly inadmissible testimony. White v. Illinois (502 U.S. 346 [1992]) represents the most extreme decision of that kind to date. The Supreme Court upheld the conviction of an alleged child molester when the only evidence against him was the victim's statements to her baby-sitter, her mother, police officers, and a doctor. The girl herself was called to the stand twice but proved unable to testify. The out-of-court statements she had made to others were then admitted. This decision proved extremely controversial and was roundly condemned by legal commentators (see Seidelson 1993, Snyder 1993, Swift 1993). Some state judiciaries, such as that of New Mexico, have simply disregarded the White decision in favor of earlier Supreme Court decisions that maintain an emphasis on face-to-face confrontation (Nichols 1996: 423).

12 The Confrontation Clause has often been interpreted as a guarantee of the defen-dant's right to cross-examine the witnesses against him. The PRVT is relatively unproblematic in this respect, since the defendant's attorney can cross-examine

Depositions are used, of course, but their admission at trial is generally problematic in a way that live testimony never is.[13] Children are sometimes allowed to testify on video or closed-circuit television when accusing an alleged abuser, for example, but in most jurisdictions this can happen only after the court makes a specific finding that it would harm the particular child in identifiable ways to be in the presence of the defendant and grants an exception to permit mediatized testimony (see Holmes 1989: 697–700).[14]

Even decisions in favor of the use of depositions generally, and of videotaped depositions in particular, reflect the law's strong preference for live witnesses. For example, the Georgia Court of Appeals judge who ruled that "the taking of the deposition of an expert witness to be used at the trial...by means of videotaping" is an acceptable practice also stressed in his decision that: "it is well to remember that the taking of a deposition...is a substitute, at best, for the actual live testimony of the witness" (*Mayor* v. *Palmerio* 135 Ga. App. 147 [1975], 150). Indeed, most of the court decisions that have allowed the use of depositions at criminal trials stipulate very clearly that this practice is acceptable only when the witness is legitimately unavailable to testify live.[15] In *Stores* v. *State* (625 P.2d 820), heard by the Supreme Court of

---

witnesses at the time the tape is made (Doret 1974: 266). The importance of cross-examination is underscored by *State* v. *Wilkinson* (64 Ohio St.2d 308, 414 N.E. 2d 261), in which an undercover drug agent's death-bed testimony recorded on video at a hospital was deemed inadmissible because the defendant's attorney had not been given sufficient notice to be there during the taping.

13 Henry H. Perritt (1994: 1074) points out that "the revised Federal Rules of Civil Procedure express a preference for videotaped depositions in jury trials over stenographic records of depositions." (For a Confrontation Clause argument in favor of videotape depositions as opposed to stenographic transcripts in criminal trials, see Stein 1981). The obstacle confronted by the PRVT is not that the judiciary is opposed to videotaped depositions but, rather, the reluctance to admit depositions at all. One exception is that some jurisdictions have made it easy for medical experts to testify on video to encourage them to participate in trials.

14 It is also the case that most of the forms of mediatized evidence mentioned at the start of this section, including the "Titanic" video, would be admissible only by order of the presiding judge.

15 As a legal term, "unavailability" refers to a variety of circumstances in which a witness cannot, will not, or does not testify. A dead witness is said to be unavailable, as is a witness who did not respond to a subpoena or refuses to speak on the stand. I quote part of the definition of unavailability found in the Federal Rules of Evidence later in the main text. In addition to justifying the use of a deposition, the unavailability of a witness enables a variety of types of testimony to be admitted that would otherwise be considered hearsay (Federal Rule of Evidence 804b).

Alaska in 1980, the court overturned a conviction in a rape case on these grounds, finding that the prosecution had not made sufficient good-faith efforts to secure at the trial the presence of the doctor who had examined the victim, whose testimony had been presented on video while she was vacationing.[16] The higher court's interpretation of the prosecution's strategy was that "the sole purpose of taking the deposition was to create former testimony to be used in lieu of live testimony. We will not sanction such an evasion of the constitutionally based preference for live testimony in open court" (827).[17] The law's preference for the live presence of witnesses, implied by the Confrontation Clause, is clear.

Writing for the dissent in *Stores* v. *State*, Justice Matthews argued that "the critical question is whether there was a significant difference between the testimony as it was actually presented to the jury on the videotape and as it might have been presented had Dr. Sydnam appeared in person at Stores' trial" (830). Justice Matthews' position was that in as much as the circumstances of the taping were similar to those of the trial (the same attorneys were present, as was a trial judge, and the witness was cross-examined), there was no reason to believe that the videotape did not provide an accurate rendition of her testimony.[18] It is interesting that Justice Connor did not argue that the doctor's testimony *would* have been different had she appeared live, only that it *might* have been, and that that performative possibility was grounds on which to reverse the original decision. Justice Connor's opinion insists on the importance of live performance to the legal

---

16 A US Supreme Court case almost exactly contemporaneous with *Stores* turned, in part, on the same question. In *Ohio* v. *Roberts* (448 U.S. 56 [1980]), the court addressed, among other evidentiary issues, the question of whether or not the prosecution had made sufficient good-faith efforts to secure a witness before introducing her testimony from a preliminary hearing. Justice Brennan's dissent focuses entirely on this question.

17 I have employed the standard format for legal citations in the first citation to the decisions I discuss. I will place only the relevant page number in the parentheses following subsequent citations.

18 The idea that admissible prior testimony should have been given under "trial-like" conditions emerges in many decisions, as does debate over whether or not the circumstances of pre-trial depositions and preliminary hearings are sufficiently trial-like for testimony given under them to be admissible. This issue, too, presents a difficulty for the PRVT. Its supporters frequently emphasize the efficiency of being able to videotape witnesses outside the courtroom, whenever and wherever is most convenient. Challengers argue that it is difficult to maintain sufficiently trial-like conditions in these circumstances.

proceeding: the witness's live presence before the jury and the possibility that something could happen in "the maniacally charged present" of the trial that did not happen on the videotape are issues of sufficient moment to require the reversal of a rape conviction.

Interpreted in this way, the Confrontation Clause would seem to be a major hurdle for the PRVT, since all testimony would take the form, technically, of prerecorded depositions. Another aspect of the Confrontation Clause also creates difficulty for the PRVT. The Clause has been interpreted as supporting "jury observation of witness demeanor during confrontation to determine credibility and elicit truth" (Armstrong 1976: 570). At first glance, this seems relatively unproblematic: the defendant could be present during the taping of testimony, thus confronting the witness, and the jury would observe the witness's demeanor when shown the tape in the courtroom. But if the Confrontation Clause is interpreted as meaning that the confrontation of witness and accused must take place *in the jury's presence*, then the PRVT has encountered an obstacle it cannot overcome, for to have the jury present during the taping of testimony would be equivalent to staging a live trial![19]

There is reason to believe that the Sixth Amendment does indeed demand that confrontation take place live, before the jury. In *Maryland v. Craig* (497 U.S. 836 [1990]) the Supreme Court concluded that allowing a victim of child abuse to testify by closed-circuit television was acceptable because "the judge, jury, and defendant [were] able to view (albeit by video monitor) the demeanor (and body) of the witness as he or she testifie[d]" (quoted in Nichols 1996: 415–16). The key words here are "albeit" and "as." The first word implies that observing a witness by means of television is acceptable primarily because it is better than not observing the witness at all, and further implies that direct, live observation would be even better. The "as" clearly indicates that the Court interprets the Confrontation Clause to mean that the jury's observation of the witness is supposed to be *simultaneous* with the testimony, thus suggesting that confrontation is not just something to be seen by a jury at some point after it occurred, but something that should occur live, in the presence of the jury.

To pursue further the ways in which liveness is fundamental to trial proceedings, I will turn to what the law says about the nature of testimony itself. A textbook analysis of the legal concept of hearsay describes

---

19 I am indebted to Armstrong (1976) for the direction of my argument concerning the constitutionality of the PRVT.

the function of witnesses as the "recordation and recollection" of perceived events; this process of the storage and retrieval of memories is the basis for in-court testimony (Graham 1992: 262). To give testimony is to perform recollection, the retrieval of memory, in the present moment of the trial. The text of Federal Rule of Evidence 804a offers further support for this characterization of the witness function. The Rule presents the following definition of "unavailability as a witness," which is the necessary condition for the introduction of a deposition into a trial:

"Unavailability as a witness" includes situations in which the declarant –...

(3) testifies to a lack of memory of the subject matter of the declarant's statement; or
(4) is unable to be present or to testify at the hearing because of death or then existing physical or mental illness.[20]

In other words, from the point of view of the federal courts, a witness who is unable to perform memory in the courtroom is indistinguishable from a dead witness or a deranged one.[21]

In his dissenting opinion in *United States* v. *Owens* (108 S. Ct. 838 [1988]), a case concerning John Foster, a savagely beaten prison guard who had identified his assailant while in the hospital but, subsequently, could not remember the attack, though he could remember making the identification, Justice Brennan suggests that in as much as Foster had had no memory of his assailant at the time of the trial, he had not even been present in the courtroom:

20 The alert reader will have noticed by this point that I have drawn my examples from the realm of criminal law even though most of the PRVTs that actually took place were civil trials. It is the case that the Sixth Amendment right to confrontation applies only to criminal proceedings. As I mentioned earlier, there were criminal PRVTs, and its early advocates did not limit its use to civil cases. Where the use of depositions and the availability of witnesses are concerned, the guidelines in the Federal Rules of Civil Procedure are very similar to those· in the Federal Rules of Evidence that govern criminal trials. According to Federal Rule of Civil Procedure 32.V.a., depositions can be used only when a witness is unavailable, and unavailability is defined there in the same terms as in the Federal Rules of Evidence.

21 The legal system's dependence on memory is illustrated differently by the law's ambiguity where false claims of memory lapse are concerned. As David Greenwald (1993: 194) has pointed out, judges have a tendency to treat witnesses whom they suspect of such a false claim as fully present and available for cross-examination and impeachment despite their technical unavailability.

> respondent's sole accuser was the John Foster who, on May 5,
> 1982, identified respondent as his attacker. This John Foster,
> however, did not testify at respondent's trial: the profound
> memory loss he suffered...prevented him from affirming,
> explaining, or elaborating upon his out-of-court statement just
> as surely and completely as...his death would have. (846)

In Brennan's analysis, it is not because certain contents had been
erased from Foster's memory that he was "unavailable as a witness."
Foster had retrieved and articulated those contents while in the
hospital; they were known and had served as the basis for a trial.
Rather, it was Foster's inability to *perform* the retrieval of those memories *in the present moment of the trial*, to "affirm, explain, or elaborate
upon" what he had said earlier and outside the courtroom, that led
Brennan to declare that the trial court should have considered Foster
to be functionally dead and his hospital bed identification inadmissible
hearsay.[22]

In the interest of intellectual honesty, I have to underline that
Brennan's opinion was the dissenting one and that the Court found
that the admission of Foster's identification of his assailant had been
proper despite his loss of memory. At first glance, this circumstance
problematizes my thesis: if the performance of memory retrieval is the
crucial feature of testimony, how could the Court accept the testimony
of an amnesiac witness? Justice Scalia, writing for the majority, found
that as long as cross-examination of Foster had been possible, there was
no Sixth Amendment violation, despite Foster's "unavailability as a
witness" due to memory loss at the time of the trial. His argument was
that "meaningful cross-examination...is not destroyed by the witness'
assertion of memory loss, which is often the very result sought to be
produced by cross-examination" (838).

---

22 I would base an analysis of the legal system's ultimate lack of enthusiasm for the
psycho-therapeutic theory of repressed memory – in which an unconscious memory
of past abuse is said to rise to consciousness, leading to law suits and trials – on this
notion that testimony is supposed to be a recollection of memory in the present
moment of the trial. In repressed memory cases, the act of retrieving the memory is
the very thing that prompts legal action. Therefore, there is no way in which that
memory can be seen to be retrieved as a fresh recollection during the trial itself.
This is only a partial explanation, of course; the psycho-therapeutic community
itself lost faith in the concept, as did many patients, who sued their therapists for
malpractice. For a good summary of the rise and fall of the concept of repressed
memory in the legal and psychological contexts, see MacNamara (1995).

Regardless of its merits as law, which are open to question,[23] Scalia's opinion supports my contention that the performance of recollection is the essence of testimony. In Scalia's view, to assert memory loss in the courtroom *is* to perform recollection, albeit in a negative way that makes the opposing attorney's job very easy. If testimony is the performance of recollection, the purpose of cross-examination is to discredit that performance specifically by showing that it has no legitimate claim to being a performance of recollection, whether by demonstrating that the accuracy of the witness's memory is open to question or by showing that the witness has, in fact, no memory of the events at issue. There is no disagreement between Brennan and Scalia on the theoretical issue of whether testimony is a performance of recollection. Rather, they disagree on the question of whether John Foster should be described as having failed to give such a performance (Brennan) or as having given a performance that helped the other side (Scalia).

Federal Rule of Evidence 612, concerning the use of documents to "refresh [the witness's] memory" in the courtroom, also clearly illustrates the premium placed within the legal discourse on the idea that testimony is a present performance of memory retrieval. Such documents may be used only to stimulate the witness's *"independent recollection"* of the issue at hand; they may not function as scripts from which witnesses recount their recollections (Rothstein 1981: 49). The judge must be persuaded that "the witness's statement, springing from active, current (though revived) recollection will be the evidence" (Rothstein 1981: 45). If the judge feels that the witness is testifying "from what purports to be a revived present memory when his testimony

---

23 Claire Seltz (1988: 867, 897–8) offers a thoroughgoing critique of Scalia's decision, arguing that "the Court's reasoning is erroneous, extreme, and not indicative of legislative history or precedent" and creates "the illogical possibility that all out-of-court identifications of any cooperative witnesses, regardless of the value of the cross-examination achieved, will be admissible at trial." Although far gentler in tone, Greenwald's analysis of the case is also critical of the decision, which he faults for invoking a false precedent and misinterpreting an ambiguity in the Federal Rules of Evidence (1993: 178, 186). Although Seltz and Greenwald agree that the *Owens* decision displays faulty legal logic and sets a dangerous precedent, neither argues that the court came to the wrong conclusion concerning the particular case. Both commentators agree that because Foster retained partial memory of the circumstances of his attack and identification, he could be effectively cross-examined concerning the basis and credibility of that identification and that Owens therefore suffered no Sixth Amendment violation (Seltz 1988: 888–90, Greenwald 1993: 179). As Greenwald (1993: 179, 187) notes, a case in which the witness could not even remember making the identification would demand a different analysis.

is actually a reflection, conscious or unconscious, of what he has read rather than what he remembers," the judge has the right "to reject such testimony by finding that the writing did not in fact revive the witness's recollection" (Graham 1992: 213). In fact, the introduction of such a writing can be justified only by a specific, and fairly elaborate, performance:

> In order to use a writing to refresh a recollection of the witness, that witness must exhibit both a lack of present memory and a need for the aid of the writing for recall. The witness must testify that he cannot remember the fact sought to be elicited. Until it is shown that the memory of the witness needs the aid of memoranda to refresh it, there can be no recourse thereto.
>
> (*American Jurisprudence* 1992: 773)[24]

The judge and jury must see the witness fail to recall the fact, and they must see his memory refreshed at that very moment.[25] To constitute valid testimony, the witness's statements must be persuasive as present performances of memory retrieval.

The foregoing analyses show that the PRVT fought an inevitably losing battle against a fundamental premise of American jurisprudence: that a trial is an ontologically live event. The hurdles placed in the way of using depositions, the emphasis on presenting live witnesses, the definition of testimony as a performance of memory retrieval in the courtroom at the present moment of the trial and of availability in terms of the witness's ability to undertake that performance, all demonstrate the centrality of this premise. The legal system has no adversion to incorporating representational technologies into its proceedings, but accepts only incursions of mediatization that do not violate the liveness of the trial. It should be clear that this respect for liveness is ideological and that it is rooted in an unexamined belief that live confrontation can somehow give rise to the truth in ways that recorded

---

24 It is worth emphasizing the irony that this thoroughly scripted moment is part of a performance of memory retrieval that the court ultimately must find to be convincingly spontaneous and unscripted.

25 Some American jurisdictions forcibly extend the same logic to the process by which a verdict is reached by forbidding jurors from taking written notes on the trial. Their decision-making thus becomes a performance of memory retrieval guaranteed to be unprompted by written texts (see Hibbitts 1992: 895).

representations cannot (a claim similar to Eric Bogosian's comments on live performance and mass media I quoted in Chapter 1). David M. Doret (1974: 250) states, for example, that "the very confrontation between witness and jury serves to elicit truth and expose falsehood." Perritt (1994: 1093) argues for a limited use of the PRVT for cases in which "a high proportion of the total trial evidence involves experts and demonstrative evidence" but not for those in which "a high proportion of the trial evidence involves individual witnesses whose veracity is being challenged."[26] This proposal again reflects the assumption that liveness equals truth.[27] This assumption is highly questionable: advocates for the PRVT made the point that testimony taped before the trial may be fresher in the witness's memory and, therefore, more accurate than what the witness recalls at trial. While logical, this claim misses the point, which is that the essence of testimony is not the information recalled but the performance of recalling it in the courtroom, before the accused and the jury. In this context, the replacement of the trial itself by a videotape is simply an impossibility. The PRVT trial tape becomes, in fact, evidence that functions that should take place in the courtroom at the time of the trial had already happened at the wrong time and in the wrong place.

Many of the questions raised about the validity of the PRVT reflect the traditional assumptions about the nature of live performance discussed in Chapters 1 and 2. John A. Shutkin (1973: 381) asks whether witnesses on video would have the same presence as live witnesses: "it is...doubtful whether a television production could ever attain the impact of a stage presentation. This impact...seems undeniably to be the product of the live performance." (Shutkin acknowledges, at least, that the "impact" to which he refers is "intangible and

---

26 In fact, the Michigan State researchers found that jurors were no better able to detect dissembling at a live trial than a mediatized one. They also found that jurors are generally very poor lie detectors, regardless of the form of the testimony (Miller and Fontes 1979: 205).

27 Collins and Skover (1992: 532) claim that the transition from oral culture to print culture entailed a progressive distrust of orality in the law. Referring to the English Statute of Frauds (1677), they state: "by equating perjury with orality, and truthfulness with writing, the statute reflected the legal mindset associated with the typographic age." I am arguing the opposite here, of course, that modern American law associates live, oral testimony with truth and recorded testimony with fraud. It is true that the live performance of testimony takes place in order to be recorded in a (usually) written record of the trial, which then represents the historical truth of the trial from that point on. The written record is nevertheless assumed to have been preceded by a live trial, which is its precondition. The authority of the written document derives from its presumed accuracy as a transcription of the live event.

immeasurable.") Doret (1974: 258) makes an equally unsubstantiated claim: "much of the power of the trial as a medium of social communication derives from the visibility of the different participants at a single, centralized forum." He offers no explanation as to why that forum must be a live trial. These statements, which are rooted in presumed ontological differences between live and mediatized representations of precisely the kind I critiqued in Chapter 2, beg the questions of just what kind of presence live performance possesses, how that presence differs from mediatized representations, and just what presence and the temporal and spatial simultaneity invoked by Doret contribute to the legal process.

Ultimately, the advocates of the PRVT themselves acknowledged that liveness is fundamental to jurisprudence. As a counterpoint to the initial outpouring of utopian claims for the PRVT in the early 1970s, further advocacy in the 1980s and 1990s promotes the idea that the primary value of the PRVT is as a way of clearing the docket of relatively simple, minor cases so that more complex and important cases can be tried live and get the attention they deserve. McCrystal argued in the 1980s that the PRVT works best in tandem with a "dual docket system," which was put into practice in Ohio, consisting of a "live docket" and a "prerecorded docket."[28] "Factually simple cases such as automobile accidents, slip and falls, landlord–tenant actions, workers' compensation, and intentional torts are assigned to the videotape docket as soon as the case is at issue" thus freeing up the court's time and energies for the more complex cases that must be tried live (McCrystal and Maschari 1983: 71).[29] The history of the PRVT is roughly comparable to that of the relationship between theatre and television discussed in Chapter 2. In both cases, the mediatized form was proposed as an equivalent replacement for the live form. But whereas the televisual has very largely succeeded in supplanting the live in many of its former arenas, the legal system, despite the incursion of mediatization it has inevitably undergone, has proven to champion

28 Rule 3.02 of the Erie County Rules of Practice of the Court of Common Pleas states that cases assigned to the videotape docket "will usually arise out of auto collisions, contracts, collections or other cases which in the court's opinion are adaptable to the videotape medium" (reproduced in McCrystal 1983: 122).

29 Judge Richard B. Klein of Philadelphia advocates a comparably limited use of the PRVT in criminal cases: "I draw the line on video trials in criminal cases unless the prosecutor certifies the sentence cannot be more than a year in jail" (quoted in Perritts 1994: 1084).

liveness in its fundamental procedures. The later line of argument adopted by PRVT advocates transforms the PRVT from a substitute for the live trial into an expedient designed to enhance the prestige of the live event. No longer the harbinger of a new paradigm of mediatized legal practice, the PRVT was pressed into the service of the existing paradigm, the paradigm of live performance.[30]

You don't own me: performance and copyright

If consideration of the privileging of liveness within legal procedure, and of the nature of testimony, prompted further reflection on the traditional values attributed to live performance, a look at copyright and intellectual property law will provoke renewed consideration of the ontology of live performance and its position within a cultural economy dominated by reproduction. Copyright is in many ways an ideal context in which to raise the latter issue since copyright law itself is a direct result of the development of technologies of reproduction and consequent economic changes. "[T]he [English] copyright act of 1710 is a sign not only of print technology's capacity to increase the rate of production of copies of a book but also of the profitability that generates disputes, litigation and lawyers" (Saunders 1992: 39).[31] In order to be protected under Title 17 of the United States Code, otherwise known as the 1976 Copyright Act, a work must be "fixed in a tangible medium of expression" that renders it replicable (that is what *copy*right means, after all). The definition of creation in Title 17 reflects this requirement: "A work is created when it is fixed in a copy...for the first time" (section 101). As far as copyright law is concerned, a work exists legally only in so far as it has been replicated; if a work has not been reproduced, it has not yet been created. There are no "originals" under copyright law: "The term 'copies' includes the material object...in which the work is first fixed" (section 101). Yet again, we find ourselves in the realm of Baudrillard's simulacrum: every "copy-rightable" work is always already a reproduction of itself.

30 The failure of the PRVT may support Jean Baudrillard's assertion, cited in Chapter 3, that simulation threatens the foundations of law. The American legal system's rejection of the televisually simulated trial might be seen as a successful effort to contain that threat.

31 Saunders (1992) provides a good overview of the development of copyright law in England, France, Germany, and the US. For a brief, practical summary of the history of copyright in England and the US, see Miller and Davis (1990: 280–7).

Title 17 is also a work of performance theory.[32] Historically, copyright law has refused to grant to live performance the status of intellectual property. The Copyright Clause of the United States Constitution (Article I, section 8, clause 8) gives Congress the power to secure "to Authors...the exclusive Right to their respective Writings." Although over the years Congress and the courts have shown themselves to be willing to construe the concept of a "Writing" quite broadly as "any physical rendering of the fruits of creative, intellectual or aesthetic labor" (*Goldstein* v. *California* [1973] as quoted in Miller and Davis 1990: 304), they have never granted that status to "intangible expression," which is to say, *performed* expression.[33] The copyright statute's definition of fixation states that "a work is 'fixed'...when its embodiment...is sufficiently permanent or stable to permit it to be perceived, reproduced, or otherwise communicated for a period of more than transitory duration" (section 101). Live performance, which exists only in the transitory present moment, is therefore excluded. Similarly, the statutory definition of "publication" states explicitly that in as much as " 'publication' is the distribution of copies...of a work to the public...a public performance or display of a work does not of itself constitute publication" (section 101) presumably because a performance is assumed to be a unique, nonrepeatable

---

32 Obviously, the context in which the relationship between copyright and performance is most frequently discussed is that of the rights of authors of plays and other performance texts. Title 17 grants to authors an exclusive right "to do and to authorize" public performances of their works (section 106.4). There have been some interesting controversies over the years focusing on playwrights who wish to assert their rights against productions whose interpretations of their work they dislike. (I discuss one such dispute against the background of changing information technologies in Auslander 1992a.) Because I am concerned here with the copyright status of performance *per se*, I will not address the issues arising from disputes over textual interpretation.

33 It is important to stress that I am focusing here on the federal copyright statute. It is possible for individual states to recognize intangible expression as property under common law or to enact statutes that offer such protection. Since state law cannot conflict with federal statute, states cannot extend copyright protection to performances but can formulate other ways of treating performance as intellectual property. This has been done chiefly through the concept of the right of publicity, recognized by many states. I discuss this concept and its relation to copyright below. For a good overview of state law protection of live performances, see Meltzer (1982: 1278–80). Meltzer (1982: 1297) argues, however, that "piecemeal state law protection of performance interests inadequately compensates entertainers."

event, not an object that can be copied.[34] Although Title 17 specifically mentions "choreographic works" as one type of protectable work of authorship (section 102a), this is true only for choreographic works that have been notated or otherwise recorded.[35] A dance that exists only as a live performance or a speech that was presented to an audience but never written down or recorded cannot be copyrighted (Miller and Davis 1990: 303). A performance that exists for no more than a transitory period is neither a publication nor protectable under copyright, and therefore cannot be owned as intellectual property.[36]

The hazards the concept of fixation creates for performance (and performers) are illustrated by the much-publicized case of *Bright Tunes Music Corp.* v. *Harrisongs Music, Ltd.* (420 F. Supp. 177 [1976]), in which former Beatle George Harrison was sued for copyright infringement because his song "My Sweet Lord" strongly resembles the earlier song "He's So Fine." The question of whether the two songs are

34 In a report presented to the American Bar Association, a committee looking into "problems of creators of works of fine and applied arts" makes the following observation: "Although the exhibition of a motion picture or television film does not in and of itself constitute publication, offering to distribute copies of the picture or film to a group of persons for purposes of public performance would constitute publication" (American Bar Association 1981: 6). By analogy, even though a public performance of a play does not constitute publication, making the play available for production (by placing it with a script service, for example) presumably would constitute publication even if the play were being circulated in manuscript form and were "unpublished" in the sense of never having been printed by a publishing company.

35 According to Adaline J. Hilgard (1994: 766–7), the fixation requirement is particularly vexing for choreographers because "none of the available means of fixation – video, written notation, or computer graphics – is entirely satisfactory." She also notes that some choreographers fear that fixing their works will either transform them into "museum pieces" or make it easier for others to pirate them. (See also Van Camp 1994: 67–72 on the problems of fixing choreography.) To some degree, choreographers prefer to rely on the dance-world custom of ostracizing choreographers who steal from others rather than depending on copyright protection. Perhaps for these reasons, the federal copyright statute's protection of choreographic works has been tested only once, in *Horgan* v. *Macmillan, Inc.* (1986), a case that was settled before being decided on appeal. I discuss *Horgan*, and Hilgard's analysis of it, below.

36 Julie Van Camp (1994: 70–2) takes note of a suggestion advanced in the context of choreographic copyright "that the United States adopt the approach of German copyright law, in which protection begins at the moment of creation of the work, prior to any fixation" since dancers' ability to transmit choreography as oral tradition is evidence that the setting of a dance on the bodies of the dancers is fixation enough to prove the existence of a work. As Van Camp indicates, the practical problems of litigating infringement claims in the absence of an independent record of the choreography are enormous.

"substantially similar" (the legal standard for copyright infringement) hinged in part on the presence of a "unique grace note" in Harrison's song that had also appeared in the earlier piece. As the judge recounts in his decision, this grace note appears on the first recording of Harrison's song, made by Billy Preston, and on the sheet music prepared from that recording, but not on Harrison's own, much better-known recording or the sheet music derived from it (180). Even though it is likely that the success of Harrison's own recording of the song was what prompted the suit (following the principle that "Where there's a hit, there's a writ"), the judge took the first fixation of the song, Preston's recording, to be the object under scrutiny. According to Harrison's testimony, the presence or absence of that particular note on Preston's recording was attributable to performative accident: "[Billy Preston] might have put that there on every take, but it just might have been on one take, or he might have varied it on different takes at different places" (181). It was Harrison's misfortune that the particular take on which the sheet music deposited for U.S. copyright was based included the incriminating note. According to the judge, Harrison himself takes a performative view of music: he "regards his song as that which he sings at the particular moment he is singing it and not something that is written on a piece of paper" (180). Copyright, however, acknowledges only fixed texts, not intangible performances. The result in the Harrison case was that one moment of performance, frozen in textual form, became the song "My Sweet Lord" in the eyes of the law.

Columbia Broadcasting System, Inc. v. DeCosta (377 F. 2d 315 [1967]) is a good case to examine in this context because it offers a particularly clear illustration of the legal status of live performance. Victor DeCosta, a Rhode Island mechanic with an enthusiasm for the Old West, developed a cowboy character he called Paladin, which he performed at "parades, the openings and finales of rodeos, auctions, horse shows," and other events. He would also distribute photographs of himself in costume and a business card reading "Have Gun Will Travel, Wire Paladin, N. Court St., Cranston, R.I." (316). After he had performed this character for ten years, he saw a television program called *Have Gun Will Travel* in which the main character, played by Richard Boone, was a cowboy called Paladin whose costume, business card, and personal idiosyncrasies (e.g., his use of a chess knight as an adornment and of a derringer in shoot-outs) were identical with those created by DeCosta, save for the address on the card. DeCosta sued the Columbia Broadcasting Corporation (CBS) for pirating his character and won a judgment that was reversed on appeal.

The appellate judge did not reverse the jury's decision because he felt that no piracy had taken place. To the contrary, Judge Coffin sympathized with DeCosta and agreed with the jury that the resemblances between the two Paladins were more than just coincidence and that CBS had stolen the Paladin character from DeCosta (317). He nevertheless reversed the decision, on the grounds that the federal copyright statute protects only works that can be reduced to "some identifiable, durable, material form" and that "the plaintiff's creation, being a personal characterization, was not reduced and could not be reduced to such a form" (320). Because DeCosta's Paladin existed only as a live performance, he could not prevail, despite the striking resemblances between his character and the television show's. The judge observed that DeCosta could have sued CBS for duplicating his business card, the one fixed and tangible artifact of his performance, but since he had never copyrighted the card, he had no cause of action (321).[37]

When live performances are fixed through writing, recording, or documentation, only the underlying text is protected against unauthorized usage, not the live performance as a text. For example, a videotape of choreography may be submitted to the Copyright Office as part of a registration. Although the choreography itself (the underlying text, in this instance) is thus protected against copying, the particular performance of that choreography on the tape is not protected. While Balanchine (as an "author") might be able to copyright his choreography of *The Nutcracker*, no dancer could copyright his particular interpretation or performance of the Mouse King in Balanchine's ballet, nor could the New York City Ballet copyright the company's performance on that tape. A similar limitation would apply to live theatrical productions, many elements of which – the script, set and costume designs, choreography, music and lyrics – can be copyrighted, but the performance itself, including the staging and the interpretation of characters, cannot be. A letter from the US Copyright Office concerning a director's application for copyright in his staging of a play states: "reference to 'stage directions' in an application...does not imply any protection...for the actions dictated by

---

37 Under the 1976 revision of the copyright statute, registration is no longer required in order for a work to enjoy copyright protection. Any work of authorship is automatically copyrighted. A work does have to be registered if a claim of infringement is to be brought, however. I cite the relevant section and discuss this requirement below, in the main text. After the 1976 revision took effect, DeCosta could have won a judgment for CBS's infringement of the copyright in his business card, provided that he registered it before filing suit.

them. The authorship on the application in this case is 'text of stage directions.' We understand this to represent a claim in the text" (quoted in Freemal 1996: 1022). This letter makes it abundantly evident that while the director could copyright a text describing his stage directions, and thus protect himself against unauthorized copying of that text, he could not copyright the execution of those directions in live performances.[38]

Live performance is excluded from copyright protection because of the belief that, as an unfixed mode of cultural production, it cannot be copied and therefore lies outside the economy of reproduction. Glossing Raymond Williams and Walter Benjamin, Celia Lury (1993: 15, 18) describes the historical shift from cultural production dominated by *repetition* to the dominance of *replication*[39] in a way that makes this assumption explicit:

38 It may seem strange that copyright protects choreography, but not stage directions, from unauthorized performances since the execution of choreography does not seem like a very different activity from the execution of stage directions. Both are fundamentally the realization of a set of instructions for movement, expression, the interpretation of a character, and so on. One simple but crucial difference, however, is that choreography is expressly protected under the federal copyright statute. Stage directions are not, and it is difficult to see under what category of copyrightable expressions they might fall. It has been argued that stage directions are analogous to choreography and should therefore enjoy the same protection. As Beth Freemal (1996) points out in her thorough discussion of this question, however, stage directions are dependent on another text (the play) in a way that choreography is not. Even if a dance is set to music, the dance retains its integrity in the absence of the music. But if the play text is removed and stage direction is left to stand on its own, of what does it consist? This also presents a problem for the fixation of stage directions: how can a director notate or fix her directions without reproducing the play text, in which she does not hold the copyright? (Choreography can be notated or fixed without reproducing the musical score.) A play that consists only of stage directions (Beckett's *Act Without Words* comes to mind) presents no problem. In such a case, the stage directions are coextensive with the dramatic work and can be copyrighted as such. In a case where the direction is based on an existing text by an author other than the director, however, the director's contribution can be seen only as a derivative work based on the play. Under American law, the copyright in derivative works is owned by the copyright holder in the primary work. If the playwright holds the copyright in a play, then the playwright, not the director of the play, would hold the copyright in stage direction as a derivative work.

39 Lury's terms "repetition" and "replication" are equivalent to Attali's (1985) terms "representation" and "repetition," respectively. I cite Attali's terminology and historical scheme in Chapter 2.

the dependence [of early cultural forms] upon "inherent, constituted physical resources" means not only that the artist's physical presence in front of an audience is required for a cultural work to come into being, but that the work's "material" existence is coterminous with its performance....Within this class of means of cultural production, then, copying takes the form of physical or bodily repetition....[O]nce the art work has a fixed material form in which the signs of the creative labor are imbedded, it can...be copied by someone other than the originating artist. It is this possibility – what Benjamin referred to as mechanical reproduction – [that] will here be called replication.

In this historical overview, live performance is the cultural mode associated with the era prior to the arrival of the technologies of reproduction that brought copyright law into being. In arguing that because live performance is not fixed in a material form it can be repeated but not replicated, Lury reproduces the ontological assumptions about live performance that I addressed in Chapter 2. However, my argument there concerning the possibility of mass-producing live performance problematizes both this distinction and the exclusion of live performance from copyright. It is apparent, for example, that a production such as *Tamara* was made to "be copied by someone other than the originating artist[s]"; that is, it was intended to be replicated, not repeated, even though the replications take the form of live performances. From this point of view, it becomes possible to imagine that these live productions could be copyrightable, despite the general exclusion of live performance from copyright protection.

That the copyright statute does not presently grant standing to live performance as intellectual property is very clear. A close examination of copyright also reveals that even in instances where performances have been recorded, the performance captured on the recording is not copyrightable in itself. In the case of a sound recording, any underlying texts and, since 1971, the recording itself may be copyrighted, but the *performance* on the recording cannot be. In *Supreme Records* v. *Decca Records*, one record company sued another for producing a recording of a song that supposedly imitated the first company's recording of the same song.[40] The judge found, however, that the first company could

---

40 *Supreme Records* (1950) is fascinating for reasons that go beyond my focus here. In its decision, the court compares the two recordings and notes "that the Supreme

not assert a "right of ownership in a musical arrangement," by which
he meant not just an instrumental or vocal score but the whole style of
the performance on the record (909). *Supreme Records* was decided well
before the 1976 revision of the copyright statute, which includes the
following, more extensive limitation:

> The exclusive rights of the owner of copyright in a sound
> recording...do not extend to the making or duplication of
> another sound recording that consists entirely of an indepen-
> dent fixation of other sounds, even though such sounds
> imitate or simulate those in the copyrighted sound recording.
> (section 114b)

Thus, it is unlawful to duplicate a recording in which you do not hold
the copyright, yet it is perfectly legal to replicate the performance on
that recording in order to make your own recording of it.[41] This
example shows that even a performance that has been fixed and
rendered replicable through reproduction is not protected by copyright.
Virtually every component of a sound recording can be protected,

record is clearly identified as 'a race or blues and rhythm' recording, while the Decca
record is 'popular.'" The judge characterizes the "race" recording as inferior to the
"popular" one, which he describes as possessing "clearer intonation and expression"
and making use of a "more precise, complex and better organized orchestral background" (912). Anyone familiar with the vexed history of race relations in
American popular music might wonder to what extent the judge's characterization
of the "race" record as inferior was a product of musical racism. More important,
perhaps, is the possibility that this case constitutes an attempt to use the legal
system to redress the problem of White artists' "covering" successful recordings by
Black artists and reaping the benefits of the Black artists' efforts by virtue of the
superior distribution and air play granted to "popular" (i.e., White) recordings. This
problem would become even more acute with the advent of the rock and roll era in
1955, especially given the propensity of White artists and their producers to fail to
pay royalties to Black songwriters. For a summary discussion of this situation, see
Szatmary (1991: 27–31).

41 Although it may seem extraordinary that the law explicitly permits the imitation of
existing sound works, this clause reflects the underlying principles of copyright as
they pertain to written texts. The copyright statute protects "original works of
authorship" (section 102a). As Miller and Davis note, however:

> a work of originality need not be novel. An author can claim copyright in a work as
> long as he created it himself, even if a thousand people created it before him.
> Originality does not imply novelty; it only implies that the copyright claimant did
> not copy from someone else.

> (Miller and Davis 1990: 290)

including the underlying text and the recording itself. The only thing that cannot be is the *performance* of the text or materials in question, which can be imitated with impunity.[42] Whether live or recorded, performance *qua* performance cannot be copyrighted.

The copyright statute's refusal to recognize performance as intellectual property has been articulated broadly in the statutory concept of fixation and in terms of specific performance genres through case law. Writing in 1950, one appellate judge observed that "there is a line of cases which holds that what we may call generically by the French word representation, – which means to perform, act, impersonate, characterize, and is broader than the corresponding English word, – is not copyrightable" (*Supreme Records* v. *Decca Records* [90 F. Supp. 904 (1950)], 909). Until a 1971 amendment to the law, for example, sound recordings were uncopyrightable because they were considered, in the

In principle, if a writer were to produce a book that was identical, word for word, with another, previously copyrighted book and could prove that he/she had had no access to the earlier book, and that her work was purely the result of independent effort, she could have a copyright in her book, despite its lack of novelty. Similarly, as long as the producer of a recording does not copy an existing recording but makes a new recording that sounds identical to the existing one, the new recording is copyrightable as an "independent fixation." Although the two circumstances are not identical (in the case of the book, the resemblance between the older and newer texts must be coincidental; this is not the case for identical sound recordings), the concept of "independent fixation" can be understood as the correlative of an "original work of authorship" in the realm of sound recording. In both cases, the fact that the later object lacks novelty is no obstacle to its being copyrighted, as long as that lack of novelty is not due to illicit copying of the protected object.

42 The practical ramifications of this clause were brought home to me by a compact disk entitled *Back to Rock N Roll*, an anthology of American pop songs from the 1960s. Most of the recordings on the disk are recreations of the original recordings by the same singers, who have earned their livings for the past twenty-five years by performing their early hits. Keep in mind that the owner of the copyright in a sound recording need not be the performer; considering the practices of the music and film industries, it is in fact unusual for performers to own the copyrights to their own recordings. If the copyright law permitted the owner of the copyright in a sound recording to prevent others from making another recording that sounds the same, the performers on this disk could be deprived of a significant portion of their livelihood. This clause also permits musical artists who traffic in pastiche, such as the Manhattan Transfer and Bette Midler (about whom more below), to make records that do, indeed, sound like other records; it allows performers to record who, by whatever trick of nature, sound exactly like performers who recorded before them; and it presumably discourages recording artists from litigating over matters of style. (My examples derive primarily from musical recordings but the principle extends to all types of sound recordings.)

words of a 1912 decision, "captured performances" (Gaines 1991: 131, 270 n. 80). *Supreme Records* applies this doctrine to theatrical perfor-mance: "the mere portrayal of a character by an actor in a play which is the creation of another is not of itself an independent creation" and therefore cannot enjoy copyright protection (908). The most often cited reason why copyright protection does not apply to performance is that to grant a performer exclusive rights to particular performed gestures or intonations would severely limit the vocabulary available to other performers and thus "impede rather than promote the useful arts" (*Booth* v. *Colgate-Palmolive* [1973] as quoted in Gaines 1991: 124). If such a right of ownership in performance existed:

> we would have to hold that Mr. Charles Laughton, for instance, could claim the right to forbid anyone else from imitating his creative mannerisms in his famous characteriza-tion of Henry VIII, or Sir Laurence Olivier could prohibit anyone else from adopting some of the innovations which he brought to the performance of Hamlet.
> (*Supreme Records, Inc. v. Decca Records, Inc.*, 909).[43]

Section 1101, added to the Copyright Act in 1997, provides for a very limited copyright in performance. This section prohibits "fix[ing] the sounds and images of a live musical performance in a copy or phonorecord" "without the consent of the performer or performers involved" and the unauthorized reproduction, transmission, or distribu-tion of "the sounds or sounds and images of a live musical performance." This addition to the law is distinctive because it is the only part of the federal statute to refer explicitly to performers as having copyrights in their performances. It clearly applies only to musicians, however. More important in this context, it prohibits only unauthorized *recordings* of live performances: it does not prohibit the live recreation of a previous performance. Whereas Section 1101 would prohibit me from making a video of a Rolling Stones concert without their permission, it would not prohibit me from recreating their concert as a live performance (as

---

43 This view of performance is not universal among American legal thinkers. Cheryl Hodgson (1975: 569–72), for example, argues that as the expression of an idea, performance could qualify as a "writing" in the expanded sense of that concept accepted by copyright. Unlike the *Supreme Records* court, Hodgson also feels that a performer's interpretation of a text (a song or a role) can be isolated from the text itself and deserves recognition as a writing.

long as I pay royalties for using their songs, of course). Section 1101 protects live musical performance only in so far as it can be mediatized; it does not protect live performance in and of itself.

There have also been a few decisions that seem to impute to performers a copyright in their performances. In *Baltimore Orioles* v. *Major League Baseball Players* (805 F. 2d663 [7th Cir. 1986]), the court decided that baseball players' performances in game broadcasts "created a copyrightable interest" (Helfing 1997: 10). In *Fleet* v. *CBS* (50 Cal. App. 4th 1911[2d Dist. 1977]), a case in which actors who were not paid for appearing in a film attempted to block release of the film by arguing that the distributor did not have the right to use their names or likenesses to publicize the film, the court concluded that the actors' "individual performances in the film…were copyrightable" as "dramatic works" (quoted in Helfing 1997: 10). Clearly, these decisions fly in the face of the historical view of performance's relation to copyright, and they are probably isolated instances. It is once again the case that the decisions apply only to specific mediatizations of performances, not to the performances themselves. That is, the *Fleet* decision would give performers ownership rights only in the particular portions of a specific film-text in which they appeared. Recreations of their performances in other media would not be affected.[44] Assuming that these decisions are valid, they show once again that only fixed performances are copyrightable; live performance is not.

There have been a number of other decisions over the years in which performers apparently have been determined to have rights of ownership in their performances, live and recorded. *Goldin* v. *Clarion Photoplays* (195 N.Y.S. 455; 202 AD 1 [1922]), for example, is a case in which the magician who invented the "Sawing a Lady in Half" illusion

---

44 Helfing (1997: 10) argues that *Baltimore Orioles* did not hold that the players' performances were copyrightable, "only that the telecast of a baseball game is copyrightable" and that "the copyright interest arises, not from the performances in themselves, but from the players' 'creative contribution' to the telecast." The irony of both *Fleet* and *Baltimore Orioles* is that arguments that appear to support performers' ownership interests in their performances were used to justify finding against the performers. The actors in *Fleet* sued under California's right of publicity statute. In finding that their performances were copyrightable, the judge also invalidated their suit, since the federal copyright statute preempts the state-level right of publicity. Under this interpretation of the case, the actors would have had to sue all over again in federal court. In *Baltimore Orioles*, the contribution of the baseball players to the copyrighted game broadcast was determined to be "work for hire" owned by the owner of the copyright in the telecast as a whole.

successfully sued to protect his exclusive right to perform it. In 1928, Charlie Chaplin won a decision against another actor, Charles Amador, for imitating his Little Tramp character in films. Bert Lahr won a judgment against a company that used a voice that sounded like his in a television commercial (*Lahr v. Adell Chemical Co.* 300 F.2d 256 [1st Cir. 1962]). An important case is *Midler v. Ford Motor Company* (1988), in which singer Bette Midler sued the automobile company and its advertising agency for using a singer who sounded exactly like Midler in a commercial. She lost her initial case but won on appeal.[45]

It is important to observe that although the cases I just cited all had the effect of extending legal protection to specific performances (a magic trick, a distinctive character) or performance styles (speaking and singing voices), none of these cases actually establishes a performer's right of ownership in performance as a work of authorship. Each was decided on a different basis, none under the copyright statute. In *Chaplin v. Amador* (93 Cal. App. 358, 269 P. 544 [1928]), the court stated explicitly that:

> the case of plaintiff does not depend on his right to the exclu-
> sive use of the role, garb, and mannerisms, etc.; it is based
> upon fraud and deception. The right of action in such a case
> arises from the fraudulent purpose and conduct of appellant
> and injury caused to the plaintiff thereby, and the deception
> to the public. (269 P. 546)

This theory of the case arose from the fact that not only had Amador imitated the Little Tramp, he had also billed himself in the films as Charlie Aplin. The decision stemmed from the conclusion that Amador had practiced fraud and was guilty of "unfair competition in business," not from the theory that Chaplin had a copyright in his performance as the Little Tramp. The original dismissal of *Lahr* v. *Adell Chemical* was reversed on a similar basis: the appeals court found that

---

45 As Judge Noonan noted in his decision, the commercial in which a voice like Midler's was used was part of a series known within the agency as "The Yuppie Campaign" in which "the aim was to make an emotional connection with Yuppies, bringing back memories of when they were in college" in the 1970s. The agency used a different song in each commercial, and tried to recruit the artist who had originally popularized it to rerecord it. When Midler declined to rerecord "Do You Want To Dance," a song she had originally recorded in 1973, the agency employed Ula Hedwig, who had once worked for Midler as a back-up singer, to imitate Midler's voice for the commercial (849 F.2d 460 [1988], 461).

using a voice that sounded like Lahr's could constitute "passing off" and, therefore, unfair competition. The decision in *Goldin* also was based, in part, on grounds of unfair competition. Clarion Photoplays had made a film revealing how the illusion was achieved; the court found against the company on grounds of unfair competition, since distributing the film would render Goldin's illusion worthless and thus deprive him of "the fruits of his ingenuity, expense, and labor" (202 AD 1, 4).[46]

Midler v. Ford Motor Company (849 F.2d 460 [1988]) likewise does not hold that Midler has a copyright in her vocal style. Judge Noonan states bluntly in his decision that "a voice is not copyrightable. The sounds are not 'fixed'" (462). In this case, the decision was made on the basis of a California statute enshrining what has come to be called the right of publicity – Civil Code, Section 990b, also known as the Celebrity Rights Act – originally designed to allow the estate of a deceased celebrity to continue to control the use of the name, voice, signature, photograph, and likeness of that celebrity.[47] Judge Noonan interpreted this statute as protecting a living celebrity's identity or personhood and found that Midler has a property right not in her voice or performance but in her identity, her self. "A voice is as distinctive and personal as a face," he wrote. "The singer manifests herself in the song. To impersonate her voice is to pirate her identity" (463).[48]

---

46 In addition to unfair competition and related concepts in business law, performances can sometimes be protected as trademarks or service marks: "Under certain circumstances, it may be possible to register a comedian's tag-line, name or stage name (or name of his 'persona') as a service mark identifying the comedian or the entertainment services provided by the comedian" (Nelson and Friedman 1993: 256).

47 For an entertaining overview of several right of publicity cases brought and decided under this statute, see Weinstein (1997). For a cultural analysis of *Midler*, see Auslander (1992a).

48 In *Sinatra* v. *Goodyear Tire and Rubber Co.* (435 F.2d 711 [1970]), Nancy Sinatra lost her case against the company and its advertising agency for using a recording of "These Boots are Made for Walking" that sounded like her own. Since Sinatra did not have the benefit of California's Celebrity Rights statute, she advanced a different argument: "that the song has been so popularized by the plaintiff that her name is identified with it;...that said song...has acquired a 'secondary meaning'" (712). "Secondary meaning" is a concept derived from trademark law referring to "a mark [that] has been used so long that it has come to be synonymous with the goods or services with which it is connected" (Miller and Davis 1990: 165). Sinatra argued, by analogy, that the close association of the song with her performance of it means that the song inevitably refers to her. Had this right been recognized, Sinatra would have had control over all performances of the song, since any rendition of

143

Performers have the right to be protected from fraud and unfair business practices; they may even have property rights in their identities. None of these rights is equivalent, however, to a copyright in performance.

The central difference between copyright and the right of publicity is that while the former protects works of authorship, the latter protects personhood and, therefore, applies only to those whose persons have market value, to celebrities.[49] Judge Noonan's decision carefully spells out Midler's claim to celebrity by summarizing her career, quoting her reviews, and indicating her status as a cultural icon appealing to baby boomers. In the last paragraph of the decision, he states:

> We need not and do not go so far as to hold that every imitation of a voice to advertise merchandise is actionable. We hold only that when a distinctive voice of a professional singer is widely known and is deliberately imitated in order to sell a product, the sellers have appropriated what is not theirs. (463)

This implies that even if an advertising agency set out deliberately to replicate the voice of an unknown singer in a commercial, that singer

"These Boots are Made for Walking" would presumably evoke her as a secondary meaning. The central difference between Sinatra's argument and Midler's is that whereas Sinatra was claiming a kind of ownership in the song itself as a consequence of her having executed a famous performance of it, Midler's claim was based only on her proprietorship of her voice. The appellate judge upheld the original decision against Sinatra because granting her the right to control performance of the song on these grounds would conflict with the federally sanctioned rights of the copyright holders in the song to do so. "Moreover," the judge observed, "the inherent difficulty of protecting or policing a 'performance' or the creation of a performer in handling copyrighted material licensed to another imposes problems of supervision that are almost impossible for a court of equity" (717–18). For a detailed analysis of *Sinatra* and a comparison of it with *Midler*, see Gaines (1991: 105–42).

49 A conceptually convoluted case illustrates this point well. In *Onassis v. Christian Dior – New York, Inc.* (122 Misc.2d 603 [1984]), Jacqueline Kennedy Onassis sued Christian Dior for using a model who looked like Onassis in a magazine advertisement. The model had done nothing to make herself look like Onassis – she simply bore a striking natural resemblance to the other woman. Onassis won her case. As a celebrity, her appearance is her property to exploit, even when it is actually another person's own appearance. For a full discussion of this case, see Gaines (1991: 84–104).

would not enjoy the same rights as Midler because that singer's identity, unlike Midler's, has no generally established value.[50]

Jane Gaines (1991: 142) observes that the *Midler* decision "signaled
a new development in intellectual property law, one that had been
evolving since the fifties but that was not recognized in common law
until the early seventies: the right of publicity paradigm." The origins
of this development can be traced back even further in case law.[51] The
illusionist in *Goldin* v. *Clarion Photoplays*, for instance, was able to
control the performance of the "Sawing a Lady in Half" illusion
because the illusion and its title "have become identified with plaintiff's name to such an extent that theatre managers and the public
immediately connected the two" (202 AD 1, 3). *DeCosta*, too, can be
seen as a step in the evolution of the right of publicity paradigm and
has nuances that are worth examining in that light.

In his *DeCosta* decision, Judge Coffin did not discount the possibility
that a character could be copyrighted and even imagines "a procedure

---

50 *Tom Waits* v. *Frito-Lay, Inc.* (978 F.2d 1093 [9th cir. 1992]), in which singer Waits
successfully sued the snack food company over a commercial employing a singer
whose voice sounded like his, builds on *Midler* and may signal a new development.
Waits is significant in part because it did not involve a song Waits himself had actually recorded, only his vocal sound and style. More important, the court found that
Waits's case could be considered not only in terms of right of publicity, but also in
terms of trademark infringement. "By expanding the possible theories of recovery
from a state law tort action to a Federal…trademark infringement action, *Waits*
theoretically permits performers anywhere in the country a cause of action"
(McEwen 1994: 134). The *Waits* decision may mean that performers outside of
states that have right of publicity statutes can look to federal law for protection of
their performing styles as trademarks. If so, it will also expand the right to protect
sound and style beyond celebrities, since ownership of a trademark is not dependent
on fame. Jill A. Phillips (1991) emphasizes that *Waits* still does not assert a copyright in performance.
51 See Apflebaum (1983: 1570–4), Gaines (1991: 187–91), Levine (1980: 130–8), and
Wohl (1988: 447–50) for overviews of the right of publicity and its origins. Gaines,
Levine, and Wohl discuss the right of publicity in relation to the right to privacy,
while Apflebaum compares right of publicity with copyright. Whereas Levine and
Wohl argue for broad construal of the right of publicity, Apflebaum (1983: 1593)
claims that right of publicity can only be appropriately used to protect "works of
authorship not fixed in tangible form." In Apflebaum's view, all other applications of
right of publicity are preempted by federal copyright statute. Gaines suggests that
the right of publicity may not have evolved organically through common law but
may have been codified to justify existing economic practices in the entertainment
industry, then provided with a genealogy in case law after the fact. If so, I am
contributing to the latter process in the discussion that follows.

for registering 'characters' by filing pictorial and narrative description [of them] in an identifiable, durable, and material form" with the Copyright Office.[52] Why, then, does he say not only that DeCosta could not prevail because he had not "reduced his creation to a fixed form" (Miller and Davis 1990: 305) but also that "the plaintiff's creation, being a personal characterization...*could not* be reduced to such a form" (320; my emphasis)? The answer lies in the judge's use of the phrase "personal characterization." In discussing this matter, the judge reveals himself to be a fairly sophisticated performance theorist, conversant with the concept of "everyday life performance." "All human beings – and a good part of the animal kingdom – create characters every day of their lives," writes Coffin, but he goes on to say that the kind of character people often invent "for their own and others' amusement" "is so slight a thing as not to warrant protection by any law...to the extent that a creation may be ineffable, we think it ineligible for protection against copying simpliciter under either state or federal law" (320).

The judge's reasoning concerning everyday life performance is sound: to create a situation in which one person could seek legal remedy because another had copied his Halloween costume or his humorous performance at the office water cooler clearly would be intolerable. This reasoning extends logically to professional performance as well. What is interesting in *DeCosta*, however, is the judge's refusal to treat DeCosta's creation as anything more than a "personal characterization" on the order of a Halloween costume, even though it turned out to be considerably more than that to CBS. Coffin notes that, in the original trial, DeCosta's attorneys had cited:

> several cases...around the general proposition that it is an actionable wrong to appropriate and exploit the product of another's creative effort; but all seem to involve distinguishable wrongs of at least equal or even superior significance.

---

52 Only characters that are very specific in their development can be copyrighted:

> The general idea of a character is unprotected. Stock figures, prototypes, or stereotypical figures likewise are unprotected....Characters become more protected as they become more detailed. But the attribution of general qualities – such as strength – or emotional features – such as compassion – is not sufficient to gain copyright protection.
>
> (Miller and Davis 1990: 344–5)

> Most rest on the tort of "passing off": appropriation not of the creation but of the value attached to it by public association...by misleading the public into thinking that the defendant's offering is the product of the plaintiff's established skill. (317–8)

Certainly, there was no "passing off" in this instance: unlike Amador's implying that he was Charlie Chaplin, CBS had no reason to state or imply that its Paladin was DeCosta because DeCosta's name and reputation were of no value to CBS. Although Coffin does not express this conclusion, it is hard to believe that it played no role in his formulation of the concept of "personal characterization." I suspect that if DeCosta's performance had been professional rather than avocational and he had become famous for it (like the illusionist in *Goldin*), the result of the appeal would have been different even before the advent of the right of publicity paradigm, because then CBS unquestionably would have poached something of established value. The irony of *DeCosta* is that the plaintiff could have prevailed had he proved that CBS had poached a creation of established value but, because DeCosta was not a celebrity, the value of his creation could be proved only by the fact that CBS found it worthy of poaching. The *Midler* decision makes it even clearer that a present-day DeCosta could expect to have a right of ownership in his performance only if he were a celebrity and CBS had something to gain by appropriating his identity, not the character he created.

In a discussion of whether ordinary people can benefit from the right of publicity, Gaines finds that the law enshrines a paradox.

> Before exploitation...the ordinary person and the unknown actor can be said to have a right of publicity that, in its dormancy, is both there and not there. It is inherent *at the same time as it must be produced by exploitation*. What I mean is that in current legal thought a person does not have publicity rights in him or herself unless, at one time or another in the course of a career, he or she has transferred these rights to another party.
>
> (Gaines 1991: 190, original emphasis)

An author does not have to be well known, or even published, to enjoy copyright protection for his/her work but a performer must be sufficiently famous so that someone else would seek to purchase her identity to enjoy protection of her performance under the right of publicity paradigm. Even then, that protection is not of the performance as a work, but as an extension of the performer's identity, construed as having value in itself. Although it is not clear that it is desirable to formulate a general property right in performance, the success of the right of publicity paradigm suggests that any attempt to do so would have to take the tack that all performances are manifestations of the performer's self and that, therefore, the unlicensed use of any performance is an appropriation of the performer's property in her identity.[53]

53 There has been a successful movement within American law to extend the rights of visual artists over their productions, modeled on the European legal concept of *droit moral* (usually translated as "moral rights" though the concept has more to do with the artist's morale than with morality). Inasmuch as *droit moral* derives from a conception of the work of art as an extension of the artist's personality, not a work created by but separate from the artist, it bears a certain resemblance to the American legal doctrine of right of publicity. Whereas the right of publicity emphasizes economic interests, however, *droit moral* equates damage to the work of art with damage to the psyche and reputation of the artist. (For a general discussion of *droit moral* and comparison with American law, see DuBoff 1984: 224–39. For a more theoretical and historical comparison of *droit moral* with copyright, see Saunders 1992.)

Droit moral is understandably very attractive to artists, in part because it gives them the right to control the integrity of their work, "to prevent their works from being altered, distorted or destroyed" (DuBoff 1984: 233). A 1990 addition to Title 17 extended these rights to visual artists (Visual Artists Rights Act of 1990, section 106a). Their extension to performing artists would be highly problematic, however. To take but one example, it is conceivable that a film actor could argue that the director and editor altered, and thus distorted and destroyed, his performance in post-production. A successful claim could result in financial penalties to the film-makers or an injunction against any release of the film.

Performers who are, like most actors, musicians, and dancers, in the business of interpreting texts created by others certainly should hesitate before supporting *droit moral* legislation for playwrights, composers, choreographers, etc. Under *droit moral*, an author need only claim that a performance of her text distorts it to block public presentation of that performance. Opponents of the imposition of *droit moral* on American law stress the impossibility of defining an objective standard for distortion, and the consequent potential for capriciousness on the parts of authors (or their heirs) in determining which uses of a text are acceptable and which are not (Saunders 1992: 207).

Proposals to implement *droit moral* for American authors of performed texts seem to me not to avoid the pitfall of embracing overly subjective criteria. One writer suggests that "professional performing groups...should be required to obtain the specific written approval of the creator or the creator's agent before departing from the creator's intentions in significant ways" (Burlingame 1991: 10). This plan allows the creator complete control over how the work is presented and interpreted and it disregards any possibility that the performers, too, may have rights as artists.

This is a highly problematic position from the perspective of acting and performance theory, in which the relationship between the performer's identity and her performance is much thornier and more ambiguous than the law would seem to allow.[54] While some performers may see their performances as manifestations of identity, others may prefer to see their performances more as "works of authorship" separate from themselves. Arguably, the ambiguity of the relationship between self and other is at the heart of performance; to eliminate that ambiguity in favor of defining performance as necessarily a manifestation of the performer's self would be a reductive enterprise. In saying this, I am

Another approach tries to harmonize *droit moral* with the First Amendment by distinguishing protected and unprotected speech: "where an interpretive artist incorporates speech [understood in a broad sense as interpretation] into a performance of an author's work that is consistent with the author's message or the author's expression of that message, the First Amendment protects the interpretive artist's speech and prevents the government from regulating it." Predictably, speech that is not consistent with the author's message would be unprotected and subject to regulation (Konrad 1991: 1608). This proposal, too, gives too much power to the author and not enough to interpreters. To Konrad's credit, the legal recourse he recommends involves neither a financial penalty nor an injunction against presenting the offending work, but a "labeling remedy." "A labeling remedy for an integrity right violation would involve a court ordering the producer and/or the interpretive artist to indicate in the performance's credits and/or advertisements that the interpretive artist has modified the author's work against the wishes of the author" (Konrad 1991: 1641). In this way, the author's personality rights would be respected without curtailing the activities of the interpreters.

My own proposal, which is more radical than either of the two discussed here and favors interpreters rather than authors, is to extend the concept of "compulsory license" from the realm of music into those of dramatic and other performing arts. This doctrine derives from early copyright legislation concerning sound recording. It holds that the composer of a piece of music has an absolute right to determine who makes the first recording of that piece (section 115). Once the composer has licensed one recording of the piece, however, anyone else who wishes has the right to make subsequent recordings of it in whatever style and interpreted howsoever they see fit, provided they pay statutory licensing and royalty fees (Miller and Davis: 1990: 314). Although I'm sure there would be problems to be confronted were this doctrine applied to dramatic and other performed texts, I feel that it would ultimately serve the interests of free and creative expression far better than an Americanized *droit moral*.

54 In a comparative discussion of the relation of self to performance in the theories of Stanislavski, Brecht, and Grotowski, I suggest that although that relationship is configured differently in each case, each theorist grounds performance in a concept of "self" that precedes performance. My deconstruction of these theories finds that all of those "selves" are, in fact, products of the performance theories they are said to ground (Auslander 1997: 28–38).

not suggesting that the law is wrong about the nature of performance, though it would surely benefit from a review of performance theory. The more important point is that the law, through its particular historical evolution, has constructed the concepts of performance and performer, and therefore of performers' rights, in particular ways that may not accord with the ways that acting and performance theory have constructed these terms through their own historical evolutions.

The suspicions of theorists who see performance's evanescence as a site of resistance to a cultural economy based in reproduction may seem justified by the vagaries of some of the decisions I've cited. George Harrison certainly learned the hard way that copyright law has no respect for what Henry Sayre (1989) has called the "aesthetic of impermanence." The lesson of *DeCosta* is that, in a capitalist representational economy, the entity legally defined as the "author" of a creation is the one who can extract profit from it.[55] *Midler* and related cases raise troubling questions about intellectual property rights that seem to accrue only to a celebrity elite. Given these considerations, it is easy to understand the appeal of seeing performance as a discourse that escapes and resists the terms of this cultural economy. That sword is double-edged, however, for it is also not difficult to sympathize with performers who might want to put that economy to work for themselves by acquiring greater control over their creations, even though that would mean sullying their performative purity.

Copyright law shares with some performance theorists the premise that live performance exists only in the present and has no copy, that it is constituted by an ontology of disappearance (Phelan 1993a: 146): that is why it is not protectable under copyright. To copyright law, an undocumented performance is less than invisible: in as much as it has no copy, it was never created; it does not exist at all. As we have seen, even performance that has been fixed through reproduction is not actually governed by copyright – only the rights in the underlying texts and the right to reproduce the fixation are protected. Decisions in which performers appear to have been accorded rights of ownership in their performances turn out to have been made on other grounds, whether those of fraud, unfair competition, or the right of publicity, not on the basis of an idea that a performance as such is ownable. It is fair to say, then, that because live performance cannot be copyrighted, it escapes ownership, commodification, and other processes of regula-

---

55 For an outstanding analysis of entertainment law as a product of and a means of sustaining capitalism, see Gaines (1991).

tion within a reproductive capitalist economy. Whether that makes performance a site of meaningful resistance to that economy is more problematic. If performance may be said to slip through the legal net of copyright, it does so because that net was designed specifically not to catch it. Whatever resistance performance's ontology of disappearance may enable has been allowed it by the very cultural and political discourses it is said to resist.

As noted at the start of this chapter, some performance theorists see performance's evanescence and its existence only in spectatorial memory as placing performance outside the purview of reproduction and regulation. The relationship of the view of memory suggested by these performance theorists to the concept of memory implicit in copyright law would seem to be one of opposition. As Pavis suggests, the version of performance that lives beyond the moment is distorted and inaccurate, a product of "the spectator's more or less distracted perception." Phelan valorizes the unreliability of spectatorial memory because it gives rise to unrecuperably subjective versions of performance that are faithful to performance's ontology of disappearance. Copyright law, by contrast, valorizes technological memory (fixation) because it provides an ostensibly reliable record of the protected object against which claims of infringement may be judged objectively: either the questionable object is "substantially similar" to the protected one or it is not.[56] Upon closer examination, however, it becomes clear that this opposition between performance theory and copyright law is only apparent, for copyright finally privileges human memory over technological memory as well. Even when a performance is fixed in tangible form, the tangible version has no absolute authority. If a question of copyright infringement were to come up, it would not be possible to resolve that question simply and self-evidently by looking at the reproduction of the performance. In order to enter into legal discourse, the performance must be retrieved from the technological memory-form in which it is preserved and subjected to the vagaries of human memory and interpretation.[57]

56 The binary opposition between unreliable human memory and reliable technological memory I am using here is generated by the juxtaposition of Phelan and Pavis with copyright law, not from my own epistemology. If anything, I find technological memory, especially in the form of computer hard drives, to be every bit as unreliable and subject to degradation as human memory.

57 As we saw from the Rodney King trials, this also holds true for criminal or civil trials in which videotaped evidence is used. The reproduction of the event at issue is not permitted to "speak for itself." Rather, it is tested against the memories of the witnesses and the discursive construction of the videotaped evidence that emerges from the live courtroom performance is what counts.

In *Horgan* v. *Macmillan, Inc.* (1986), the estate of George Balanchine sued a publishing company for printing photographs of *The Nutcracker* that the estate claimed violated the copyright in his choreography, a videotape of which he had submitted along with his copyright application. "The trial court stated that choreography is essentially the movement of steps in a dance and that photographs merely catch dancers at specific instants in time. Therefore, the court reasoned, photographs could not capture movement, which is the essence of choreography" (Hilgard 1994: 770–1). But the appellate court felt that the trial court had not employed the appropriate standard for infringement and sent the case back to be tried on its merits. The appellate court proposed two theories of how photographs might infringe on choreography, the second of which is of interest here.[58] "The court stated that a photograph could elicit in the imagination of a person who had recently seen a performance the flow of movement immediately preceding and following the split second recorded in the photograph" (Hilgard 1994: 776). Although the case was settled before it was decided on appeal, *Horgan* is the only extant decision in a copyright infringement case involving choreography under the 1976 statute. One legal scholar suggests that "the court's approach would provide a choreographer with a claim based on an observer's recall of the movement surrounding the moment captured in the photograph" (Hilgard 1994: 780–1).[59] In this interpretation of *Horgan*, spectatorial memory is far from being out of the reach of regulatory processes; in fact, it is pressed into service by the law. (Even if the deposited videotape, rather than spectatorial memory, were used to decide the case, the comparison between the photographs and the video would still be made by means of human memory, for no human being could look at the video and the photos simultaneously.) When it comes to the evaluation of copyright infringement claims, human memory is not the safe

---

58 Elisa A. Alcabes (1987) recommends addressing the difficult question of whether still photographs can infringe the copyrights in performances by simply adding to the law a rule under which all unauthorized photographs of performances would be presumed to be infringing derivative works. This seems rather a reductive solution to an intriguing theoretical problem.

59 Hilgard (1994: 787) writes disapprovingly of this decision. She finds substantial fault with the *Horgan* court and suggests an alternate standard for infringement of choreography: "an artist must copy both the movement and timing of a piece for a court to find copyright infringement." This would mean that no static representation of dance movement in photography or painting could infringe the copyright on the choreography depicted.

haven from regulation and control that Phelan proposes. Rather, it becomes a *mechanism for the enforcement of regulation*.[60] Performance's presumed ontological resistance to objectification does not make performance a privileged site of ideological resistance to a cultural economy based in capital and reproduction. If performance persists only as spectatorial memory, then it persists in precisely the form in which it can be useful to the law that regulates the circulation of cultural objects as commodities.

Not only is memory an agent of control, it is a site of regulation as well. In *Bright Tunes Music Corp.* v. *Harrisongs Music, Ltd*, the court did not find that Harrison had deliberately plagiarized the earlier song but concluded that "his subconscious knew…a song his conscious mind did not remember.…This is, under the law, infringement of copyright, and is no less so even though subconsciously accomplished" (180–1). In such cases, memory and other psychic operations are subject to policing. The very undependability of memory becomes the object of legal surveillance. Even the processes by which subconscious materials enter into consciousness and the relation between the subconscious and memory become matters of legal scrutiny. In Harrison's case, a subconscious memory of a performance manifest itself in his own performance in a way that rendered him subject to legal discipline.

Law and remembrance

In the previous sections of this chapter, I showed that the workings of memory are integral to two areas of jurisprudence. Testimony is understood specifically as a performance of memory retrieval in the present moment of the trial. Copyright infringement claims may police the memories of accused infringers and draw on spectatorial memory as a means of adjudication. Arguably, memory is the very foundation of law, not just in the sense that Anglo–American common law is "an inscription of the past in the present" (Goodrich 1990: 36) but in the larger sense Peter Goodrich invokes when summarizing the thought of a late 16th-century legal scholar:

---

60 Gaines (1991: 117–18) suggests that one reason sound recordings originally were not recognized under copyright law is because it was thought that the unreliability of aural memory would make the resolution of claims of infringement overly subjective; this further reinforces my point.

memory governs law not as a series of established particulari-
ties, precedents that will always differ from circumstance to
infinite circumstance, but as "essential law," as a method of
handling, defining and dividing a system of argument....
Memory establishes legal institutions and not the banal specificity of individual cases.

(Goodrich 1990: 35)

Legal memory, then, is not just a matter of being able to cite precedents relevant to specific circumstances. Memory is the deep structure
of a language of law whose utterances take the form of specific acts of
recollection.

Inasmuch as memory is brought into the legal discourse as both a
policed site and a mechanism of regulation, Phelan's proposition that
memory eludes regulation and control, cited at the beginning of this
chapter, seems true only of materials stored in memory *and never
retrieved* from it. As long as a memory remains stored, it apparently has
no engagement with mechanisms of regulation and control. But once a
memory is retrieved, it can no longer claim to take up a position
outside the reach of those mechanisms; it becomes both a subject and a
means of regulation and control. If a witness cannot or will not retrieve
memories of the matter at issue, the court considers that witness to be
unavailable to the legal discourse and, therefore, to be equivalent to a
dead witness. If George Harrison had not retrieved "He's So Fine" from
his memory, even subconsciously, his psychic processes would not have
been the subject of a court decision. "Visibility is a trap,..." Phelan
warns, "it summons surveillance and the law" (1993a: 6). Although
Phelan is referring here to visibility politics, not to memory, the
making present of memories surely must run the same risk – once they
emerge from the safe haven of memory, recollections become visible
and, therefore, subject to surveillance and to being pressed into service
as testimony. It would seem that as soon as a memory is retrieved, it
becomes available to the law.

The question that emerges from this analysis is: at what point in the
process of memory retrieval does this risk actually appear? Does a
memory become visible and, thus, summon the law, simply by being
retrieved, or is visibility the legacy of the moment at which the
retrieved memory explicitly enters into discourse? In other words, is it
possible for a memory to remain safe from surveillance at some
moment after it has been retrieved but before it has been entered into
discourse? My argument is that there is no such moment, that memory
itself solicits discourse. This idea is staged by copyright law. Title 17

states that a copy of a work need not be deposited with the Copyright Office for that work to receive copyright protection, but a copy must be deposited to support a claim of infringement (sections 407a, 411a). The sole purpose of storing a copy of the work in the governmental memory bank is to enter it into (legal) discourse.

In a provocative passage, Goodrich (1990: 9–10) provides a context for considering the question of when memory may be said to enter into discourse and thus summon the law:

> The path of the law is that of experience, in the words of one American judge. Could we not take that to mean that we live the law, that what is interesting and at the same time frightening about the law is precisely that it is integral to experience, that it is everywhere present, not as command or facile rule but rather as an architecture of daily life, a law of the street, an insidious imaginary. In terms of any phenomenology of the law in its forms of daily life, we would need to study the images of possibility, the imagery, the motive and affective bonds that tie the legal subject quite willingly, though not necessarily happily, to the limits of law, to this biography, to this persona, to this body and these organs.
>
> (Goodrich 1990: 9–10)

Goodrich's Foucauldian suggestion that law is not a secondary overlay on individual experience but a constituent of that experience itself has important implications. From the perspective afforded by Goodrich's account, it becomes clear that the experiences stored in memory were themselves shaped in relation to the law as part of the phenomenology of daily life.

Perhaps Goodrich's reference to the legal subject's persona can be taken to suggest that the psychic functions of memory storage and retrieval (or, in legal parlance, recordation and recollection) also do not occur outside the context of law as a constituent of experience. In view of Goodrich's discussion of the phenomenology of law, it is clear that memories do not summon the law by becoming visible or by being entered into discourse, because there is no moment at which a memory exists prior to its inscription in and by the law. The content of any memory has already been shaped by law as part of the phenomenology of daily life. In that sense, all memory is inhabited by the structures of law, is always already entered into legal discourse.

The extent to which memory is both embedded in and structured by legal discourse problematizes it as a site of resistance to that same discourse. Much the same can be said of liveness, the ontological quality some performance theorists see as placing performance beyond the reach of regulation. This is true only in the limited sense that live performances cannot be copyrighted. To the extent that the law itself embraces live performance at a procedural level, however, liveness, like memory, enters into the service of the law. It is perhaps for this reason that Jacques Derrida (1978 [1966]: 247) suggests that in order for performance to escape objectification, "its act must be forgotten, actively forgotten." Unlike Pavis and Phelan, both of whom seem to see memory as functioning outside of reproduction, at least where performance is concerned, Derrida suggests that the recording of an event in memory is itself a form of reproduction. The memory thus assumes the form in which it can be appropriated by such regulatory agencies as the law. In order to escape regulation and the economy of reproduction, performance must not only disappear, it must also be excluded from memory.

As I have described it here, the relationship of performance to current American jurisprudence is complex, especially when considered through two different bodies of law. One way of summarizing these complexities is to compare the implications of a copyright case for the legal status of performance with those of a case focused on evidentiary issues. George Harrison's argument in *Bright Tunes* that a song is not a fixed text but an evanescent performance fell on deaf ears, with the result that the textualized version of one performance of his song became the song as far as the law was concerned. When Justice Connor argued in *Stores* that the fixed (videotaped) version of the doctor's testimony was not an acceptable substitute for her live presence, he seemed to respect the ontology of performance in a way that copyright does not. In the former case, the possibility of what I have called performative accident is effaced: the song is identified with a written text, regardless of how that text came into existence. In the latter instance, performative accident is valorized: the doctor's testimony is valid only if given under circumstances allowing for such accident. Despite this apparent contradiction, the argument that performance ontologically resists fixation is accepted at a fundamental level by both branches of the law. Because it cannot be fixed, performance has no standing under copyright. Therefore, a cultural object such as "My Sweet Lord" cannot be defined *as a performance* for the purposes of copyright litigation. The same recognition, that performance cannot be fixed without ceasing to be performative, yields the procedural preference for live testimony over videotaped depositions.

In a mediatized culture, the legal arena may be one of the few sites left where liveness continues to be valued.

The fact that the grounding of performance in an ontology of liveness and disappearance is as fundamental to the understanding of performance in and of the law as it is to many accounts of performance emerging from performance theory problematizes the desire to see that ontology as a source of resistance to reproduction and regulation. I have shown here that liveness – performance in the present – and memory are privileged terms within the procedural discourse of law, and central mechanisms by which law, including the laws that govern the economy of reproduction, is actualized. In a double gesture of recuperation, which is based in the same understanding of the ontology of performance as that advocated by some performance theorists, American law denies performance legal standing as intellectual property and recuperates it as central to the legal process itself.

5

CONCLUSION

My project here – analyzing the situation of live performance in a mediatized culture – has entailed documenting many of the ways in which mediatization impinges upon live events. Almost all live performances now incorporate the technology of reproduction, at the very least in the use of electric amplification, and sometimes to the point where they are hardly live at all. But the influence of mediatization on live events is not simply a matter of equipment. Some live performances, such as certain Broadway plays and many sports events, are now literally made for television: the live event itself is shaped to the demands of mediatization. Others, like Madonna's concerts and Disney's *Beauty and the Beast*, recreate mediatized performances in a live setting.

In many instances, the incursion of the mediatized into the live has followed a particular historical pattern. Initially, the mediatized form is modeled on the live form, but it eventually usurps the live form's position in the cultural economy. The live form then starts to replicate the mediatized form. This pattern is apparent in the historical relationship of theatre and television. Those involved in early television production first took the replication of the theatre spectator's visual experience as their objective. And the cultural discourse surrounding television successfully defined the new medium as delivering the same experience as the theatre, only under conditions better suited to postwar suburban culture. This understanding of television contributed to its ability to displace the theatre within the cultural economy of the postwar period. I have argued here that, since the late 1940s, live theatre has become more and more like television and other mediatized cultural forms. To the extent that live performances now emulate mediatized representations, they have become second-hand recreations of themselves as refracted through mediatization.

This historical dynamic does not occur in a vacuum, of course. It is bound up with the audience's perception and expectations, which shape and are shaped by technological change and the uses of technology influenced by capital investment. As Jacques Attali (1985) shows, an economy based in repetition and the mass reproduction of cultural objects emerged when the production of unique cultural objects was no longer profitable. Analyzing audience desires when mediatized culture was in its infancy, Walter Benjamin (1986 [1936]) concluded that audiences were responding to the perceptual possibilities offered by the film medium. What this new mass audience wanted, in Benjamin's view, was a relationship to cultural objects defined by proximity and intimacy. He saw the desire for reproducible cultural objects as symptomatic of these needs. Building on Benjamin's analysis, I have suggested that our current concepts of proximity and intimacy derive from television. The incursion of mediatization into live events can be understood as a means of making those events respond to the need for televisual intimacy, thus fulfilling desires and expectations shaped by mediatized representations.

At various points, I have described the relationship between the live and the mediatized as competitive, conflictual, and agonistic. I must stress, however, that I consider this relation of opposition to exist only at the level of a cultural economy that responds to changing historical and technological circumstances. It is not an opposition rooted in essential differences between the live and the mediatized. Some contemporary performance practitioners and theorists like Eric Bogosian and Peggy Phelan derive a notion of live performance as a socially and politically oppositional discourse from ostensible ontological differences between live and mediatized representations. I have argued here that the qualities performance theorists frequently cite to demonstrate that live performance forms are ontologically different from mediatized forms turn out, upon close examination, to provide little basis for convincing distinctions. Mediatized forms like film and video can be shown to have the same ontological characteristics as live performance, and live performance can be used in ways indistinguishable from the uses generally associated with mediatized forms. Therefore, ontological analysis does not provide a basis for privileging live performance as an oppositional discourse.

In rejecting the argument for ontological differences between live and mediatized cultural forms, I suggested that the best way of thinking about that relationship is to look at the meanings and uses of live performance in specific cultural contexts. To that end, I offered a detailed analysis of the relationship between live and recorded performances in the culture of rock music. The historical narrative of the relationship between theatre and television applies as well to the general relationship between popular music and sound recording. Live performance ceased long ago to be the primary experience of popular music, with the result that most live performances of popular music now seek to replicate the music on the recordings. Even in the case of a musical genre like jazz, where the artist is expected to produce a performance different from the recorded one, the recording is the standard according to which the live performance is judged.

The particular relationship of live and recorded performances in rock culture revolved around a complex articulation of the concept of authenticity that was central to the rock ideology of the 1960s and 1970s. I have argued here that rock authenticity is a concept that depends on a specific interaction of recordings and live performances rather than the nomination of one or the other as authentic. The primary experience of the music is as a recording; the function of live performance is to authenticate the sound on the recording. In rock culture, live performance is a secondary experience of the music but is nevertheless indispensable, since the primary experience cannot be validated without it. Although some rock fans do insist that live music is authentic in a way that recorded music is not, the relationship of live and mediatized performances in rock culture was never actually a relation of opposition in which the live was seen as authentic and the recorded as inauthentic. Rather, authenticity was produced through a dialectical or symbiotic relationship between live and mediatized representations of the music, in which neither the recording nor the live concert could be perceived as authentic in and of itself.

Arguably, as mediatization furthered its incursion into rock with the advent of music video, rock's ideology of authenticity lost its sway. In yet another iteration of the historical narrative I have proposed, music video displaced live performance in its relationship to sound recordings by taking over live performance's authenticating function. A relationship that had previously centered on a couple became a threesome: live performance of rock did not cease to exist, but was reduced to replicating and, thus, authenticating the *video* rather than the music itself. The importance of both live performance and the authenticity it certified have diminished considerably in rock culture. Rock ideology exists now only as a simulation deployed by the music industry. Through *MTV Unplugged* – with its emphasis on liveness and acoustic musicianship – and the strategic awarding of Grammys, the industry simulates the ideological distinctions on which rock culture is based (e.g., the distinction between the authentic and the inauthentic), thus maintaining its power as the arbiter of those distinctions.

After devoting most of this book to examining the status of live performance in cultural realms over which mediatization has achieved dominion, I turned to one social realm that has offered significant resistance to the incursion of mediatization: the legal arena. By discussing the failure of the prerecorded videotape trial to take root, I showed that the assumption that a trial is an ontologically live event is embedded so deeply in the discourse of American law that the mediatized trial simply could not become the dominant form. To demonstrate the centrality of live performance to legal procedure, I discussed both the system's strong preference for live testimony and the ways in which testimony is defined as a live performance of memory-retrieval in the present moment of the trial.

It is ironic that the legal system may be the one place in a mediatized culture in which live performance retains its traditional functions and values, since some performance theorists claim that live performance's ontology of disappearance and its persistence only in memory allow it to escape the reach of regulation and, thus, make it a site of resistance to the law. In examining intellectual property law, we can see that this is true to a limited degree. Although the law has increasingly approached the idea of making performance "ownable" as a cultural commodity through the development of the right of publicity, that area of law governs performance only if it is seen as a part of the performer's self. Live performance's temporal evanescence does remove it from the purview of copyright law. Even where performances are recorded, the underlying text is copyrighted but not the *performance* of the text. Therefore, it is fair to say that performance *qua* performance has so far escaped legal definition as a cultural commodity and is unregulated to that extent.

However, the notion that performance's disappearance into memory exempts it from regulation is untenable. As I showed, memory is both a site policed by the law and a central mechanism of law enforcement. The workings of memory themselves can be the objects of legal discipline, as George Harrison learned from the lawsuit over "My Sweet Lord." Far from providing a safe haven from regulation, spectatorial memory can be brought into legal discourse to determine whether a performance has infringed a copyright. Most significant of all, live performance and memory both enter the service of the law in the form of testimony, the live performance of memory retrieval. Given all the ways in which the legal system subjects memory to surveillance, adjudicates its operation, and presses it into service as an agent of legal procedure, the suggestion that memory is a realm exempt from regulation is clearly erroneous.

A colleague told me recently that my historical narrative describing the relationship between the live and the mediatized brought to her mind an image of two mirrors facing each other and bouncing an image back and forth between them. If the relationship between the live and the mediatized could be understood as the infinite regress this image suggests, then one would expect that after live performances had become more like mediatized ones, mediatized performances would start to resemble live performances that had internalized mediatization. Subsequent live performances would mirror those mediatized representations, and so on. To think about the relationship between the live and the mediatized in this way is implicitly to assume that each category has comparable cultural standing, that each has an equally strong interest in reflecting the other. But my view of cultural economy holds that at any given historical moment, there are dominant forms that enjoy much greater cultural presence, prestige, and power than other forms. Nondominant forms will tend to become more like the dominant ones but not the other way around. At present, television is the dominant cultural form. Since television usurped the theatre's position in the cultural economy, theatre has become more like television. But has television gone on to become more like theatre-as-television? That Chapters 2 and 3 both end with the suggestion that the way live performance is perceived and the cultural prestige accorded to it are generational issues indicates that the relationship between the live and the mediatized is a volatile question subject to significant change over time. If the cultural prestige of live performance were to increase in the future, a kind of back-and-forth exchange among different cultural forms might well occur. That seems unlikely, however. Currently, mediatized forms enjoy far more cultural presence and prestige – and profitability – than live forms. In many instances, live performances are produced either as replications of mediatized representations or as raw materials for subsequent mediatization. As I have argued here, any change in the near future is likely to be toward a further diminution of the symbolic capital associated with live events.

BIBLIOGRAPHY

Alcabes, Elisa A. (1987) "Unauthorized photographs of theatrical works: do they infringe the copyright?" *Columbia Law Review*, 87, 5: 1032–47.

Altman, Rick (1986) "Television/Sound," in *Studies in Entertainment: Critical Approaches to Mass Culture*, Tania Modleski (ed.), Bloomington: Indiana University Press, pp. 39–54.

American Bar Association (1981) *Committee Report: Division III, Committee No. 304*.

American Jurisprudence (1992) *Witnesses*, 2nd edn, vol. 81, Rochester, NY: Lawyers Cooperative Publishing.

Apflebaum, Marc. J. (1983) "Copyright and the right of publicity: one pea in two pods?" *Georgetown Law Journal*, 71: 1567–94.

Armstrong, James J. (1976) "The criminal videotape trial: serious constitutional questions," *Oregon Law Review*, 55: 567–85.

Attali, Jacques (1985) *Noise: The Political Economy of Music*, Brian Massumi (trans.), Minneapolis: University of Minnesota Press.

Auslander, Philip (1992a) "Intellectual property meets the cyborg: performance and the cultural politics of technology," *Performing Arts Journal*, 14, 1: 30–42.

—— (1992b) *Presence and Resistance: Postmodernism and Cultural Politics in Contemporary American Performance*, Ann Arbor, MI: University of Michigan Press.

—— (1993) *American Experimental Theater: A Critical Introduction*, New York: University Arts Resources.

—— (1997) *From Acting to Performance: Essays in Modernism and Postmodernism*, London, New York: Routledge.

Banks, Jack (1996) *Monopoly Television: MTV's Quest to Control the Music*, Boulder, CO: Westview Press.

Barker, David (1987 [1985]) "Television production techniques as communication," in *Television: The Critical View*, 4th edn, Horace Newcomb (ed.), New York: Oxford University Press, pp. 179–96.

Barnouw, Erik (1990) *Tube of Plenty: The Evolution of American Television*, 2nd revised edn, New York: Oxford University Press.

Barthes, Roland (1977) *Image – Music – Text*, Stephen Heath (trans.), New York: Hill and Wang.

Baudrillard, Jean (1981) *For a Critique of the Political Economy of the Sign*, Charles Levin (trans.), St. Louis, MO: Telos Press.

—— (1983) *Simulations*, Paul Foss, Paul Patton, and Philip Beitchman (trans.), New York: Semiotext(e).

—— (1990) *Seduction*, Brian Singer (trans.), New York: St Martin's Press.

Baumol, William J. and Bowen, William G. (1966) *Performing Arts: The Economic Dilemma*, New York: The Twentieth Century Fund.

Beadle, Jeremy J. (1993) *Will Pop Eat Itself? Pop Music in the Soundbite Era*, London: Faber and Faber.

Belanger, Paul (1946) "Television ballet," *Television*, May: 8–13.

Benjamin, Walter (1986 [1936]) "The work of art in the age of mechanical reproduction," Harry Zohn (trans.), in *Video Culture: A Critical Investigation*, John G. Hanhardt (ed.), Layton, UT: Peregrine Smith Books, pp. 27–52.

Berland, Jody (1993) "Sound, image and social space: music video and media reconstruction," in *Sound and Vision: The Music Video Reader*, Simon Frith, Andrew Goodwin, and Lawrence Grossberg (eds), London, New York: Routledge, pp. 25–43.

Blau, Herbert (1982) *Blooded Thought: Occasions of Theatre*, New York: PAJ Press.

—— (1990) *The Audience*, Baltimore: Johns Hopkins University Press.

—— (1992). *To All Appearances: Ideology and Performance*, New York, London: Routledge.

—— (1996) Contribution to "Forum on Interdisciplinarity", *PMLA*, 111, 2: 274–5.

Blossom, Roberts (1966) "On filmstage," *TDR: Tulane Drama Review*, 11, 1: 68–72.

Bogosian, Eric (1994) *Pounding Nails in the Floor With My Forehead*, New York: Theatre Communications Group.

Bolen, Murray (1950) *Fundamentals of Television*, Hollywood: Hollywood Radio Publishers.

Bolter, Jay David and Grusin, Richard (1996) "Remediation," *Configurations*, 3: 311–58.

Bolz, Norbert and van Reijen, Willem (1996) *Walter Benjamin*, Laimdota Mazzarins (trans.), Atlantic Highlands, NJ: Humanities Press.

Brennan, Thomas E. (1972) "Videotape – the Michigan experience," *The Hastings Law Journal*, 24: 1–7.

Bretz, Rudy (1953) *Techniques of Television Production*, New York: McGraw-Hill.

Brewster, Ben and Jacobs, Lea (1997) *Theatre to Cinema: Stage Pictorialism and the Early Feature Film*, Oxford, New York: Oxford University Press.

Burger, Hans (1940) "Through the television camera," *Theatre Arts*, 1 March: 206–9.

Burlingame, Beverly Ray (1991) "Moral rights: all the world's *not* a stage," *Entertainment, Publishing and the Arts Handbook, 1991*, John David Viera and Robert Thorne (eds), Deerfield, IL: Clark Boardman Callaghan, pp. 3–15.

Burnett, Robert (1996) *The Global Jukebox: The International Music Industry*, London, New York: Routledge.

Butler, Judith (1993) *Bodies that Matter: On the Discursive Limits of "Sex"*, New York, London: Routledge.

Cafarelli, Carl (1997) "An informal history of bubblegum music," *Goldmine* 437 (25 April 1997): 16–19+.

Carroll, Noël (1998) A *Philosophy of Mass Art*, Oxford: Oxford University Press.

Case, Sue-Ellen (1996) *The Domain-Matrix: Performing Lesbian at the End of Print Culture*, Bloomington: Indiana University Press.

Causey, Matthew (forthcoming) "Postorganic performance: the appearance of theatre in virtual environments," in *The Texts of Cyberspace*, Marie-Laure Ryan (ed.), Bloomington: Indiana University Press.

Cavell, Stanley (1982) "The fact of television," *Daedalus*, 111, 4: 75–96.

Chin, Daryl (1991) "From popular to pop: the arts in/of commerce," *Performing Arts Journal*, 37: 5–20.

Clarida, Robert (1993) "Did Milli Vanilli do the mashed potato? Lanham Act responses to misattribution in the music industry," in *Entertainment, Publishing and the Arts Handbook, 1993–4*, John David Viera and Robert Thorne (eds), New York: Clark Boardman Callaghan, pp. 185–217.

Collins, Ronald L. K. and Skover, David M. (1992) "Paratexts," *Stanford Law Review*, 44, 3: 509–52.

Connor, Steven (1989) *Postmodernist Culture: An Introduction to Theories of the Contemporary*, Oxford: Basil Blackwell.

Cook, Bruce (1973) *Listen to the Blues*, New York: Scribner's Sons.

Cook, Nicholas (1995–6) "Music minus one: rock, theory and performance," *New Formations*, 27: 23–41.

Copeland, Roger (1990) "The presence of mediation," *TDR: The Journal of Performance Studies*, 34, 4: 28–44.

Crimp, Douglas (1993 [1980]) "The photographic activity of postmodernism," in *Postmodernism: A Reader*, Thomas Docherty (ed.), New York: Columbia University Press, pp. 172–9.

Croyder, Leslie Ann (1982) "Ohio court hears first murder trial," *Trial*, 18, 6: 12.

Cubitt, Sean (1991) *Timeshift: On Video Culture*, London, New York: Routledge.

—— (1994) "Laurie Anderson: myth, management and platitude," in *Art Has No History! The Making and Unmaking of Modern Art*, John Roberts (ed.), London, New York: Verso, pp. 278–96.

Curtis, Jim (1987) *Rock Eras: Interpretations of Music and Society, 1954–1984*, Bowling Green, OH: Bowling Green State University Popular Press.

Daum, Meghan (1997) "Virtual love," *The New Yorker*, 25 August and 1 September: 80–9.

Densmore, John (1991) *Riders on the Storm: My Life with Jim Morrison and the Doors* (audiobook), n. p.: Seven Wolves Publishing.

Derrida, Jacques (1978 [1966]) "The theater of cruelty and the closure of representation," in *Writing and Difference*, Alan Bass (trans.), Chicago: University of Chicago Press, pp. 232–50.

Dienst, Richard (1994) *Still Life in Real Time: Theory After Television*, Durham, NC: Duke University Press.

Doret, David M. (1974) "Trial by videotape – can justice be seen to be done?" *Temple Law Quarterly*, 47, 2: 228–68.

Douglas, Susan J. (1997) "Girls 'n' spice: all things nice?" *The Nation*, 25 August and 1 September: 21–4.

DuBoff, Leonard D. (1984) *Art Law in a Nutshell*, St. Paul: West Publishing Co.

Dunlap, Orrin E., Jr. (1947) *Understanding Television*, New York: Greenberg.

Dupuy, Judy (1945) *Television Show Business*, Schenectady: General Electric.

Durant, Alan (1985) "Rock revolution or time-no-changes: visions of change and continuity in rock music," in *Popular Music 5: Continuity and Change*, Richard Middleton and David Horn (eds), Cambridge: Cambridge University Press, pp. 97–121.

Eisenberg, Evan (1987) *The Recording Angel*, New York: Penguin.

Eisenstein, Sergei M. (1988 [1923]) "The montage of attractions," in *Selected Works*, vol. I, *Writings, 1922–34*, Richard Taylor (ed. and trans.), London: BFI; Bloomington: Indiana University Press.

Esslin, Martin (ed.) (1977) *The Encyclopedia of World Theater*, New York: Charles Scribner's Sons.

Ferrer, Jose (1949) "Television no terror," *Theatre Arts*, April: 46–7.

Feuer, Jane (1983) "The concept of live television: ontology as ideology," in *Regarding Television*, E. Ann Kaplan (ed.), Frederick, MD: University Publications of America, pp. 12–22.

Forced Entertainment (1996) "A decade of forced entertainment," *Performance Research*, 1, 1: 73–88.

Freemal, Beth (1996) "Theatre, stage directions & copyright law," *Chicago-Kent Law Review*, 71, 3: 1017–40.

Friedlander, Paul (1996) *Rock and Roll: A Social History*, Boulder, CO: Westview Press.

Frith, Simon (1988a) *Music for Pleasure*, London: Routledge.

—— (1988b) "Picking up the pieces," in *Facing the Music*, Simon Frith (ed.), New York: Pantheon, pp. 88–130.

—— (1996) *Performing Rites: On the Value of Popular Music*, Cambridge: Harvard University Press.

Fry, Tony (1993) "Introduction," *R U A TV?: Heidegger and the Televisual*, Tony Fry (ed.), Sydney: Power Publications, pp. 11–23.

Fuchs, Elinor (1996) *The Death of Character: Perspectives on Theater after Modernism*, Bloomington, IN: Indiana University Press.

Gaar, Gillian G. (1992) *She's A Rebel: The History of Women in Rock & Roll*, Seattle, WA: Seal Press.

Gaines, Jane (1991) *Contested Culture: The Image, the Voice, and the Law*, Chapel Hill, NC: University of North Carolina Press.

Goldman, Albert (1992) *Sound Bites*, New York: Random House.

Goldsmith, Alfred N. (1937) "Television among the visual arts," *Television: Collected Addresses and Papers*, 2: 51–6.

Gomery, Douglas (1985) "Theatre television: the missing link of technological change in the U.S. motion picture industry," *The Velvet Light Trap*, 21: 54–61.

Goodrich, Peter (1990) *Languages of Law: From Logics of Memory to Nomadic Masks*, London: Weidenfeld and Nicolson.

Goodwin, Andrew (1990) "Sample and hold: pop music in the digital age of reproduction," in *On Record: Rock, Pop, and the Written Word*, Simon Frith and Andrew Goodwin (eds), New York: Pantheon, pp. 258–73.

—— (1993) *Dancing in the Distraction Factory: Music Television and Popular Culture*, London: Routledge.

Gracyk, Theodore (1996) *Rhythm and Noise: An Aesthetics of Rock*, Durham, NC: Duke University Press.

—— (1997) "Listening to music: performances and recordings," *The Journal of Aesthetics and Art Criticism*, 55, 2: 139–50.

Graham, Michael H. (1992) *Federal Rules of Evidence in a Nutshell*, 3rd edn, St. Paul: West Publishing Co.

Greenwald, David (1993) "The forgetful witness," *University of Chicago Law Review*, 60: 167–95.

Gross, David (1986) "Culture, politics, and 'lifestyle' in the 1960s," in *Race, Politics, and Culture: Critical Essays on the Radicalism of the 1960s*, Adolph Reed, Jr. (ed.), New York: Greenwood Press, pp. 99–117.

Grossberg, Lawrence (1988) " 'You [still] have to fight for your right to party': music television as billboards of post-modern difference," *Popular Music*, 7, 3: 315–32.

—— (1992) *We Gotta Get Out of this Place: Popular Conservatism and Post-modern Culture*, New York, London: Routledge.

—— (1993) "The media economy of rock culture: cinema, postmodernity and authenticity," in *Sound and Vision: The Music Video Reader*, Simon Frith, Andrew Goodwin and Lawrence Grossberg (eds), London, New York: Routledge, pp. 185–209.

—— (1994) "Is anybody listening? Does anybody care? On talking about 'the state of rock,'" in *Microphone Fiends: Youth Music, Youth Culture*, Andrew Ross and Tricia Rose (eds), New York, London: Routledge, pp. 41–58.

Hall, Russell (1997) "Alice Cooper," *Goldmine*, 23, 21: 14–15.

Heath, Stephen and Skirrow, Gillian (1977) "Television, a world in action," *Screen* 18, 2: 7–59.

Helfing, Robert F. (1997) "Drama trauma," in *Establishing Presence: Advance-ments in Intellectual Property Law*, special section of *The Los Angeles Daily Journal*, 110, 79 (24 April): S10–11, S34.

Hibbitts, Bernard J. (1992) "'Coming to our senses': communication and legal expression in performance cultures, *Emory Law Journal*, 41, 4: 873–960.

—— (1995) "Making motions: the embodiment of law in gesture," *Journal of Contemporary Legal Issues*, 6: 51–81.

Hickey, Dave (1996) "Those cool American blondes," in *Alex Katz Under The Stars: American Landscapes 1951–1995*, New York: Institute for Contempo-rary Art/P.S. 1 Museum, pp. 43–8.

Hilgard, Adaline J. (1994) "Can choreography and copyright waltz together in the wake of *Horgan v. MacMillan, Inc.*?" *University of California at Davis Law Review*, 27: 757–89.

Hodgson, Cheryl L. (1975) "Intellectual property – performer's style – a quest for ascertainment, recognition, and protection," *Denver Law Journal*, 52: 561–94.

Holmes, Stephanie Ann (1989) "'Lights, camera, action': videotaping and closed-circuit television procedures coyly confront the Sixth Amendment," *South Carolina Law Review*, 40, 3: 693–731.

Hopkins, Jerry (1983) *Hit and Run: The Jimi Hendrix Story*, New York: Perigree Books.

Hunter, Mary (1949) "The stage director in television," *Theatre Arts*, May: 46–7.

Jameson, Fredric (1991) *Postmodernism or The Cultural Logic of Late Capitalism*, Durham, NC: Duke University Press.

Johnson, Randal (1993) "Pierre Bourdieu on art, literature, and culture," in Pierre Bourdieu, *The Field of Cultural Production*, New York: Columbia University Press, pp. 1–25.

Jones, Robert Edmond (1941) *The Dramatic Imagination*, New York: Duell, Sloan and Pearce.

Kaplan, E. Ann (1987) *Rocking Around the Clock: Music Television, Postmod-ernism, and Consumer Culture*, New York, London: Methuen.

Katsh, M. Ethan (1989) *The Electronic Media & the Transformation of Law*, New York: Oxford University Press.

Kirby, Michael (1984 [1972]) "On acting and not-acting," in *The Art of Perfor-mance*, Gregory Battcock and Robert Nickas (eds), New York: Dutton, pp. 97–117.

Konrad, Otto W. (1991) "A federal recognition of performance art author moral rights," *Washington and Lee Law Review*, 48, 4: 1579–643.

Kroker, Arthur, Kroker, Marilouise, and Cook, David (1989) *The Panic Ency-clopedia: The Definitive Guide to the Postmodern Scene*, New York: St. Martin's Press.

Laing, Dave (1991) "A voice without a face: popular music and the phono-graph in the 1890s," *Popular Music*, 10, 1: 1–9.

Lederer, Fredric I. (1994) "Technology comes to the courtroom, and,..." *Emory Law Journal*, 43, 3: 1095–122.

Levine, Marla E. (1980) "The right of publicity as a means of protecting performer's style," *Loyola of Los Angeles Law Review*, 14, 129–63.

Lohr, Lenox R. (1940) *Television Broadcasting: Production, Economics, Technique*, New York: McGraw-Hill.

Lury, Celia (1993) *Cultural Rights: Technology, Legality and Personality*, London: Routledge.

MacNamara, Mark (1995) "Fade away: the rise and fall of the repressed-memory theory in the courtroom," *California Lawyer*, 15, 3: 36–41, 86.

Marshall, John McClellan (1984) "Medium v. message: The Videotape Civil Trial," *Texas Bar Journal*, July 1984: 852–5.

Martin, Christopher (1993) "Traditional criticism of popular music and the making of a lip-synching scandal," *Popular Music and Society*, 17, 4: 63–81.

McCrystal, James L. (1972) "The judge's critique," contribution to "First Videotape Trial: experiment in Ohio: a symposium by the participants," *Defense Law Journal*, 21: 268–71.

—— (1983) "Prerecorded testimony," in *Video Techniques in Trial and Pretrial*, Fred I. Heller (ed.), New York: Practising Law Institute, pp. 105–28.

McCrystal, James L. and Maschari, Ann B. (1983 [1981]), "Electronic recording of deposition testimony saves money," *For the Defense*, July 1981, reprinted in *Video Technology: Its Use and Application in Law*, Fred I. Heller (ed.), New York: Practising Law Institute, pp. 180–2.

—— (1983) "PRVTT: A lifeline for the jury system," *Trial*, March: 70–3, 100.

—— (1984 [1983]), "In video veritas: the jury no longer need disregard the prerecorded taped trial," *The Judges Journal*, 22, 31, reprinted in *Video Technology: Its Use and Application in Law*, Fred I. Heller (ed.), New York: Practising Law Institute, pp. 241–50

McCrystal, James L. and Young, James L. (1973) "Pre-recorded videotape trials – an Ohio innovation," *Brooklyn Law Review*, 39: 560–6.

McEwen, Richard (1994) "The Frito Bandito's last stand: *Waits* rocks performer's rights into the media age," *Journal of Law and Commerce*, 14, 1: 123–40.

McKenzie, Jon (1997) "Laurie Anderson for dummies," *TDR: The Journal of Performance Studies*, 41, 2: 30–50.

McLuhan, Marshall (1964) *Understanding Media: The Extensions of Man*, 2nd edn, New York: New American Library.

Meltzer, Amy R. (1982) "A new approach to an entertainer's right of performance," *Washington University Law Quarterly*, 59, 4: 1269–303.

Meltzer, Richard (1987 [1970]) *The Aesthetics of Rock*, New York: Da Capo.

Meyer, Ursula (1972) *Conceptual Art*, New York: E. P. Dutton.

Meyerhold, Vsevolod (1969 [1930]) "The reconstruction of the theatre," in *Meyerhold on Theatre*, Edward Braun (ed. and trans.), New York: Hill and Wang.

Miller, Arthur R., and Davis, Michael H. (1990) *Intellectual Property: Patents, Trademarks, and Copyright in a Nutshell*, 2nd edn, St Paul: West Publishing Co.

Miller, Gerald R. and Fontes, Norman E. (1979) *Videotape On Trial: A View from the Jury Box*, Beverly Hills: Sage Publications.

Molderings, Herbert (1984) "*Life is No Performance*: performance by Jochen Gerz," in *The Art of Performance: A Critical Anthology*, Gregory Battcock and Robert Nickas (eds), New York: E. P. Dutton, pp.166–80.

Morrill, Alan E. (1970) "Enter – the video tape trial," *John Marshall Journal of Practice and Procedures*, 3, 2: 237–59.

Morse, Margaret (1998) *Virtualities: Television, Media Art, and Cyberculture*, Bloomington: Indiana University Press.

Murray, Thomas J. (1972a) Prefatory note to "First Videotape Trial: experiment in Ohio: a symposium by the participants," *Defense Law Journal*, 21: 267–8.

—— (1972b) Counsel for the plaintiff's contribution to "First Videotape Trial: experiment in Ohio: a symposium by the participants," *Defense Law Journal*, 21: 271–4.

Nance, Scott (1993) *Music You Can See! The MTV Story*, Las Vegas, NV: Pioneer Books.

Negus, Keith (1997) *Popular Music in Theory*, Hanover, NH, London: Wesleyan University Press.

Nelson, Peter Martin and Friedman, Dawn G. (1993) "Representing comedians: how to protect your client's material," in *Entertainment, Publishing and the Arts Handbook, 1993–4*, John David Viera and Robert Thorne (eds), New York: Clark Boardman Callaghan, pp. 249–60.

Newman, Charles (1985) *The Post-Modern Aura: The Act of Fiction in an Age of Inflation*, Evanston, IL: Northwestern University Press.

Nichols, Carolyn M. (1996) "The interpretation of the Confrontation Clause," *New Mexico Law Review*, 26, 3: 393–431.

Palmer, Robert (1995) *Rock & Roll: An Unruly History*, New York: Harmony Books.

Pavis, Patrice (1992) "Theatre and the media: specificity and interference," in *Theatre at the Crossroads of Culture*, Loren Kruger (trans.), London, New York: Routledge, pp. 99–135.

Perritt, Henry H.Jr., (1994) "Video depositions, transcripts and trials," *Emory Law Journal*, 43, 3: 1071–93.

Phelan, Peggy (1993a) *Unmarked: The Politics of Performance*, London, New York: Routledge.

—— (1993b) "Preface: Arresting performances of sexual and racial difference: toward a theory of performative film," *Women & Performance: A Journal of Feminist Theory*, 6, 2: 5–10.

Phillips, Jill A. (1991) "Performance rights: protecting a performer's style," *The Wayne Law Review*, 37, 3: 1683–98.

Poggi, Jack (1968) *Theater in America: The Impact of Economic Forces, 1870–1967*, Ithaca, NY: Cornell University Press.

Porcello, Thomas (1991) "The ethics of digital audio-sampling: engineers' discourse," *Popular Music*, 10, 1: 69–84.

Reynolds, Kay (1942) "Television – Marvel into Medium," *Theatre Arts*, February: 121–6.

Ritchie, Michael (1994) *Please Stand By: A Prehistory of Television*, Woodstock, NY: The Overlook Press.

Robertson, Elizabeth M. (1979) *Juror Response to Prerecorded Videotape Trials*, NBS Special Publication 480–30, Washington, DC, National Bureau of Standards, US Department of Commerce.

Rose, Brian G. (1986) *Television and the Performing Arts*, New York: Greenwood Press.

Rothstein, Paul F. (1981) *Evidence in a Nutshell: State and Federal Rules*, 2nd edn, St Paul: West Publishing Co.

Saltz, David (1997) "The art of interaction: interactivity, performativity, and computers," *The Journal of Aesthetics and Art Criticism*, 55, 2: 117–27.

Saunders, David (1992) *Authorship and Copyright*, London: Routledge.

Sayre, Henry (1989) *The Object of Performance*, Chicago: University of Chicago Press.

Schipper, Henry (1992) *Broken Record: The Inside Story of the Grammy Awards*, New York: Birch Lane Press.

Seabrook, John (1997) "Big Ben," *The New Yorker*, 73, 7 (7 April 1977): 78–87.

Seidelson, David E. (1993) "The Confrontation Clause and the Supreme Court: from 'Faded Parchment' to Slough," *Widener Journal of Public Law*, 3, 1: 477–508.

Seltz, Claire L. (1988) "Casenote: *United States* v. *Owens*, 108 S. Ct. 838 (1988)," *Journal of Criminal Law and Criminology*, 79: 866–98.

Shapiro, Harry and Glebbeek, Caesar (1990) *Jimi Hendrix: Electric Gypsy*, New York: St. Martin's Press.

Sherman, Rorie (1993) "And now, the power of tape," *National Law Journal*, 15, 23 (8 February): 1, 30.

Shuker, Roy (1994) *Understanding Popular Music*, London, New York: Routledge.

Shutkin, John A. (1973) "Videotape trials: legal and practical implications," *Columbia Journal of Law and Social Problems*, 9, 8: 363–93.

Snyder, Barbara Rook (1993) "Defining the contours of unavailability and reliability for the Confrontation Clause," *Capital University Law Review*, 22, 1: 189–206.

Sontag, Susan (1966) "Film and theatre," *TDR: Tulane Drama Review*, 11, 1: 24–37.

Spigel, Lynn (1992) *Make Room For TV: Television and the Family Ideal in Postwar America*, Chicago: University of Chicago Press.

Stein, Marshall D. (1981) "Criminal trial by paper deposition vs. the right of confrontation," *Boston Bar Journal*, April: 18–27.

Sudjic, Deyan (1990) *Cult Heroes*, New York: W. W. Norton.

Swift, Eleanor (1993) "Smoke and mirrors: the failure of the Supreme Court's accuracy rationale in *White v. Illinois* requires a new look at confrontation," *Capital University Law Review*, 22, 1: 145–88.

Szatmary, David P. (1991) *Rockin' In Time: A Social History of Rock-and-Roll*, 2nd edn, Englewood Cliffs, NJ: Prentice-Hall.

Thaler, Paul (1994) *The Watchful Eye: American Justice in the Age of Trial Television*, Westport, CT: Praeger.

Théberge, Paul (1997) *Any Sound You Can Imagine: Making Music/Consuming Technology*, Hanover, NH, London: Wesleyan University Press.

Tichi, Cecilia (1991) *Electronic Hearth: Creating an American Television Culture*, New York: Oxford University Press.

Toth, Csaba (1997) "Like cancer in the system: industrial gothic, nine inch nails, and videotape," *Gothic: Transmutations of Horror in Late Twentieth Century Art*, Christoph Grunenberg (ed.), Cambridge, MA: The MIT Press.

Van Camp, Julie (1994) "Copyright of choreographic works," in *Entertainment, Publishing and the Arts Handbook, 1994–5*, John David Viera and Robert Thorne (eds), New York: Clark Boardman Callaghan, pp. 59–92.

Vardac, A. Nicholas (1949) *Stage to Screen: Theatrical Method from Garrick to Griffith*, Cambridge, MA: Harvard University Press.

von Hoffman, Nicholas (1995) "Broadway plugs into the computer age," *Architectural Digest*, 52, 11: 130–4.

Wade, Robert J. (1944) "Television backgrounds," *Theatre Arts*, 28: 728–32.

Watts, Raymond N. (1972) Counsel for the defendant's contribution to "First videotape trial: experiment in Ohio: a symposium by the participants," *Defense Law Journal*, 21: 274–8.

Weinstein, Jerome E. (1997) "What do robots, James Dean and Doritos corn chips have in common?" in *Entertainment, Publishing and the Arts Handbook, 1997–8*, John David Viera and Robert Thorne (eds), New York: Clark Boardman Callaghan, pp. 225–37.

Whiteley, Sheila (1992) *The Space Between the Notes: Rock and the Counter-Culture*, London, New York: Routledge.

Whitman, Willson (1937) *Bread and Circuses: A Study of Federal Theatre*, New York: Oxford University Press.

Williams, Raymond (1992 [1974]) *Television: Technology and Cultural Form*, Hanover: Wesleyan University Press.

Wohl, Leonard A. (1988) "The right of publicity and vocal larceny: sounding off on sound-alikes," *Fordham Law Review*, 57: 445–62.

Wright, Edward A. (1958) *A Primer for Playgoers*, Englewood Cliffs, NJ: Prentice-Hall.

Wurtzler, Steve (1992) "She sang live, but the microphone was turned off: the live, the recorded, and the *subject* of representation," in *Sound Theory Sound Practice*, Rick Altman (ed.), New York, London: Routledge, pp. 87–103.

Youngblood, Gene (1970) *Expanded Cinema*, New York: E. P. Dutton.

INDEX

INDEX